Progress Chart

This chart lists all the topics in the book. Once you have completed each page, stick a sticker in the correct box below.

Page	Topic	Sticker	Page	Topic	Sticker	Page	Topic	Sticker
2	Reading and writing numbers		13	Adding two numbers		24	Real-life problems	
3	Multiplying and dividing by 10		14	Subtracting three-digit numbers		25	Real-life problems	
4	Ordering sets of large numbers		15	Subtracting three-digit numbers		26	Areas of rectangles and squares	
5	Rounding numbers		16	Adding decimals		27	Problems involving time	
6	Identifying patterns		17	Adding decimals		28	Bar graphs	
7	Recognizing multiples of 6, 7, and 8		18	Subtracting decimals		29	Probability	
8	Factors of numbers 1 to 30		19	Subtracting decimals		30	Triangles	
9	Recognizing equivalent fractions		20	Multiplying by one-digit numbers		31	Expanded form	
10	Ordering sets of numbers		21	Multiplying by one-digit numbers		32	Speed trials	
11	Rounding decimals		22	Division with remainders		33	All the 3s	
12	Adding two numbers		23	Division with remainders		34	All the 3s again	

Page	Topic	Sticker	Page	Topic	Sticker	Page	Topic	Sticker
77	Naming polygons		91	Congruency		105	Probability	
78	Adding decimals		92	Lines of symmetry		106	Column addition	
79	Adding decimals		93	Writing equivalent number sentences		107	Column addition	
80	Subtracting decimals		94	Multiplying and dividing		108	Adding fractions	
81	Subtracting decimals		95	Ordering sets of measures		109	Adding fractions	
82	Multiplying by one-digit numbers		96	Decimal models		110	Subtracting fractions	
83	Multiplying by one-digit numbers		97	Identifying patterns		111	Subtracting fractions	
84	Division with remainders		98	Products with odd and even numbers		112	Multiplying by two-digit numbers	
85	Division with remainders		99	Squares of numbers		113	Multiplying by two-digit numbers	
86	Real-life problems		100	Factors of numbers from 66 to 100		114	Dividing by one-digit numbers	
87	Real-life problems		101	Renaming fractions		115	Dividing by one-digit numbers	
88	Perimeters of squares and rectangles		102	Ordering sets of decimals		116	Real-life problems	
89	Problems involving time		103	Symmetry		117	Real-life problems	
90	Using bar graphs		104	Comparing areas		118	Problems involving time	

Well done! With the help of the X-Men, Spider-Man, the Fantastic Four, and other Marvel heroes and villains, you can now count yourself a math expert!

MARVEL
HEROES

Math
Made Easy

Grade 4: ages 9–10
Workbook

Consultant
Alison Tribley

LONDON, NEW YORK, MUNICH,
MELBOURNE, AND DELHI

Reading and writing numbers

Write each of these numbers in words.

146,289 in words is **One hundred forty-six thousand, two hundred eighty-nine**

Two million, three hundred ten thousand, five hundred sixty is **2,310,560**

Write each of these numbers in words.

146,209

407,543

245,107

Write each of these in numbers.

Four hundred fifteen thousand, thirty-two

Six hundred ninety-four thousand, seven hundred eleven

Seven hundred nine thousand, two hundred three

Write each of these numbers in words.

9,307,012

2,024,390

8,908,434

Write each of these numbers in words.

Try these!   One million, two hundred fifty-one

Three million, forty thousand, four hundred four

Nine million, three hundred two thousand, one hundred one

Multiplying and dividing by 10

Write the answer in the box.

22 x 10 = **220**

50 ÷ 10 = **5**

Write the product in the box.

26 x 10 =   43 x 10 =   55 x 10 =

66 x 10 =   33 x 10 =   47 x 10 =

137 x 10 =   936 x 10 =   284 x 10 =

634 x 10 =   821 x 10 =   473 x 10 =

Write the quotient in the box.

40 ÷ 10 =   20 ÷ 10 =   50 ÷ 10 =

60 ÷ 10 =   70 ÷ 10 =   580 ÷ 10 =

130 ÷ 10 =   270 ÷ 10 =   100 ÷ 10 =

540 ÷ 10 =   980 ÷ 10 =   710 ÷ 10 =

Write the number that has been multiplied by 10 in the box.

x 10 = 470   x 10 = 640   x 10 = 740

x 10 = 790   x 10 = 100   x 10 = 830

x 10 = 7,140   x 10 = 3,060   x 10 = 5,290

Write the quotient in the box.

30 ÷ 10 =   20 ÷ 10 =   90 ÷ 10 =

70 ÷ 10 =   50 ÷ 10 =   580 ÷ 10 =

310 ÷ 10 =   270 ÷ 10 =   100 ÷ 10 =

Ordering sets of large numbers

Write these numbers in order, from least to greatest.

3,322	526	304	42	2,240	440
42	304	440	526	2,240	3,322

I'm the greatest!

Write the numbers in each row in order, from least to greatest.

320	195	945	402	910	986

308	640	380	805	364	910

259	349	25	1,000	619	100

20,501	36,821	2,501	45,601	40,561	25,001

Write the numbers in each row in order, from least to greatest.

984,000	8,840,000	8,900	98,240	7,560	75,600

301,550	6,405,000	6,450,000	64,500	31,500	3,150

7,000,100	70,100	7,100,000	710	710,000	7,100

CLAIRTON
Population
85,440

DISTRICT X
Population
8,440

SAPIEN TOWN
Population
8,404,420

WESTCHESTER COUNTY
Population
8,440,042

Which town has:

The second-smallest population?

The smallest population?

The second-largest population?

Rounding numbers

Some of these numbers are BIG!

Round each number to the nearest ten.

14		81		45		63	
57		58		49		35	
82		47		22		62	
46		26		85		99	
33		51		68		29	

Round each number to the nearest hundred.

286		224		825		460	
539		329		378		937	
772		255		449		612	
116		750		618		990	

Round each number to the nearest thousand.

4,240		3,500		9,940		1,051	
8,945		5,050		5,530		4,850	
6,200		7,250		6,499		8,450	
12,501		8,762		6,500		4,292	

Identifying patterns

Continue each pattern.

Steps of 8:	6	14	22	30	38
Steps of 14:	20	34	48	62	76

I'm BIG on patterns. Can you do these?

Continue each pattern.

4	34	64					
10	61	112					
48	100	152					
20	37	54					
25	100	175			400		
25	45	65					165
8	107	206					
7	25	43					
22	72	122		222			
60	165	270					
13	37	61			133		
11	30	49					
32	48	64					
36	126	216			486		
32	54	76					186
26	127	228					
12	72	132					432
32	50	68					

Recognizing multiples of 6, 7, and 8

Circle the multiples of 6. For example, 6 x 2 = 12, so circle 12.

8   (12)   15   (18)   20   (24)

Circle the multiples of 6.

20	32	62	6	42	34
24	10	38	72	16	60
14	22	44	8	30	18
66	64	52	25	54	28

Circle the multiples of 7.

27	34	49	36	47	35
21	60	58	19	56	26
28	73	40	46	23	63
18	25	14	37	69	27

Circle the multiples of 8.

50	32	62	12	16	25
56	18	38	28	60	24
34	72	48	44	82	14
22	54	70	40	64	80

Circle the number that is a multiple of 6 and 7.

| 24 | 35 | 42 | 62 | 70 | 72 |

Circle the numbers that are multiples of both 6 and 8.

| 16 | 24 | 28 | 48 | 54 | 60 |

Try to work through these at lightning speed.

Factors of numbers from 1 to 30

Factors are numbers that divide evenly into a larger number.

Circle the factors of 4   ①   ②   3   ④

Write all the factors of each number.

The factors of 15 are

The factors of 12 are

The factors of 9 are

The factors of 20 are

The factors of 30 are

The factors of 22 are

The factors of 24 are

The factors of 26 are

Circle all the factors of each number.

Which numbers are factors of 14?   1 2 3 5 7 9 12 14

Which numbers are factors of 13?   1 3 4 5 6 7 8 9 10 12 13

Which numbers are factors of 7?   1 2 3 4 5 6 7

Which numbers are factors of 11?   1 2 3 4 5 6 7 8 9 10 11

Which numbers are factors of 6?   1 2 3 4 5 6

Which numbers are factors of 8?   1 2 3 4 5 6 7 8

Which numbers are factors of 17?   1 2 5 7 8 9 11 17

Which numbers are factors of 18?   1 2 3 4 5 6 8 9 10 12 18

Some numbers only have factors of 1 and themselves; they are called prime numbers. Write down all the prime numbers that are less than 30.

Recognizing equivalent fractions

Make each pair of fractions equal by writing a number in the box.

$$\frac{1}{2}\,^{\times 2}_{\times 2} = \frac{2}{4} \qquad \frac{1}{3}\,^{\times 3}_{\times 3} = \frac{3}{9}$$

Make each pair of fractions equal by writing a number in the box.

$$\frac{1}{5} = \frac{\square}{20} \qquad \frac{3}{4} = \frac{\square}{16} \qquad \frac{1}{3} = \frac{\square}{12}$$

$$\frac{2}{3} = \frac{\square}{9} \qquad \frac{6}{12} = \frac{\square}{8} \qquad \frac{4}{8} = \frac{\square}{2}$$

$$\frac{1}{2} = \frac{\square}{4} \qquad \frac{4}{12} = \frac{\square}{6} \qquad \frac{3}{5} = \frac{\square}{10}$$

$$\frac{1}{4} = \frac{\square}{8} \qquad \frac{6}{18} = \frac{\square}{9} \qquad \frac{4}{16} = \frac{\square}{4}$$

$$\frac{3}{9} = \frac{9}{\square} \qquad \frac{4}{10} = \frac{2}{\square} \qquad \frac{3}{4} = \frac{15}{\square}$$

$$\frac{4}{16} = \frac{2}{\square} \qquad \frac{9}{12} = \frac{3}{\square} \qquad \frac{6}{12} = \frac{2}{\square}$$

$$\frac{3}{5} = \frac{6}{\square} \qquad \frac{2}{6} = \frac{1}{\square} \qquad \frac{9}{12} = \frac{3}{\square}$$

Make each pair of fractions equal by writing a number in the box.

$$\frac{1}{2} = \frac{\square}{4} = \frac{3}{\square} = \frac{\square}{8} = \frac{\square}{10} = \frac{6}{\square}$$

$$\frac{1}{4} = \frac{2}{\square} = \frac{\square}{12} = \frac{4}{\square} = \frac{5}{\square} = \frac{\square}{24}$$

$$\frac{3}{4} = \frac{6}{\square} = \frac{\square}{12} = \frac{12}{\square} = \frac{\square}{20} = \frac{18}{\square}$$

$$\frac{1}{3} = \frac{\square}{6} = \frac{3}{\square} = \frac{4}{\square} = \frac{\square}{15} = \frac{6}{\square}$$

$$\frac{1}{5} = \frac{\square}{10} = \frac{\square}{15} = \frac{4}{\square} = \frac{5}{\square} = \frac{\square}{30}$$

$$\frac{2}{3} = \frac{\square}{6} = \frac{\square}{9} = \frac{8}{\square} = \frac{10}{\square} = \frac{12}{\square}$$

Ordering sets of numbers

Write the numbers in order, from least to greatest.

$2 \qquad 1\frac{1}{4} \qquad \frac{3}{4} \qquad \frac{1}{4} \qquad \frac{1}{2}$

$\boxed{\frac{1}{4}} \qquad \boxed{\frac{1}{2}} \qquad \boxed{\frac{3}{4}} \qquad \boxed{1\frac{1}{4}} \qquad \boxed{2}$

Write the numbers in order, from least to greatest.

2	$1\frac{1}{4}$	$3\frac{1}{2}$	$1\frac{1}{2}$	$2\frac{1}{2}$					
2	$1\frac{1}{2}$	1	$2\frac{1}{4}$	3					
4	$2\frac{1}{2}$	$1\frac{3}{4}$	$1\frac{1}{4}$	$3\frac{1}{2}$					
$6\frac{1}{2}$	$4\frac{1}{4}$	$1\frac{1}{2}$	$1\frac{1}{4}$	$2\frac{3}{4}$					
$4\frac{1}{4}$	$3\frac{1}{2}$	$2\frac{3}{4}$	$2\frac{1}{2}$	$3\frac{1}{4}$					
$3\frac{2}{3}$	$3\frac{1}{2}$	$3\frac{3}{4}$	$3\frac{1}{4}$	$4\frac{1}{4}$					
$3\frac{3}{4}$	$3\frac{1}{3}$	$4\frac{1}{4}$	$3\frac{2}{3}$	$3\frac{1}{2}$					
$6\frac{1}{2}$	$5\frac{2}{3}$	$6\frac{3}{4}$	$6\frac{1}{4}$	$5\frac{1}{2}$					
$13\frac{1}{2}$	$14\frac{3}{4}$	$14\frac{1}{2}$	$13\frac{3}{4}$	$12\frac{3}{4}$					
$10\frac{1}{5}$	$9\frac{3}{4}$	$10\frac{1}{2}$	$9\frac{1}{5}$	$9\frac{1}{2}$					
$7\frac{1}{3}$	$9\frac{3}{4}$	$10\frac{1}{2}$	$9\frac{1}{5}$	$9\frac{1}{2}$					

Rounding decimals

Round each decimal to the nearest whole number.

3.4	3
5.7	6
4.5	5

If the whole number has 5 after it, round to the next greatest whole number.

Get these done now!

Round each decimal to the nearest whole number.

1.1		6.2		7.3		4.8	
2.8		5.8		8.6		3.7	
1.3		3.2		8.5		6.4	
6.5		4.7		0.9		2.1	

Round each decimal to the nearest whole number.

22.2		14.8		27.5		33.8	
56.2		37.8		48.2		56.7	
75.4		81.8		66.5		71.6	
98.3		42.1		19.9		36.4	

Round each decimal to the nearest whole number.

110.4		126.3		107.1		111.9	
275.3		352.7		444.4		398.7	
359.8		276.8		348.3		599.8	
673.4		785.6		543.2		987.4	
867.2		686.8		743.2		845.5	

Adding two numbers

Find each sum.

```
  211        1
+ 214      482
  425    + 573
         1,055
```

I KNOW you can work it out!

Remember to regroup if you have to.

Find each sum.

```
  224        452        612
+ 365      + 227      + 345
_____      _____      _____
```

```
  485        563        535
+ 606      + 147      + 187
```

Write the answer in the box.

313 + 237 =   635 + 267 =

Write the missing number in the box.

```
  3 6 2      2   6      7   1      7 3 9
+ 4 1 9    + 5 8 1    + 2 6 4    + 2 4
  7   1      8 4 7        9 6        7 9
```

Find each sum.

Blade destroys 107 vampires in one night and 103 vampires the following night. How many vampires has he destroyed altogether?

Daredevil rounds up 134 criminals in one week. The next week, he rounds up 241. How many criminals has he rounded up during those two weeks?

Adding two numbers

Find each sum.

$$\begin{array}{r} 1{,}234 \\ +\ 5{,}642 \\ \hline 6{,}876 \end{array} \qquad \begin{array}{r} 3{,}794 \\ +\ 5{,}125 \\ \hline 8{,}919 \end{array}$$

Remember to regroup if you need to.

Find each sum.

$$\begin{array}{r} 2{,}552 \\ +\ 3{,}214 \\ \hline \end{array} \qquad \begin{array}{r} 5{,}325 \\ +\ 2{,}653 \\ \hline \end{array} \qquad \begin{array}{r} 2{,}471 \\ +\ 4{,}238 \\ \hline \end{array}$$

$$\begin{array}{r} 3{,}749 \\ +\ 2{,}471 \\ \hline \end{array} \qquad \begin{array}{r} 4{,}675 \\ +\ 3{,}916 \\ \hline \end{array} \qquad \begin{array}{r} 8{,}482 \\ +\ 1{,}349 \\ \hline \end{array}$$

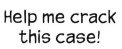

Help me crack this case!

Write the answer in the box.

2,431 + 4,621 =

1,342 + 3,264 =

1,738 + 4,261 =

2,013 + 3,642 =

Write the missing number in the box.

$$\begin{array}{r} \boxed{\ }\ 741 \\ +\ 2{,}94\boxed{\ } \\ \hline 6{,}684 \end{array} \qquad \begin{array}{r} \boxed{\ }\ 652 \\ +\ 3{,}2\boxed{\ }4 \\ \hline 4{,}926 \end{array} \qquad \begin{array}{r} 3{,}642 \\ +\ \boxed{\ }\ 83 \\ \hline 8{,}473 \end{array}$$

Find each sum.

On Monday, Phoenix helped 2,521 people to safety, and the Colossus helped 2,443 people. How many people did they help on Monday?

On Saturday, Nightcrawler rescued 4,476 people, and Wolverine rescued 3,478 people on Sunday. How many people did they rescue that weekend?

Subtracting three-digit numbers

Write the difference between the lines. Regroup if needed.

```
    644
  - 223
    421
```

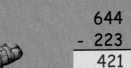

```
   6 11
   4̸7̸1 cm
  - 252 cm
    219 cm
```

Do you know the difference?

Write the difference between the lines.

```
    363          578          745          693
  - 151        - 334        - 524        - 481
  _____       _____       _____       _____
```

```
   480 ft       559 ft       750 ft       472 ft
 - 130 ft     - 218 ft     - 640 ft     - 362 ft
 _____     _____     _____     _____
```

Write the difference in the box.

364 - 122 = _____   799 - 354 = _____

$776 - $515 = _____ $840 - $730 = _____

$684 - $574 = _____ $220 - $120 = _____

Write the difference between the lines.

```
    463          584          661          494
  - 145        - 237        - 342        - 185
  _____       _____       _____       _____
```

```
    325          837          468          852
  - 116        - 719        - 209        - 329
  _____       _____       _____       _____
```

Find the answer to each problem.

Spider-Man shoots 234 webs, but 127
are destroyed. How many webs are left?   _____

Spider-Man has 860 web cartridges. 420
are stolen. How many cartridges remain?   _____

Subtracting three-digit numbers

Write the difference between the lines.

624 m	419 m	747 m
- 263 m	- 137 m	- 456 m

614	826	521	815 m
- 407	- 727	- 355	- 193 m

Write the difference in the box.

516 - 308 =

748 - 339 =

631 - 542 =

477 - 198 =

Write the difference between the lines.

535	715	312	924
- 247	- 518	- 113	- 528

Write the missing numbers in the box.

7 2 3	6 ☐ 2	4 ☐ 6	5 3 2
- 1 2 ☐	- 3 1 7	- 3 1 7	- ☐ 5
5 9 5	3 4 5	9 9	3 4 7

Find the answer to each problem.

Mister Fantastic gets $137 million to fund his starship project. The project costs $260 million. How much more funding does he need?

There are 664 people involved in the starship project. 276 are building computers. How many are taking part in other activities?

15

Adding decimals

Write the answer between the lines. Line up the decimal points. Write zeros as needed.

$6.25
+ $2.60
$8.85

3.35 m
+ 3.50 m
6.85 m

Write the answer between the lines.

$3.25
+ $4.50
_____

$6.50
+ $2.25
_____

$3.35
+ $1.50
_____

$6.55
+ $2.45
_____

$4.15
+ $4.75
_____

$3.50
+ $3.95
_____

4.50 m
+ 2.35 m
_____

3.60 m
+ 4.15 m
_____

7.30 m
+ 1.65 m
_____

7.15 m
+ 2.20 m
_____

3.30 m
+ 6.55 m
_____

5.20 m
+ 1.75 m
_____

You have to be good at math to time travel.

Write the sum in the box.

$6.25 + $3.30 =

$7.15 + $2.50 =

$6.35 + $2.30 =

$6.20 + $2.65 =

$3.45 + $6.10 =

$7.45 + $1.50 =

Find the answer to each problem.

On Monday Doctor Strange travels forward in time by 1.90 days. On Tuesday he fast forwards another 4.75 days. How many days ahead is he now?

Doctor Strange travels another 2.13 days forward. How many days ahead is he now?

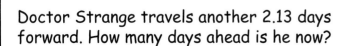

Adding decimals

Write the answer between the lines. Line up the decimal points. Write zeros as needed.

$3.35
+ $5.55
$8.90

4.45 m
+ 1.25 m
5.70 m

Write the sum between the lines.

$3.35	$7.60	$4.45
+ $5.55	+ $3.25	+ $1.50
_____	_____	_____

| $4.55 | $7.15 | $3.50 |
| + $4.35 | + $2.75 | + $2.95 |

| 4.50 m | 5.60 m | 3.30 m |
| + 2.35 m | + 2.05 m | + 1.55 m |

| 7.25 m | 4.40 m | 6.30 m |
| + 2.20 m | + 6.55 m | + 1.75 m |

ROOOAR! I need your help to figure out these sums!

Write the sum in the box.

$4.75 + $3.30 = $1.50 + $4.15 = $5.45 + $2.30 =

$3.20 + $2.55 = $6.10 + $2.45 = $8.35 + $1.40 =

Work out the answer for each problem.

Max buys two Marvel comics that cost $3.55 and $2.95. How much does he spend?

Max buys two different comics that cost $3.25 and $2.75. How much does he spend altogether?

Subtracting decimals

Write the difference between the lines.

These sums are real beasts!

$7.55
- $2.20
$5.35

5.60 m
- 2.60 m
3.00 m

Write the difference between the lines.

$9.45
- $3.30

$7.60
- $7.20

$7.55
- $2.30

$6.35
- $3.25

$5.95
- $1.75

$6.55
- $2.40

Write the difference between the lines.

3.90 m
- 1.40 m

8.75 m
- 3.35 m

9.20 m
- 3.20 m

8.55 m
- 1.15 m

4.15 m
- 2.00 m

3.55 m
- 2.40 m

Write the difference in the box.

$6.15 - $1.10 =

$5.55 - $2.50 =

$7.75 - $4.30 =

$8.85 - $6.05 =

8.55 m - 2.30 m =

6.15 m - 4.05 m =

Find the answer to the problem.

Karen is given $15.00 for her birthday.
She buys an Avengers book for $9.55.
How much money does she have left?

If Karen had been given $12.00 for her birthday,
how much would she have left after buying the
Avengers book?

Subtracting decimals

Write the difference between the lines. Line up the decimal points. Write zeros as needed.

$$\begin{array}{r} {}^{5\ 13} \\ \$6.\cancel{35} \\ +\ \$2.40 \\ \hline \$3.95 \end{array}$$

$$\begin{array}{r} {}^{6\ 12} \\ 7.25\ m \\ +\ 1.65\ m \\ \hline 5.60\ m \end{array}$$

Write the difference between the lines.

$5.65 - $2.75	$7.45 - $3.65	$6.85 - $4.75
$3.15 - $1.25	$7.50 - $2.90	$4.15 - $1.75

I can handle whatever you throw at me!

Write the difference between the lines.

4.35 m - 2.55 m	7.25 m - 2.55 m	4.85 m - 2.95 m
5.45 m - 2.65 m	8.25 m - 2.30 m	7.30 m - 3.50 m

Write the difference in the box.

$6.25 - $3.50 =

$4.35 - $2.55 =

$8.20 - $3.30 =

$7.40 - $3.80 =

6.45 m - 2.55 m =

7.35 m - 3.55 m =

Find the answer to the problem.

Blade's sword is 3.55 metres long. He breaks off a piece 0.75 metres long. How long is his sword now?

I'm gonna make you pay for breaking my sword....

Multiplying by one-digit numbers

Find each product.
Multiply the ones.
Regroup if needed,
then multiply the tens.

$$\begin{array}{r} 22 \\ \times 2 \\ \hline 44 \end{array} \qquad \begin{array}{r} \overset{1}{2}6 \\ \times 3 \\ \hline 78 \end{array} \qquad \begin{array}{r} \overset{1}{4}4 \\ \times 4 \\ \hline 176 \end{array}$$

Find each product.

$$\begin{array}{r} 37 \\ \times 2 \\ \hline \end{array} \qquad \begin{array}{r} 19 \\ \times 2 \\ \hline \end{array} \qquad \begin{array}{r} 16 \\ \times 4 \\ \hline \end{array} \qquad \begin{array}{r} 32 \\ \times 3 \\ \hline \end{array}$$

$$\begin{array}{r} 21 \\ \times 3 \\ \hline \end{array} \qquad \begin{array}{r} 25 \\ \times 4 \\ \hline \end{array} \qquad \begin{array}{r} 16 \\ \times 6 \\ \hline \end{array} \qquad \begin{array}{r} 33 \\ \times 5 \\ \hline \end{array}$$

I've got a favor to ask! Help me find each product.

$$\begin{array}{r} 39 \\ \times 2 \\ \hline \end{array} \qquad \begin{array}{r} 24 \\ \times 2 \\ \hline \end{array} \qquad \begin{array}{r} 41 \\ \times 2 \\ \hline \end{array} \qquad \begin{array}{r} 36 \\ \times 3 \\ \hline \end{array}$$

$$\begin{array}{r} 29 \\ \times 3 \\ \hline \end{array} \qquad \begin{array}{r} 35 \\ \times 2 \\ \hline \end{array} \qquad \begin{array}{r} 28 \\ \times 3 \\ \hline \end{array} \qquad \begin{array}{r} 26 \\ \times 6 \\ \hline \end{array}$$

$$\begin{array}{r} 10 \\ \times 6 \\ \hline \end{array} \qquad \begin{array}{r} 30 \\ \times 2 \\ \hline \end{array} \qquad \begin{array}{r} 20 \\ \times 4 \\ \hline \end{array} \qquad \begin{array}{r} 50 \\ \times 3 \\ \hline \end{array}$$

Find the answer to each problem.

Magneto flies through the air at 150 miles per hour. Storm can fly at twice that speed. How fast can Storm travel?

Magneto's helmet is 30 cm tall. How tall will a pile of 4 helmets be?

Multiplying by one-digit numbers

Find each product.
Multiply the ones.
Regroup if needed,
then multiply the tens.

$$\begin{array}{r} 43 \\ \times\ 3 \\ \hline 129 \end{array} \qquad \overset{3}{\begin{array}{r} 76 \\ \times\ 6 \\ \hline 456 \end{array}} \qquad \overset{3}{\begin{array}{r} 35 \\ \times\ 7 \\ \hline 245 \end{array}}$$

Get me the products NOW!

Find each product.

$$\begin{array}{r} 46 \\ \times\ 8 \\ \hline \end{array} \qquad \begin{array}{r} 48 \\ \times\ 5 \\ \hline \end{array} \qquad \begin{array}{r} 40 \\ \times\ 7 \\ \hline \end{array} \qquad \begin{array}{r} 32 \\ \times\ 6 \\ \hline \end{array} \qquad \begin{array}{r} 36 \\ \times\ 9 \\ \hline \end{array}$$

$$\begin{array}{r} 54 \\ \times\ 4 \\ \hline \end{array} \qquad \begin{array}{r} 55 \\ \times\ 6 \\ \hline \end{array} \qquad \begin{array}{r} 58 \\ \times\ 7 \\ \hline \end{array} \qquad \begin{array}{r} 96 \\ \times\ 3 \\ \hline \end{array} \qquad \begin{array}{r} 42 \\ \times\ 9 \\ \hline \end{array}$$

$$\begin{array}{r} 82 \\ \times\ 3 \\ \hline \end{array} \qquad \begin{array}{r} 24 \\ \times\ 9 \\ \hline \end{array} \qquad \begin{array}{r} 81 \\ \times\ 7 \\ \hline \end{array} \qquad \begin{array}{r} 64 \\ \times\ 4 \\ \hline \end{array} \qquad \begin{array}{r} 52 \\ \times\ 6 \\ \hline \end{array}$$

$$\begin{array}{r} 37 \\ \times\ 7 \\ \hline \end{array} \qquad \begin{array}{r} 40 \\ \times\ 8 \\ \hline \end{array} \qquad \begin{array}{r} 50 \\ \times\ 3 \\ \hline \end{array} \qquad \begin{array}{r} 30 \\ \times\ 7 \\ \hline \end{array} \qquad \begin{array}{r} 20 \\ \times\ 9 \\ \hline \end{array}$$

$$\begin{array}{r} 27 \\ \times\ 5 \\ \hline \end{array} \qquad \begin{array}{r} 36 \\ \times\ 4 \\ \hline \end{array} \qquad \begin{array}{r} 21 \\ \times\ 6 \\ \hline \end{array} \qquad \begin{array}{r} 42 \\ \times\ 9 \\ \hline \end{array} \qquad \begin{array}{r} 57 \\ \times\ 2 \\ \hline \end{array}$$

Find the answer to the problem.

Colossus can wreck 48 cars an hour.
How many cars can he wreck in 6 hours?

A canister belt can hold 7 gas
canisters. How many canisters
can 28 belts hold?

21

Division with remainders

Find each quotient.

$$3\overline{)17}$$ $\quad$ 5 r 2
$\quad$ 15
$\quad\quad$ 2

$$4\overline{)30}$$ $\quad$ 7 r 2
$\quad$ 28
$\quad\quad$ 2

Find each quotient.

$3\overline{)35}$ $\qquad$ $4\overline{)46}$ $\qquad$ $3\overline{)22}$ $\qquad$ $5\overline{)38}$

$4\overline{)50}$ $\qquad$ $5\overline{)37}$ $\qquad$ $5\overline{)63}$ $\qquad$ $4\overline{)58}$

$2\overline{)37}$ $\qquad$ $4\overline{)67}$ $\qquad$ $7\overline{)75}$ $\qquad$ $2\overline{)99}$

$4\overline{)59}$ $\qquad$ $5\overline{)84}$ $\qquad$ $3\overline{)76}$ $\qquad$ $5\overline{)94}$

Write the answer in the box.

What is 37 divided by 4?

What is 78 divided by 5?

What is 46 divided by 3?

What is 53 divided by 2?

22

Division with remainders

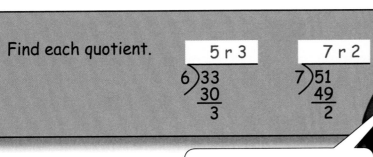

Find each quotient.

$$5 \text{ r } 3$$
$$6\overline{)33}$$
$$\underline{30}$$
$$3$$

$$7 \text{ r } 2$$
$$7\overline{)51}$$
$$\underline{49}$$
$$2$$

I'm on the case.

Find each quotient.

$6\overline{)43}$ $9\overline{)40}$ $8\overline{)75}$ $6\overline{)98}$

$7\overline{)53}$ $7\overline{)82}$ $9\overline{)53}$ $6\overline{)94}$

$7\overline{)65}$ $8\overline{)63}$ $6\overline{)26}$ $8\overline{)45}$

$9\overline{)92}$ $7\overline{)85}$ $8\overline{)66}$ $7\overline{)27}$

Write the answer in the box.

What is 97 divided by 7?

What is 84 divided by 8?

What is 75 divided by 6?

What is 64 divided by 9?

23

Real-life problems

Write the answers in the box.

Wolverine has $4.50 and he is given another $3.20. How much money does he have?

$7.70

```
  4.50
+ 3.20
  7.70
```

Longshot has 120 cards. He divides them equally among five people. How many cards does each person get?

24

```
      24
  5) 120
     10
     20
     20
      0
```

Write the answers in the box.

Daredevil buys a mask for $5.50 and a belt for $6.65. How much does he spend?

How much does he have left from $20?

The 32 children in a class donate $5 each to one of Captain America's charities. What is the total amount they raised?

Six of Thor's hammers laid end to end measure two yards. What fraction of a yard do two hammers measure?

Measure these!

Each of 5 Marvel superheroes has $18. How much do they have altogether?

If the above total were shared among 9 superheroes, how much would each have?

Real-life problems

The Goblin's glider is 16 in. wide. How wide will six gliders side by side be?

96 in.

$$\begin{array}{r} \overset{3}{16} \\ \times\ \ 6 \\ \hline 96 \end{array}$$

Rogue is 1.20 m tall. Her friend is 1.55 m tall. How much taller than Rogue is her friend?

0.35 m

$$\begin{array}{r} 1.55 \\ -\ 1.20 \\ \hline 0.35 \end{array}$$

Black Cat has a container of poison that contains 800 ml. She pours 320 ml into a glass, how much is left in the container?

One of Maggot's slugs weighs 280 g. Another weighs 130 g. How much heavier is the first slug than the smaller slug?

There are 7 shelves of Marvel comics. 5 shelves are 1.2 m long. 2 shelves are 1.5 m long. What is the total length of the 7 shelves?

Storm has read 5 pages of a 20-page comic book. If it has taken her 9 minutes, how long is it likely to take her to read the whole comic book?

If you want to get a move on, get a glider!

The Green Goblin is flying around the city. He circles the city 36 times in a minute. How many times does does he fly around the city in 30 seconds?

Areas of rectangles and squares

Find the area of this rectangle.

6 ft

24 ft²

4 ft

To find the area of a rectangle or square, multiply length (l) by width (w).
Area = l x w = 6 ft x 4 ft = 24 ft²

Find the area of these squares and rectangles.

Be careful! I'm here to check your answers.

3 in.

9 in.

in.²

4 yd

4 yd

yd²

2 ft

2 ft

ft²

8 cm

2 cm

cm²

4 in.

12 in.

in.²

5 mi

4 mi

mi²

3 yd

3 yd

yd²

26

Problems involving time

Find the answer to this problem.

The Ghost Rider leaves town at 7:30 A.M. and arrives at the next town at 10:45 A.M. How long did his journey take?

7:30 ➝ 10:30 = 3 h

10:30 ➝ 10:45 = 15 min

Total = 3 h 15 min

Find the answer to each problem.

An X-Men film starts at 7:00 P.M. and finishes at 8:45 P.M. How long is the film?

It takes Moira MacTaggert 1 hour 10 minutes to find a cure for a deadly virus. If she begins work at 10:35 A.M., at what time will she find the cure?

It takes Magneto 2 hours 25 minutes to change Earth's magnetic field. If he starts the operation at 1:25 P.M., at what time will he finish?

Gambit takes his helicopter in for repair at 7:00 A.M. It is finished at 1:50 P.M. How long did the repair take?

Professor X has to be at a meeting by 8:50 A.M. If he takes 1 hour 30 minutes to get ready, and the trip takes 35 minutes, at what time does he need to get up?

Bar graphs

Use this bar graph to answer each question.

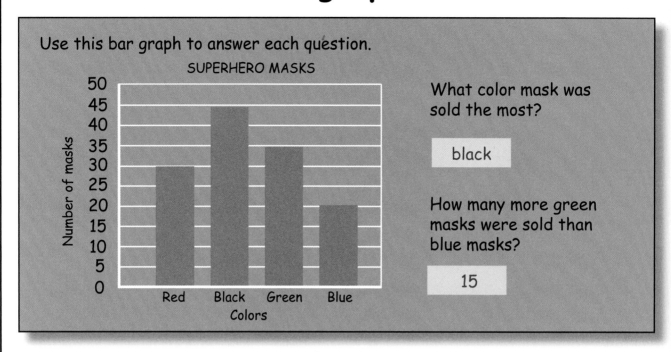

SUPERHERO MASKS

What color mask was sold the most?

black

How many more green masks were sold than blue masks?

15

Use the bar graphs to answer the questions.

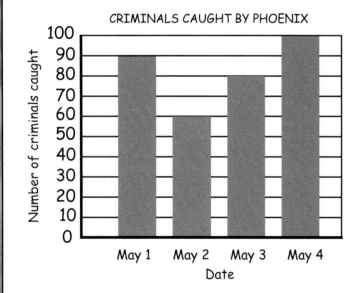

CRIMINALS CAUGHT BY PHOENIX

How many criminals did Phoenix catch on May 4?

How many more did she catch on May 3 than on May 2?

On which date were 90 criminals caught?

Can you read these graphs?

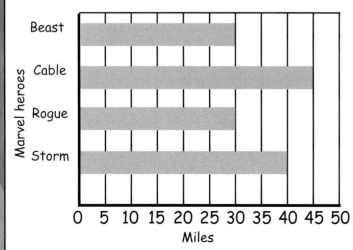

DISTANCE RUN BY MARVEL HEROES

Who ran 40 miles?

Who ran the same distance as Beast?

How much farther did Cable run than Rogue?

Probability

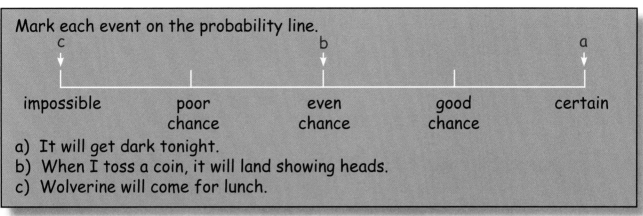

Mark each event on the probability line.

```
   c                              b                          a
   ↓                              ↓                          ↓
   ├──────────┬──────────┬──────────┬──────────┤
impossible    poor         even        good      certain
             chance       chance      chance
```

a) It will get dark tonight.
b) When I toss a coin, it will land showing heads.
c) Wolverine will come for lunch.

Mark each event on the probability line.

```
   ├──────────┬──────────┬──────────┬──────────┤
impossible    poor         even        good      certain
             chance       chance      chance
```

a) Snow will fall in July.
b) The sun will come up tomorrow.
c) A new baby will be a girl.
d) Iron Man will visit my school.
e) I will watch some television tonight.

Is anything certain in this world?

Mark each event on the probability line.

```
   ├──────────┬──────────┬──────────┬──────────┤
impossible    poor         even        good      certain
             chance       chance      chance
```

a) Magneto rolls a 6 on a number cube.
b) Magneto does not roll a 6 on a number cube.
c) Magneto rolls a number between 1 and 6.
d) Magneto rolls a 7 on a number cube.
e) Magneto rolls a 1, 2, or 3 on a number cube.

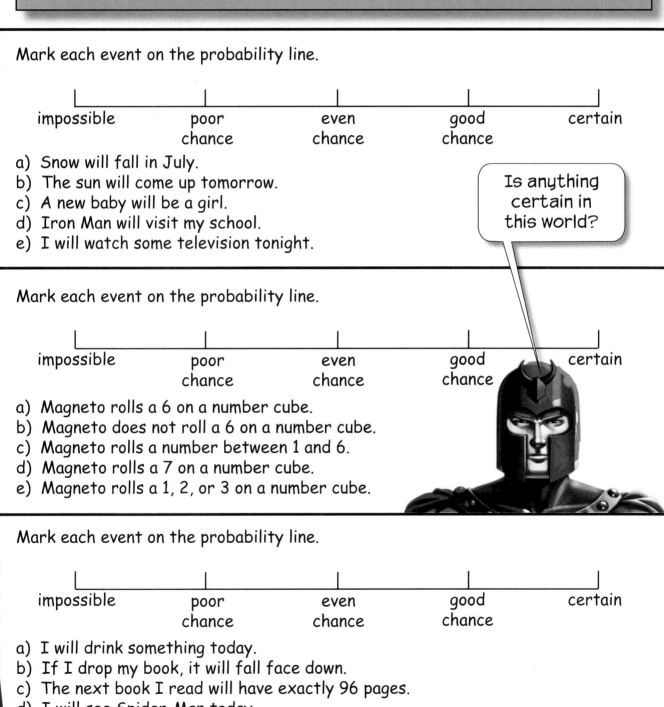

Mark each event on the probability line.

```
   ├──────────┬──────────┬──────────┬──────────┤
impossible    poor         even        good      certain
             chance       chance      chance
```

a) I will drink something today.
b) If I drop my book, it will fall face down.
c) The next book I read will have exactly 96 pages.
d) I will see Spider-Man today.
e) I will see a black car today.

Triangles

Look at these different triangles.

Hammer these triangles into shape!

Equilateral
(all sides equal;
is also isosceles)

Isosceles
(at least two
sides equal)

Scalene
(all sides
different)

Right angle
(may be isosceles or
scalene, but one angle
must be a right angle)

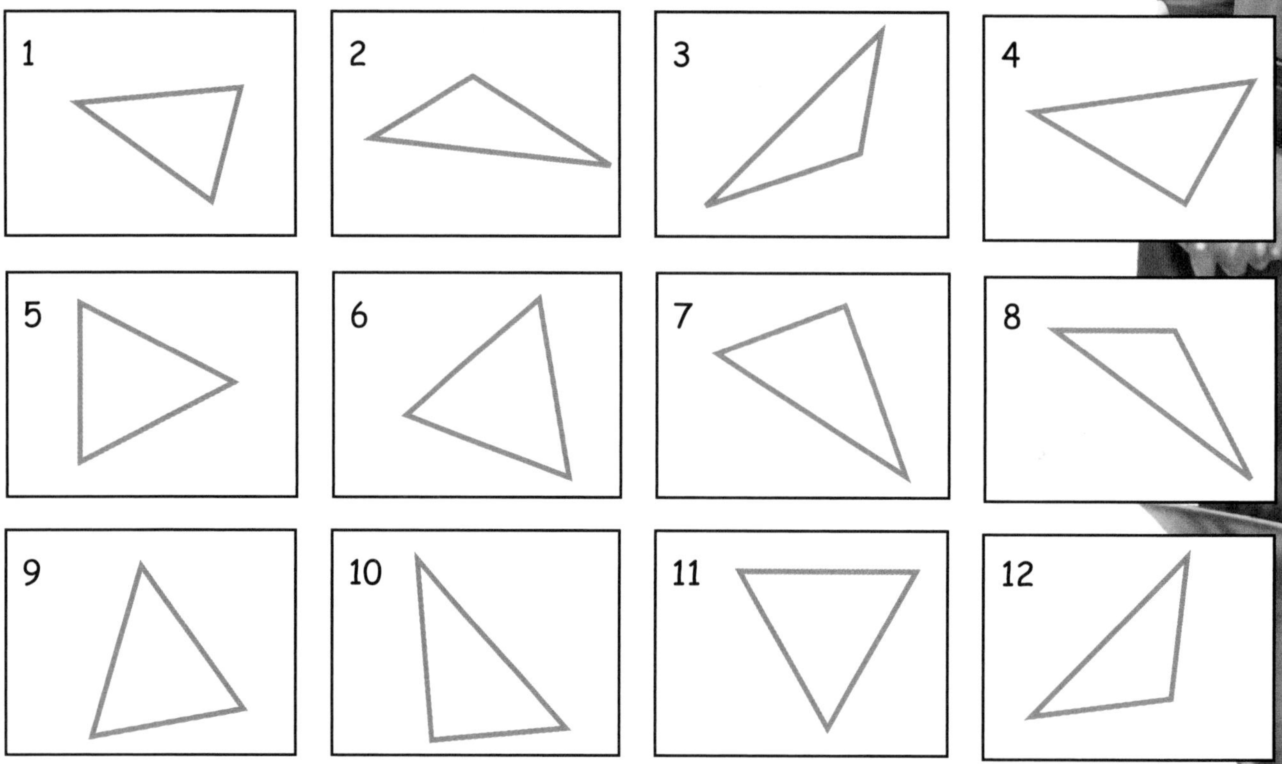

1	2	3	4

5	6	7	8

9	10	11	12

List the triangles that are:

Equilateral _____

Isoceles _____

Scalene _____

Right angle _____

30

Expanded form

What is the value of 3 in 3,208? 3,000

Write 7,143 in expanded form. (7 x 1,000) + (1 x 100) + (4 x 10) + (3 x 1)

7,000 + 100 + 40 + 3

What is the value of 3 in these numbers?

139		3,526		1,003	
37		37,641		399	

What is the value of 7 in these numbers?

927		7,423		278	
3,279		17,444		765	

What is the value of 5 in these numbers?

2,500		885		51	

Circle each number in which 6 has the value of 60.

6,782	926	860	362
161	676	865	60,000

Write these numbers in expanded form.

3,897

24,098

6,098

8,945

Speed trials

Write the answers as fast as you can, but get them right!

4 x 10 = 40   8 x 2 = 16

Write the answers as fast as you can, but get them right!

3 x 2 =	1 x 5 =	4 x 10 =	1 x 3 =
2 x 2 =	10 x 5 =	8 x 10 =	2 x 3 =
5 x 2 =	0 x 5 =	6 x 10 =	10 x 3 =
1 x 2 =	3 x 5 =	1 x 10 =	8 x 3 =
6 x 2 =	4 x 5 =	5 x 10 =	6 x 3 =
4 x 2 =	8 x 5 =	3 x 10 =	4 x 3 =
7 x 2 =	6 x 5 =	7 x 10 =	7 x 3 =
9 x 2 =	7 x 5 =	0 x 10 =	0 x 3 =
10 x 2 =	9 x 5 =	2 x 10 =	5 x 3 =
8 x 2 =	5 x 5 =	9 x 10 =	3 x 3 =
0 x 2 =	3 x 5 =	10 x 10 =	8 x 4 =
2 x 7 =	5 x 3 =	10 x 1 =	7 x 4 =
2 x 1 =	5 x 8 =	10 x 7 =	6 x 4 =
2 x 4 =	5 x 9 =	10 x 4 =	3 x 4 =
3 x 7 =	5 x 7 =	10 x 3 =	10 x 4 =
2 x 5 =	5 x 4 =	10 x 5 =	0 x 4 =
2 x 9 =	5 x 1 =	10 x 8 =	3 x 4 =
2 x 6 =	4 x 7 =	10 x 6 =	9 x 4 =
2 x 8 =	5 x 10 =	10 x 2 =	5 x 4 =
2 x 3 =	5 x 2 =	10 x 9 =	2 x 4 =

All the 3s

You will need to know these:

$1 \times 3 = 3$ $2 \times 3 = 6$ $3 \times 3 = 9$ $4 \times 3 = 12$

$5 \times 3 = 15$ $10 \times 3 = 30$

How many altogether?

6 sets of three are   six threes are $6 \times 3 =$

How many altogether?

7 sets of three are   seven threes are $7 \times 3 =$

How many altogether?

8 sets of three are   eight threes are $8 \times 3 =$

How many altogether?

9 sets of three are   nine threes are $9 \times 3 =$

All the 3s again

Cover the three times table with a sheet of paper so you can't see the numbers. Write the answers. Be as fast as you can, but get them right!

1 x 3 =	5 x 3 =	6 x 3 =
2 x 3 =	7 x 3 =	9 x 3 =
3 x 3 =	9 x 3 =	4 x 3 =
4 x 3 =	4 x 3 =	5 x 3 =
5 x 3 =	6 x 3 =	3 x 7 =
6 x 3 =	8 x 3 =	3 x 4 =
7 x 3 =	10 x 3 =	2 x 3 =
8 x 3 =	1 x 3 =	10 x 3 =
9 x 3 =	3 x 3 =	3 x 9 =
10 x 3 =	2 x 3 =	3 x 6 =
3 x 1 =	3 x 5 =	3 x 5 =
3 x 2 =	3 x 7 =	3 x 8 =
3 x 3 =	3 x 9 =	7 x 3 =
3 x 4 =	3 x 4 =	3 x 2 =
3 x 5 =	3 x 6 =	3 x 10 =
3 x 6 =	3 x 8 =	8 x 3 =
3 x 7 =	3 x 10 =	3 x 0 =
3 x 8 =	3 x 1 =	1 x 3 =
3 x 9 =	3 x 0 =	3 x 3 =
3 x 10 =	3 x 2 =	3 x 9 =

All the 4s

How many altogether?

6 sets of four are [ ]   six fours are [ ]   6 x 4 = [ ]

How many altogether?

7 sets of four are [ ]   seven fours are [ ]   7 x 4 = [ ]

How many altogether?

8 sets of four are [ ]   eight fours are [ ]   8 x 4 = [ ]

How many altogether?

9 sets of four are [ ]   nine fours are [ ]   9 x 4 = [ ]

All the 4s again

You should know all of the four times table by now.
1 x 4 = 4   2 x 4 = 8   3 x 4 = 12   4 x 4 = 16   5 x 4 = 20
6 x 4 = 24   7 x 4 = 28   8 x 4 = 32   9 x 4 = 36   10 x 4 = 40
Say these to yourself a few times.

Cover the four times table with a sheet of paper so you can't see the numbers.
Write the answers. Be as fast as you can, but get them right!

1 x 4 =	5 x 4 =	6 x 4 =
2 x 4 =	7 x 4 =	9 x 4 =
3 x 4 =	9 x 4 =	4 x 1 =
4 x 4 =	3 x 4 =	5 x 4 =
5 x 4 =	6 x 4 =	4 x 7 =
6 x 4 =	8 x 4 =	3 x 4 =
7 x 4 =	10 x 4 =	2 x 4 =
8 x 4 =	1 x 4 =	10 x 4 =
9 x 4 =	4 x 4 =	4 x 3 =
10 x 4 =	2 x 4 =	4 x 6 =
4 x 1 =	4 x 5 =	4 x 5 =
4 x 2 =	4 x 7 =	4 x 8 =
4 x 3 =	4 x 9 =	7 x 4 =
4 x 4 =	4 x 4 =	4 x 2 =
4 x 5 =	4 x 6 =	4 x 10 =
4 x 6 =	4 x 8 =	8 x 4 =
4 x 7 =	4 x 10 =	4 x 0 =
4 x 8 =	4 x 1 =	1 x 4 =
4 x 9 =	4 x 0 =	4 x 4 =
4 x 10 =	4 x 2 =	4 x 9 =

Speed trials

You should know all of the 1, 2, 3, 4, 5, and 10 times tables by now, but how quickly can you do them? Ask someone to time you as you do this page. Remember, you must be fast but also correct.

4 x 2 =	6 x 3 =	
8 x 3 =	3 x 4 =	
7 x 4 =	7 x 5 =	7 x 2 =
6 x 5 =	3 x 10 =	6 x 3 =
8 x 10 =	1 x 2 =	5 x 4 =
8 x 2 =	7 x 3 =	4 x 5 =
5 x 3 =	4 x 4 =	3 x 10 =
9 x 4 =	6 x 5 =	2 x 2 =
5 x 5 =	4 x 10 =	1 x 3 =
7 x 10 =	6 x 2 =	0 x 4 =
0 x 2 =	5 x 3 =	10 x 5 =
4 x 3 =	8 x 4 =	9 x 2 =
6 x 4 =	0 x 5 =	8 x 3 =
3 x 5 =	2 x 10 =	7 x 4 =
4 x 10 =	7 x 2 =	6 x 5 =
7 x 2 =	8 x 3 =	5 x 10 =
3 x 3 =	9 x 4 =	4 x 0 =
2 x 4 =	5 x 5 =	3 x 2 =
7 x 5 =	7 x 10 =	2 x 8 =
9 x 10 =	5 x 2 =	1 x 9 =

Some of the 6s

You should already know parts of the 6 times table because they are parts of the 1, 2, 3, 4, 5, and 10 times tables.

1 x 6 = 6   2 x 6 = 12   3 x 6 = 18

4 x 6 = 24   5 x 6 = 30   10 x 6 = 60

Find out if you can remember them quickly and correctly.

Cover the six times table with paper so you can't see the numbers. Write the answers as quickly as you can.

What are two sixes?   What are five sixes?

What are three sixes?   What are ten sixes?

What is one six?   What are four sixes?

Write the answers as quickly as you can.

How many sixes make 30?   How many sixes make 6?

How many sixes make 12?   How many sixes make 18?

How many sixes make 24?   How many sixes make 60?

Write the answers as quickly as you can.

Multiply six by three.   Multiply six by two.

Multiply six by five.   Multiply six by four.

Multiply six by one.   Multiply six by ten.

Write the answers as quickly as you can.

2 x 6 =   10 x 6 =   4 x 6 =

5 x 6 =   3 x 6 =   1 x 6 =

Daredevil uses his radar sense to detect four hidden bugs. Each eavesdropping bug emits five pulses. How many pulses are there in all?

The rest of the 6s

You need to learn these:

$$6 \times 6 = 36 \qquad 7 \times 6 = 42$$
$$8 \times 6 = 48 \qquad 9 \times 6 = 54$$

Have no fear! It's only a question of adding 6!

This work will help you remember the 6 times table.

Complete these sequences.

6   12   18   24   30

$5 \times 6 = 30$ so $6 \times 6 = 30$ plus another $6 =$

18   24   30

$6 \times 6 = 36$ so $7 \times 6 = 36$ plus another $6 =$

6   12   18   48   60

$7 \times 6 = 42$ so $8 \times 6 = 42$ plus another $6 =$

6   12   18   24   30

$8 \times 6 = 48$ so $9 \times 6 = 48$ plus another $6 =$

    24   42   60

Test yourself on the rest of the 6 times table.
Cover the above part of the page with a sheet of paper.

What are six sixes?   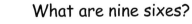   What are eight sixes?

What are seven sixes?   What are nine sixes?

$8 \times 6 =$ $7 \times 6 =$ $6 \times 6 =$ $9 \times 6 =$

39

Practice the 6s

You should know all of the 6 times table now, but how quickly can you remember it? Ask someone to time you as you do this page. Remember, you must be fast but also correct.

1 x 6 =	2 x 6 =	7 x 6 =
2 x 6 =	4 x 6 =	3 x 6 =
3 x 6 =	6 x 6 =	9 x 6 =
4 x 6 =	8 x 6 =	6 x 4 =
5 x 6 =	10 x 6 =	1 x 6 =
6 x 6 =	1 x 6 =	6 x 2 =
7 x 6 =	3 x 6 =	6 x 8 =
8 x 6 =	5 x 6 =	0 x 6 =
9 x 6 =	7 x 6 =	6 x 3 =
10 x 6 =	9 x 6 =	5 x 6 =
6 x 1 =	6 x 3 =	6 x 7 =
6 x 2 =	6 x 5 =	2 x 6 =
6 x 3 =	6 x 7 =	6 x 9 =
6 x 4 =	6 x 9 =	4 x 6 =
6 x 5 =	6 x 2 =	8 x 6 =
6 x 6 =	6 x 4 =	10 x 6 =
6 x 7 =	6 x 6 =	6 x 5 =
6 x 8 =	6 x 8 =	6 x 0 =
6 x 9 =	6 x 10 =	6 x 1 =
6 x 10 =	6 x 0 =	6 x 6 =

Speed trials

You should know all of the 1, 2, 3, 4, 5, 6, and 10 times tables by now, but how quickly can you remember them?
Ask someone to time you as you do this page.
Remember, you must be fast but also correct.

4 x 6 =	6 x 3 =	
5 x 3 =	8 x 6 =	
7 x 3 =	6 x 6 =	3 x 7 =
6 x 5 =	3 x 10 =	6 x 6 =
6 x 10 =	6 x 2 =	5 x 4 =
8 x 2 =	7 x 3 =	4 x 6 =
5 x 3 =	4 x 6 =	3 x 6 =
9 x 6 =	6 x 5 =	2 x 6 =
5 x 5 =	6 x 10 =	6 x 3 =
7 x 6 =	6 x 2 =	0 x 6 =
0 x 2 =	5 x 3 =	10 x 5 =
6 x 3 =	8 x 4 =	6 x 2 =
6 x 6 =	0 x 6 =	8 x 3 =
3 x 5 =	5 x 10 =	7 x 6 =
4 x 10 =	7 x 6 =	6 x 5 =
7 x 10 =	8 x 3 =	5 x 10 =
3 x 6 =	9 x 6 =	6 x 0 =
2 x 4 =	5 x 5 =	3 x 10 =
6 x 9 =	7 x 10 =	2 x 8 =
9 x 10 =	5 x 6 =	1 x 8 =

Some of the 7s

You should already know parts of the 7 times table because they are parts of the 1, 2, 3, 4, 5, 6, and 10 times tables.

$1 \times 7 = 7$ $2 \times 7 = 14$ $3 \times 7 = 21$ $4 \times 7 = 28$

$5 \times 7 = 35$ $6 \times 7 = 42$ $10 \times 7 = 70$

Find out if you can remember them quickly and correctly.

If you want to be fantastic, get practicing!

Cover the six times table with paper so you can't see the numbers. Write the answers as quickly as you can.

What are three sevens?   What are four sevens?

What are two sevens?   What are six sevens?

What are five sevens?   What are ten sevens?

Write the answers as quickly as you can.

How many sevens make 14?   How many sevens make 28?

How many sevens make 35?   How many sevens make 21?

How many sevens make 70?   How many sevens make 42?

Write the answers as quickly as you can.

Multiply seven by three.   Multiply seven by six.

Multiply seven by five.   Multiply seven by two.

Multiply seven by four.   Multiply seven by ten.

Write the answers as quickly as you can.

$10 \times 7 =$ $4 \times 7 =$ $5 \times 7 =$

$3 \times 7 =$ $6 \times 7 =$ $2 \times 7 =$

The Invisible Woman generates five invisible force fields. Inside each force field are seven people. How many invisible people altogether?

The rest of the 7s

You should now know all of the 1, 2, 3, 4, 5, 6, and 10 times tables. You need to learn only these parts of the seven times table.

7 x 7 = 49   7 x 8 = 56   7 x 9 = 63

ROARRR!!!!

This work will help you remember the 7 times table.

Complete these sequences.

7   14   21   28   35   42

6 x 7 = 42   so   7 x 7 = 42 plus another 7 =

21   28   35

7 x 7 = 49   so   8 x 7 = 49 plus another 7 =

7   14   21   56   70

8 x 7 = 56   so   9 x 7 = 56 plus another 7 =

7   21   28   35

Test yourself on the rest of the 7 times table.
Cover the section above with a sheet of paper.

What are seven sevens?   What are eight sevens?

What are nine sevens?   What are six sevens?

8 x 7 =   7 x 7 =   9 x 7 =   6 x 7 =

Carnage uses his symbiotic skin to generate nine snares. Each snare captures seven enemies. How many enemies has he snared in total?

Inside one of these snares, each trapped enemy carries seven sonic devices. How many sonic devices in total are inside that snare?

43

Practice the 7s

BLAZE THROUGH THESE!

You should know all of the 7 times table now, but how quickly can you remember it? Ask someone to time you as you do this page. Remember, you must be fast but correct.

1 x 7 =	2 x 7 =	7 x 6 =
2 x 7 =	4 x 7 =	3 x 7 =
3 x 7 =	6 x 7 =	9 x 7 =
4 x 7 =	8 x 7 =	7 x 4 =
5 x 7 =	10 x 7 =	1 x 7 =
6 x 7 =	1 x 7 =	7 x 2 =
7 x 7 =	3 x 7 =	7 x 8 =
8 x 7 =	5 x 7 =	0 x 7 =
9 x 7 =	7 x 7 =	7 x 3 =
10 x 7 =	9 x 7 =	5 x 7 =
7 x 1 =	7 x 3 =	7 x 7 =
7 x 2 =	7 x 5 =	2 x 7 =
7 x 3 =	7 x 7 =	7 x 9 =
7 x 4 =	7 x 9 =	4 x 7 =
7 x 5 =	7 x 2 =	8 x 7 =
7 x 6 =	7 x 4 =	10 x 7 =
7 x 7 =	7 x 6 =	7 x 5 =
7 x 8 =	7 x 8 =	7 x 0 =
7 x 9 =	7 x 10 =	7 x 1 =
7 x 10 =	7 x 0 =	6 x 7 =

Speed trials

You should know all of the 1, 2, 3, 4, 5, 6, 7, and 10 times tables now, but how quickly can you remember them? Ask someone to time you as you do this page. Remember, you must be fast but also correct.

4 x 7 =	7 x 3 =	9 x 7 =
5 x 10 =	8 x 7 =	7 x 6 =
7 x 5 =	6 x 6 =	8 x 3 =
6 x 5 =	5 x 10 =	6 x 6 =
8 x 7 =	6 x 3 =	7 x 4 =
5 x 8 =	7 x 5 =	4 x 6 =
9 x 6 =	4 x 6 =	3 x 7 =
5 x 7 =	6 x 5 =	2 x 8 =
7 x 6 =	7 x 10 =	7 x 3 =
0 x 5 =	6 x 7 =	0 x 6 =
6 x 3 =	5 x 7 =	10 x 7 =
6 x 7 =	8 x 4 =	6 x 2 =
3 x 5 =	0 x 7 =	8 x 7 =
4 x 7 =	5 x 8 =	7 x 7 =
7 x 10 =	7 x 6 =	6 x 5 =
7 x 8 =	8 x 3 =	5 x 10 =
2 x 7 =	9 x 6 =	7 x 0 =
4 x 9 =	7 x 7 =	3 x 10 =
9 x 10 =	7 x 10 =	2 x 7 =
6 x 10 =	5 x 6 =	7 x 8 =

Some of the 8s

Let's get busy. Answer these as quickly as you can.

Cover the eight times table with paper so you can't see the numbers. Write the answers as quickly as you can.

What are three eights?

What are four eights?

What are two eights?

What are six eights?

What are five eights?

What are ten eights?

Write the answers as quickly as you can.

How many eights make 16?

How many eights make 24?

How many eights make 40?

How many eights make 56?

How many eights make 80?

How many eights make 48?

Write the answers as quickly as you can.

Multiply eight by three.

Multiply eight by six.

Multiply eight by five.

Multiply eight by two.

Multiply eight by four.

Multiply eight by ten.

Write the answers as quickly as you can.

$6 \times 8 =$ $2 \times 8 =$ $7 \times 8 =$

$4 \times 8 =$ $5 \times 8 =$ $3 \times 8 =$

Kingpin buys eight newspapers to read about his enemy Daredevil. Each newspaper has six stories about Daredevil. How many stories in all?

The rest of the 8s

You need to learn only these parts of the eight times table.

8 x 8 = 64   9 x 8 = 72

This work will help you remember the 8 times table.

Complete these sequences.

8   16   24   32   40   48

7 x 8 = 56   so   8 x 8 = 56 plus another 8 =

24   32   40

8 x 8 = 64   so   9 x 8 = 64 plus another 8 =

8   16   24   64   80

8   24   40

Test yourself on the rest of the 8 times table.
Cover the section above with a sheet of paper.

What are seven eights?   What are eight eights?

What are nine eights?   What are eight sixes?

8 x 8 =   9 x 8 =   8 x 9 =   10 x 8 =

What number multiplied by 8 gives the answer 72?

A number multiplied by 8 gives the answer 64.
What is the number?

A shopkeeper arranges Doctor Strange
masks in piles of 8. How many masks will
there be in 10 piles?

How many 8s make 56?

47

Practice the 8s

You should know all of the 8 times table now, but how quickly can you remember it? Ask someone to time you as you do this page. Be fast but also correct.

1 x 8 =	2 x 8 =	8 x 6 =
2 x 8 =	4 x 8 =	3 x 8 =
3 x 8 =	6 x 8 =	9 x 8 =
4 x 8 =	8 x 8 =	8 x 4 =
5 x 8 =	10 x 8 =	1 x 8 =
6 x 8 =	1 x 8 =	8 x 2 =
7 x 8 =	3 x 8 =	7 x 8 =
8 x 8 =	5 x 8 =	0 x 8 =
9 x 8 =	7 x 8 =	8 x 3 =
10 x 8 =	9 x 8 =	5 x 8 =
8 x 1 =	8 x 3 =	8 x 8 =
8 x 2 =	8 x 5 =	2 x 8 =
8 x 3 =	8 x 7 =	8 x 9 =
8 x 4 =	8 x 9 =	4 x 8 =
8 x 5 =	8 x 2 =	8 x 6 =
8 x 6 =	8 x 4 =	10 x 8 =
8 x 7 =	8 x 6 =	8 x 5 =
8 x 8 =	8 x 8 =	8 x 0 =
8 x 9 =	8 x 10 =	8 x 1 =
8 x 10 =	8 x 0 =	6 x 8 =

Speed trials

You should know all of the 1, 2, 3, 4, 5, 6, 7, 8, and 10 times tables now, but how quickly can you remember them? Ask someone to time you as you do this page. Be fast but also correct.

Let's swing into action on this now!

4 x 8 =	7 x 8 =	
5 x 10 =	8 x 7 =	
7 x 8 =	6 x 8 =	7 x 6 =
8 x 5 =	8 x 10 =	8 x 3 =
6 x 10 =	6 x 3 =	8 x 8 =
8 x 7 =	7 x 7 =	7 x 4 =
5 x 8 =	5 x 6 =	4 x 8 =
9 x 8 =	6 x 7 =	3 x 7 =
8 x 8 =	7 x 10 =	2 x 8 =
7 x 6 =	6 x 9 =	7 x 3 =
7 x 5 =	5 x 8 =	0 x 8 =
6 x 8 =	8 x 4 =	10 x 8 =
6 x 7 =	0 x 8 =	6 x 2 =
5 x 7 =	5 x 9 =	8 x 6 =
8 x 4 =	7 x 6 =	7 x 8 =
7 x 10 =	8 x 3 =	6 x 5 =
2 x 8 =	9 x 6 =	8 x 10 =
4 x 7 =	8 x 6 =	8 x 7 =
6 x 9 =	9 x 10 =	5 x 10 =
9 x 10 =	6 x 6 =	8 x 2 =
		8 x 9 =

49

Some of the 9s

You should already know nearly all of the 9 times table because it is part of the 1, 2, 3, 4, 5, 6, 7, 8, and 10 times tables.

$1 \times 9 = 9$ $2 \times 9 = 18$ $3 \times 9 = 27$ $4 \times 9 = 36$ $5 \times 9 = 45$

$6 \times 9 = 54$ $7 \times 9 = 63$ $8 \times 9 = 72$ $10 \times 9 = 90$

Find out if you can remember them quickly and correctly.

What are three nines?   What are eight nines?

What are seven nines?   What are four nines?

What are six nines?   What are five nines?

Write the answers as quickly as you can.

How many nines equal 18?   How many nines equal 54?

How many nines equal 90?   How many nines equal 63?

How many nines equal 72?   How many nines equal 36?

Write the answers as quickly as you can.

Multiply nine by seven.   Multiply nine by ten.

Multiply nine by two.   Multiply nine by five.

Multiply nine by six.   Multiply nine by four.

Multiply nine by three.   Multiply nine by eight.

Write the answers as quickly as you can.

$6 \times 9 =$ $2 \times 9 =$

$5 \times 9 =$ $3 \times 9 =$

$0 \times 9 =$ $7 \times 9 =$

With one optic blast from my ruby quartz visor, I'll figure these out.

The rest of the 9s

You need to learn only this part of the nine times table.

$$9 \times 9 = 81$$

This work will help you remember the nine times table.

Complete these sequences.

9   18   27   36   45   54   ▢   ▢   ▢   ▢

8 x 9 = 72 so 9 x 9 = 72 plus another 9 = ▢

27   36   45   ▢   ▢   ▢   ▢   ▢

9   18   27   ▢   ▢   ▢   ▢   72   ▢   90

9   ▢   27   ▢   45   ▢   ▢   ▢   ▢   ▢

Look for a pattern in the nine times table.

1 x 9 = 09
2 x 9 = 18
3 x 9 = 27
4 x 9 = 36
5 x 9 = 45
6 x 9 = 54
7 x 9 = 63
8 x 9 = 72
9 x 9 = 81
10 x 9 = 90

I can't see any patterns. Can you?

Write down any patterns you can see. (There are more than one.)

_____
_____
_____
_____
_____
_____

Practice the 9s

HA!

You should know all of the 9 times table now, but how quickly can you remember it? Ask someone to time you as you do this page. Be fast and correct.

1 x 9 =	2 x 9 =	9 x 6 =
2 x 9 =	4 x 9 =	3 x 9 =
3 x 9 =	6 x 9 =	9 x 9 =
4 x 9 =	8 x 9 =	9 x 4 =
5 x 9 =	10 x 9 =	1 x 9 =
6 x 9 =	1 x 9 =	9 x 2 =
7 x 9 =	3 x 9 =	7 x 9 =
8 x 9 =	5 x 9 =	0 x 9 =
9 x 9 =	7 x 9 =	9 x 3 =
10 x 9 =	9 x 9 =	5 x 9 =
9 x 1 =	9 x 3 =	9 x 9 =
9 x 2 =	9 x 5 =	2 x 9 =
9 x 3 =	9 x 7 =	8 x 9 =
9 x 4 =	9 x 2 =	4 x 9 =
9 x 5 =	9 x 4 =	9 x 7 =
9 x 6 =	9 x 6 =	10 x 9 =
9 x 7 =	9 x 8 =	9 x 5 =
9 x 8 =	9 x 10 =	9 x 0 =
9 x 9 =	9 x 0 =	9 x 1 =
9 x 10 =	9 x 9 =	6 x 9 =

Speed trials

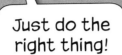

Just do the right thing!

You should know all of the times tables now, but how quickly can you remember them? Ask someone to time you as you do this page. Be fast and correct.

6 x 8 =	4 x 8 =	8 x 10 =
9 x 10 =	9 x 8 =	7 x 9 =
5 x 8 =	6 x 6 =	8 x 5 =
7 x 5 =	8 x 9 =	8 x 7 =
6 x 4 =	6 x 4 =	7 x 4 =
8 x 8 =	7 x 3 =	4 x 9 =
5 x 10 =	5 x 9 =	6 x 7 =
9 x 8 =	6 x 8 =	4 x 6 =
8 x 3 =	7 x 7 =	7 x 8 =
7 x 7 =	6 x 9 =	6 x 9 =
9 x 5 =	7 x 8 =	10 x 8 =
4 x 8 =	8 x 4 =	6 x 5 =
6 x 7 =	0 x 9 =	8 x 8 =
2 x 9 =	10 x 10 =	7 x 6 =
8 x 4 =	7 x 6 =	6 x 8 =
7 x 10 =	8 x 7 =	9 x 10 =
2 x 8 =	9 x 6 =	8 x 4 =
4 x 7 =	8 x 6 =	7 x 10 =
6 x 9 =	9 x 9 =	5 x 8 =
9 x 9 =	6 x 7 =	8 x 9 =

Times tables for division

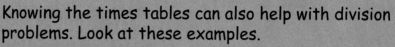

Knowing the times tables can also help with division problems. Look at these examples.

3 x 6 = 18 which means that 18 ÷ 3 = 6 and 18 ÷ 6 = 3
4 x 5 = 20 which means that 20 ÷ 4 = 5 and 20 ÷ 5 = 4
9 x 3 = 27 which means that 27 ÷ 3 = 9 and 27 ÷ 9 = 3

Help me investigate these problems and get to the truth.

Use your knowledge of the times tables to work these division problems.

5 x 8 = 40 which means that 40 ÷ 5 =   and that 40 ÷ 8 =

5 x 7 = 35 which means that 35 ÷ 5 =   and that 35 ÷ 7 =

5 x 3 = 15 which means that 15 ÷ 3 =   and that 15 ÷ 5 =

4 x 3 = 12 which means that 12 ÷ 4 =   and that 12 ÷ 3 =

3 x 10 = 30 which means that 30 ÷ 3 =   and that 30 ÷ 10 =

8 x 4 = 32 which means that 32 ÷ 4 =   and that 32 ÷ 8 =

3 x 9 = 27 which means that 27 ÷ 3 =   and that 27 ÷ 9 =

4 x 10 = 40 which means that 40 ÷ 4 =   and that 40 ÷ 10 =

These division problems help practice the 3 and 4 times tables.

28 ÷ 4 =   18 ÷ 3 =   16 ÷ 4 =

24 ÷ 4 =   27 ÷ 3 =   30 ÷ 3 =

12 ÷ 3 =   15 ÷ 3 =   20 ÷ 4 =

24 ÷ 3 =   32 ÷ 4 =   21 ÷ 3 =

How many fours in 24?   How many sevens in 28?

Divide 36 by four.   Divide 27 by nine.

How many threes in 21?   How many eights in 48?

Times tables for division

This page will help you remember times tables by dividing by 2, 3, 4, 5, and 10.

$20 \div 5 = \boxed{4}$ $18 \div 3 = \boxed{6}$ $60 \div 10 = \boxed{6}$

Complete the problems.

$40 \div 8 =$	$16 \div 2 =$	
$35 \div 5 =$	$21 \div 3 =$	
$24 \div 4 =$	$28 \div 4 =$	$14 \div 2 =$
$45 \div 5 =$	$25 \div 5 =$	$12 \div 3 =$
$10 \div 2 =$	$20 \div 10 =$	$12 \div 4 =$
$40 \div 10 =$	$20 \div 2 =$	$20 \div 2 =$
$6 \div 2 =$	$18 \div 3 =$	$20 \div 4 =$
$24 \div 3 =$	$32 \div 4 =$	$20 \div 5 =$
$30 \div 5 =$	$40 \div 5 =$	$20 \div 10 =$
$30 \div 10 =$	$80 \div 10 =$	$18 \div 2 =$
$40 \div 5 =$	$6 \div 2 =$	$18 \div 3 =$
$21 \div 3 =$	$15 \div 3 =$	$15 \div 3 =$
$14 \div 2 =$	$24 \div 4 =$	$15 \div 5 =$
$27 \div 3 =$	$15 \div 5 =$	$24 \div 3 =$
$100 \div 10 =$	$10 \div 10 =$	$24 \div 4 =$
$15 \div 5 =$	$4 \div 2 =$	$50 \div 5 =$
$15 \div 3 =$	$4 \div 4 =$	$50 \div 10 =$
$20 \div 5 =$	$10 \div 5 =$	$30 \div 3 =$
$20 \div 4 =$	$90 \div 10 =$	$30 \div 5 =$
$16 \div 2 =$	$9 \div 3 =$	$30 \div 10 =$

Times tables for division

This page will help you remember times tables by dividing by 2, 3, 4, 5, 6, and 10.

$12 \div 6$ | 2 $30 \div 6 =$ | 5 $60 \div 10 =$ | 6

Complete the problems.

	$30 \div 10 =$	$36 \div 4 =$
	$18 \div 6 =$	$35 \div 5 =$
$14 \div 2 =$	$20 \div 2 =$	$48 \div 6 =$
$18 \div 3 =$	$18 \div 6 =$	$24 \div 3 =$
$20 \div 4 =$	$24 \div 3 =$	$20 \div 2 =$
$15 \div 5 =$	$24 \div 4 =$	$30 \div 6 =$
$8 \div 2 =$	$27 \div 3 =$	$25 \div 5 =$
$15 \div 3 =$	$18 \div 2 =$	$32 \div 4 =$
$16 \div 4 =$	$18 \div 3 =$	$27 \div 3 =$
$25 \div 5 =$	$36 \div 4 =$	$16 \div 2 =$
$6 \div 6 =$	$36 \div 6 =$	$42 \div 6 =$
$10 \div 10 =$	$40 \div 5 =$	$5 \div 5 =$
$42 \div 6 =$	$100 \div 10 =$	$4 \div 4 =$
$24 \div 4 =$	$16 \div 4 =$	$28 \div 4 =$
$54 \div 6 =$	$42 \div 6 =$	$14 \div 2 =$
$90 \div 10 =$	$48 \div 6 =$	$24 \div 6 =$
$30 \div 6 =$	$32 \div 4 =$	$18 \div 6 =$
$90 \div 10 =$	$60 \div 6 =$	$54 \div 6 =$
$36 \div 6 =$	$60 \div 10 =$	$60 \div 6 =$
$50 \div 5 =$	$30 \div 6 =$	$40 \div 5 =$

Times tables for division

This page will help you remember times tables by dividing by 2, 3, 4, 5, 6, 7, and 10.

$42 \div 7 =$ 6 $21 \div 7 =$ 3 $70 \div 7 =$ 10

Complete the problems.

$56 \div 7 =$	$42 \div 7 =$	$70 \div 7 =$
$35 \div 5 =$	$18 \div 6 =$	$35 \div 5 =$
$14 \div 2 =$	$28 \div 7 =$	$35 \div 7 =$
$18 \div 6 =$	$24 \div 6 =$	$24 \div 6 =$
$20 \div 5 =$	$24 \div 4 =$	$21 \div 3 =$
$15 \div 3 =$	$24 \div 2 =$	$49 \div 7 =$
$36 \div 4 =$	$21 \div 7 =$	$42 \div 7 =$
$21 \div 7 =$	$18 \div 6 =$	$32 \div 4 =$
$18 \div 2 =$	$18 \div 3 =$	$27 \div 3 =$
$15 \div 5 =$	$49 \div 7 =$	$16 \div 4 =$
$49 \div 7 =$	$36 \div 4 =$	$42 \div 6 =$
$25 \div 5 =$	$36 \div 6 =$	$45 \div 5 =$
$7 \div 7 =$	$70 \div 7 =$	$40 \div 4 =$
$63 \div 7 =$	$24 \div 3 =$	$24 \div 3 =$
$42 \div 7 =$	$42 \div 6 =$	$14 \div 7 =$
$24 \div 6 =$	$48 \div 6 =$	$18 \div 3 =$
$54 \div 6 =$	$54 \div 6 =$	$56 \div 7 =$
$28 \div 7 =$	$60 \div 6 =$	$63 \div 7 =$
$30 \div 6 =$	$63 \div 7 =$	$48 \div 6 =$
$35 \div 7 =$	$25 \div 5 =$	$24 \div 3 =$

Times tables for division

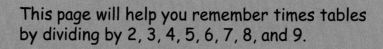

This page will help you remember times tables
by dividing by 2, 3, 4, 5, 6, 7, 8, and 9.

28 ÷ 7 = [4]   32 ÷ 8 = [4]   27 ÷ 9 = [3]

Complete the problems.

18 ÷ 6 =	72 ÷ 9 =	28 ÷ 7 =
32 ÷ 8 =	56 ÷ 7 =	45 ÷ 5 =
14 ÷ 7 =	72 ÷ 8 =	35 ÷ 7 =
18 ÷ 9 =	24 ÷ 8 =	18 ÷ 9 =
63 ÷ 7 =	27 ÷ 9 =	21 ÷ 3 =
72 ÷ 9 =	81 ÷ 9 =	56 ÷ 7 =
72 ÷ 8 =	42 ÷ 6 =	64 ÷ 8 =
56 ÷ 7 =	27 ÷ 3 =	32 ÷ 8 =
24 ÷ 6 =	14 ÷ 7 =	27 ÷ 9 =
81 ÷ 9 =	36 ÷ 4 =	16 ÷ 8 =
63 ÷ 9 =	36 ÷ 6 =	42 ÷ 6 =
45 ÷ 5 =	48 ÷ 8 =	45 ÷ 9 =
54 ÷ 9 =	21 ÷ 7 =	40 ÷ 4 =
70 ÷ 7 =	24 ÷ 3 =	24 ÷ 8 =
42 ÷ 7 =	40 ÷ 8 =	63 ÷ 7 =
30 ÷ 5 =	45 ÷ 9 =	24 ÷ 6 =
54 ÷ 6 =	54 ÷ 6 =	18 ÷ 6 =
56 ÷ 8 =	42 ÷ 7 =	56 ÷ 8 =
30 ÷ 5 =	63 ÷ 9 =	63 ÷ 9 =
35 ÷ 7 =	50 ÷ 5 =	48 ÷ 8 =

Times tables for practice grids

This is a times tables grid.

X	3	4	5	6
7	21	28	35	42
8	24	32	40	48

Square up to the task!

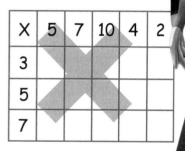

Complete each times tables grid.

X	1	3	5	7	9
2					
3					

X	4	6
6		
7		
8		

X	6	7	8	9	10
3					
4					
5					

X	5	7	10	4	2
3					
5					
7					

Don't get grid lock!

X	2	6	4	7
5				
10				

X	8	5	9	6
9				
7				

Times tables practice grids

Here are more times tables grids.

STREEEETCH your mind....

Target the right answer!

X	2	4	6
3			
7			

X	8	3	7	2
5				
6				
8				

X	2	3	4	5	7
4					
6					
8					

X	2	3	4	5
8				
9				

X	10	9	8	7
5				
7				
9				

X	3	6
2		
3		
4		
5		
6		
7		

X	2	4	6	8
1				
3				
5				
7				
9				
0				

Times tables practice grids

Here are some other times tables grids.

X	7	8	9	10
7				
8				

X	9	8	7	6	5	4
9						
8						
7						

X	2	5	7	9
4				
6				
8				

X	3	5	7
2			
8			
6			
0			
4			
7			

X	8	7	9	6
7				
9				
0				
10				
8				
6				

Line 'em up, fill in the grids, and make it snappy!

Speed trials

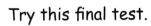

Try this final test.

64 ÷ 8 =	40 ÷ 8 =	15 ÷ 3 =
3 x 7 =	8 x 7 =	8 x 8 =
27 ÷ 3 =	6 x 8 =	14 ÷ 2 =
90 ÷ 10 =	18 ÷ 2 =	9 x 9 =
7 x 9 =	9 x 7 =	24 ÷ 4 =
6 x 8 =	36 ÷ 4 =	7 x 8 =
48 ÷ 6 =	4 x 9 =	30 ÷ 5 =
7 x 7 =	45 ÷ 5 =	6 x 6 =
9 x 5 =	8 x 5 =	42 ÷ 6 =
45 ÷ 9 =	42 ÷ 6 =	9 x 5 =
3 x 9 =	7 x 4 =	49 ÷ 7 =
56 ÷ 8 =	35 ÷ 7 =	8 x 6 =
36 ÷ 4 =	9 x 3 =	72 ÷ 8 =
24 ÷ 3 =	24 ÷ 8 =	9 x 7 =
36 ÷ 9 =	8 x 2 =	54 ÷ 9 =
6 x 7 =	36 ÷ 9 =	7 x 6 =
4 x 4 =	6 x 10 =	10 ÷ 10 =
32 ÷ 8 =	80 ÷ 10 =	7 x 7 =
49 ÷ 7 =	6 x 9 =	16 ÷ 8 =
25 ÷ 5 =	16 ÷ 2 =	7 x 9 =
56 ÷ 7 =	54 ÷ 9 =	63 ÷ 7 =

Watch the signs!

Addition, multiplication, and division

Write the missing number in the box.

$$8 + ? = 8 \qquad 5 \times ? = 5$$
$$8 + \boxed{0} = 8 \qquad 5 \times \boxed{1} = 5$$

Write the missing number in the box.

3 + ☐ = 15	17 + ☐ = 24	☐ + 7 = 19	16 + ☐ = 16
4 + ☐ = 12	12 × ☐ = 12	☐ × 9 = 9	☐ + 6 = 6
25 + ☐ = 40	35 ÷ ☐ = 5	12 + ☐ = 17	4 + ☐ = 9
☐ + 60 = 75	14 + ☐ = 21	☐ + 30 = 52	☐ + 9 = 57
5 × ☐ = 30	12 ÷ ☐ = 3	50 ÷ ☐ = 10	8 × ☐ = 48
☐ × 6 = 54	90 ÷ ☐ = 5	43 × ☐ = 430	☐ ÷ 9 = 4

Write the missing number in the box.

$3 \times (6 \times 4) = (3 \times ?) \times 4$

$(2 \times 5) \times 9 = ? \times (5 \times 9)$

$(7 \times 9) \times 3 = 7 \times (? \times 3)$

$8 \times (8 \times 7) = (8 \times 8) \times ?$

$5 \times (10 + 3) = (5 \times 10) + (? \times 3)$

$(8 + 6) \times 7 = (8 \times 7) + (6 \times ?)$

$9 \times (5 + 12) = (? \times 5) + (? \times 12)$

$(3 + 7) \times 2 = (? \times 2) + (7 \times 2)$

Place value to 10,000,000

These numbers are colossal!

How many hundreds are there in 6,000? `60` hundreds (60 x 100 = 6,000)

What is the value of the 8 in 684? `80` (Because the 8 is in the tens column.)

Write how many tens there are in:

		800		tens	400		tens	
500		tens	1,400		tens	4,600		tens
5,300		tens	1,240		tens	1,320		tens
2,700		tens	5,930		tens	4,530		tens

What is the value of the 8 in these numbers?

86		820	138
8,122		84,301	124,382

What is the value of the 3 in these numbers?

324,126	3,927,142	214,623
8,254,320	3,711,999	124,372

How many hundreds are there in:

6,500	hundreds	524,600	hundreds
18,800	hundreds	712,400	hundreds

What is the value of the 9 in these numbers?

9,214,631	2,389,147	463,946
297,034	9,110,827	105,429

Multiplying and dividing by 10

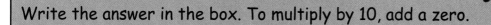

Write the answer in the box. To multiply by 10, add a zero.

42 x 10 = [420]   68 ÷ 10 = [6.8]

Jump to it!

Write the product in the box.

84 x 10 = [   ]   13 x 10 = [   ]   54 x 10 = [   ]

36 x 10 = [   ]   58 x 10 = [   ]   54 x 10 = [   ]

256 x 10 = [   ]   412 x 10 = [   ]   836 x 10 = [   ]

4,700 x 10 = [   ]   687 x 10 = [   ]   2,145 x 10 = [   ]

Write the quotient in the box. To divide by 10, move the decimal point one place left.

82 ÷ 10 = [   ]   58 ÷ 10 = [   ]   38 ÷ 10 = [   ]

19 ÷ 10 = [   ]   79 ÷ 10 = [   ]   82 ÷ 10 = [   ]

245 ÷ 10 = [   ]   367 ÷ 10 = [   ]   279 ÷ 10 = [   ]

379 ÷ 10 = [   ]   924 ÷ 10 = [   ]   674 ÷ 10 = [   ]

Find the missing factor.

[   ] x 10 = 240   [   ] x 10 = 750   [   ] x 10 = 990

[   ] x 10 = 370   [   ] x 10 = 140   [   ] x 10 = 350

[   ] x 10 = 550   [   ] x 10 = 870   [   ] x 10 = 760

Find the dividend.

[   ] ÷ 10 = 4.7   [   ] ÷ 10 = 7.8   [   ] ÷ 10 = 4.7

[   ] ÷ 10 = 25.7   [   ] ÷ 10 = 9.9   [   ] ÷ 10 = 80.7

[   ] ÷ 10 = 40.9   [   ] ÷ 10 = 67.9   [   ] ÷ 10 = 26.9

Ordering sets of measures

Sort it out!

Write these measures in order, from least to greatest.

| 4,100 km | 34 km | 1,621 km | 347 km | 6 km | 879 km |

| 6 km | 34 km | 347 km | 879 km | 1,621 km | 4,100 km |

Write these amounts in order, from least to greatest.

$416	$15,940	$1,504	$826	$37,532
7,200 mi	720 mi	27,410 mi	15 mi	247 mi
1,327 lb	9,565 lb	32,942 lb	752,247 lb	556 lb
8,940 yrs	20,316 yrs	8,520 yrs	320 yrs	4,681 yrs
14,632 kg	8,940 kg	175 kg	217,846 kg	75,126 kg
9,420 km	764 km	25,811 km	114,243 km	7,240 km
$4,212	$37,227	$1,365,240	$950	$143,822
24,091 ft	59,473 ft	1,237 ft	426 ft	837,201 ft
2,330 oz	103,427 oz	9,625 oz	847 oz	47,632 oz
7,340 m	249 m	12,746 m	32 m	17,407,321 m
$12,111	$12,493	$43	$430	$5,672

Appropriate units of measure

Choose the best units to measure the length of each item.

inches	feet	yards

notebook	car	swimming pool
inches	feet	yards

Choose the best units to measure the length of each item.

inches	feet	yards

TV set	bicycle	toothbrush	football field

shoe	backyard	canoe	fence

The height of a door is about 7 _____

The height of a pencil is about 7 _____

The height of a flagpole is about 7 _____

My seventh sense tells me that you can do this.

Choose the best units to measure the weight of each item.

ounces	pounds	tons

kitten	train	tomato	sweatshirt

hamburger	elephant	refrigerator

The weight of a tennis ball is about 2 _____

The weight of a bag of potatoes is about 5 _____

The weight of a truck is about 4 _____

Identifying patterns

Continue each pattern.

Intervals of 6:	2	8	14	20	26	32
Intervals of 3:	26	23	20	17	14	11

Continue each pattern.

0	10	20				
5	10	15				
5	7	9				
3	10	17				
4	7	10			19	
1	9	17		33		

Continue each pattern.

46	42	38				
33	29	25				
65	60	55				
50	43	36			15	
28	25	22				
49	42	35				7

Continue each pattern.

5	7	9		13		
56	53	50				
3	8	13				
47	40	33			12	
1	4	7				
81	72	63				

It's time for action!

Recognizing multiples

My heightened senses make uncovering things real easy.

Circle the multiples of ten. For example, 2 x 10 = 20, so circle 20.

14   (20)   25   (30)   47   (60)

Circle the multiples of 6.

| 20 | 24 | 56 | 72 | 26 | 35 |
| 1 | 3 | 6 | 16 | 32 | 36 |

Circle the multiples of 7.

| 14 | 17 | 35 | 27 | 47 | 49 |
| 63 | 42 | 52 | 37 | 64 | 71 |

Circle the multiples of 8.

| 18 | 54 | 64 | 35 | 72 | 8 |
| 25 | 31 | 48 | 84 | 32 | 28 |

Circle the multiples of 9.

| 64 | 81 | 36 | 35 | 33 | 98 |
| 45 | 53 | 27 | 18 | 92 | 106 |

Circle the multiples of 10.

| 44 | 37 | 30 | 29 | 50 | 100 |
| 15 | 35 | 60 | 46 | 90 | 45 |

Circle the multiples of 11.

| 45 | 33 | 87 | 98 | 99 | 60 |
| 24 | 44 | 65 | 54 | 66 | 121 |

Circle the multiples of 12.

| 23 | 34 | 48 | 74 | 24 | 60 |
| 72 | 66 | 29 | 109 | 108 | 132 |

Using information in tables

Use the table to answer the questions.

MARVEL HEROES FAVORITE SPORTS

Sport	Number of votes
Basketball	5
Soccer	10
Softball	4
Swimming	7

How many Marvel heroes voted for swimming?

7

What is the most popular sport?

soccer

Use the table to answer the questions.

APPEARANCES IN MARVEL COMICS

Character	April	May	June
Cyclops	5	9	11
Magneto	7	2	9
Rogue	3	1	12
Wolverine	8	8	10

How many times did Wolverine appear in May?

Who appeared 9 times in June?

How many times did Cyclops appear in April, May, and June?

Complete the table and answer the questions.

SUPERHERO OLYMPIC MEDALS

Superhero	Gold	Silver	Bronze	Total
Human Torch	3	4	9	16
Invisible Woman	6	6	4	
Mister Fanstastic	12	8	7	
Black Panther	10	8	10	
Spider-Man	9	5	4	
Wolverine	8	4	4	

How many more gold medals did Wolverine win than bronze medals?

Which Marvel hero won the most bronze medals?

Which Marvel hero won three times as many bronze medals as gold medals?

Am I the winner?

Coordinate graphs

Remember to write the coordinates for the x-axis first.

A   (2, 5)

B   (3, 3)

C   (5, 2)

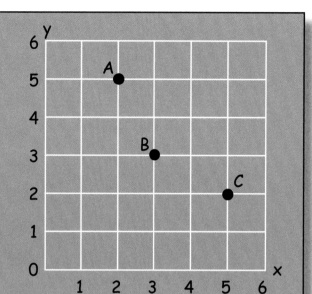

Write the coordinates for each icon.

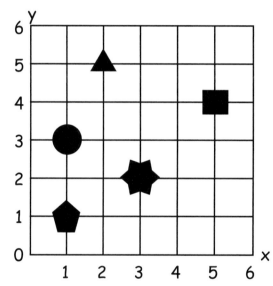

Write the coordinates for each letter.

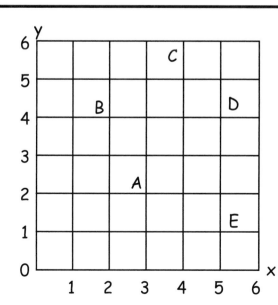

A

B

C

D

E

Surf into shape!

71

Fraction models

Write the missing numbers to show
what part is colored pale blue.

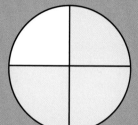

$$\frac{\boxed{3}\ \text{pale blue parts}}{\boxed{4}\ \text{parts}} = \frac{3}{4}$$

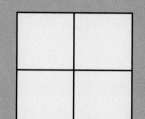

$$\frac{4}{4} = \boxed{1} \qquad \frac{2}{4} = \frac{1}{2}$$

So, pale blue part = $1\frac{1}{\boxed{2}}$

Write the missing numbers to show what part is shaded.

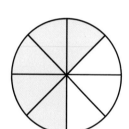

$$\frac{\underline{}}{9} \qquad \frac{2}{\underline{}}$$

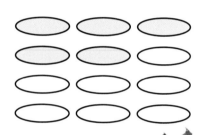

Write the fraction for the part that is shaded.

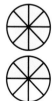
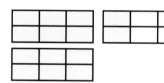

or   or   or

Write the fraction for the part that is shaded.

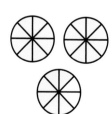

☐ ☐   or   ☐ ☐   ☐   or   ☐   ☐ ☐

72

Converting fractions and decimals

Write these fractions as decimals.

$\frac{6}{10}$ = 0.6

$\frac{4}{100}$ = 0.04

Write these decimals as fractions.

0.2 = $\frac{2}{10}$ = $\frac{1}{5}$

0.53 = $\frac{53}{100}$

Even small numbers don't escape me.

Write these fractions as decimals.

$\frac{7}{10}$ = $\frac{1}{10}$ = $\frac{3}{10}$ =

$\frac{2}{10}$ = $\frac{8}{10}$ = $\frac{5}{10}$ =

$\frac{1}{2}$ =   = $\frac{9}{10}$ = $\frac{4}{10}$ =

Write these decimals as fractions.

0.4 = $\frac{4}{}$ = $\frac{2}{}$ 0.5 = $\frac{5}{}$ = $\frac{1}{2}$ 0.6 = $\frac{6}{}$ = $\frac{3}{}$

0.7 = $\frac{7}{}$ 0.2 = $\frac{2}{}$ = $\frac{1}{}$ 0.3 = $\frac{3}{}$

0.1 = $\frac{1}{}$ 0.8 = $\frac{8}{}$ = $\frac{4}{}$ 0.9 = $\frac{9}{}$

Change these fractions to decimals.

$\frac{3}{100}$ = $\frac{1}{100}$ = $\frac{7}{100}$ =

$\frac{25}{100}$ = $\frac{15}{100}$ = $\frac{49}{100}$ =

$\frac{56}{100}$ = $\frac{24}{100}$ = $\frac{72}{100}$ =

Change these decimals to fractions.

0.83 = 0.91 = 0.73 =

0.39 = 0.43 = 0.17 =

Factors of numbers from 31 to 65

The factors of 40 are: 1   2   4   5   8   20   40

Circle the factors of 56:

(1)   (2)   3   (4)   5   6   (7)   (8)   (14)   (28)   32   (56)

Find all the factors of each number.

The factors of 31 are

The factors of 47 are

The factors of 35 are

The factors of 50 are

The factors of 42 are

The factors of 52 are

The factors of 48 are

The factors of 60 are

Find all the factors of each number if you DARE!

Circle all the factors of each number.

Which numbers are factors of 14?

1   2   3   4   5   6   7   8   9   10   11   12   13   14

Which numbers are factors of 45?

1   3   4   5   8   9   12   15   16   21   24   36   40   44   45

Which numbers are factors of 61?

1   3   4   5   6   10   15   16   18   20   24   29   30   61

Which numbers are factors of 65?

1   2   4   5   6   8   9   10   12   13   14   15   30   60   65

Some numbers have only factors of 1 and themselves. They are called prime numbers. Write all the prime numbers between 31 and 65 in the box.

Writing equivalent fractions

Make these fractions equal by writing in the missing number.

$\dfrac{20}{100} = \dfrac{\boxed{}}{10}$ $\dfrac{4}{5} = \dfrac{\boxed{}}{10}$ $\dfrac{5}{9} = \dfrac{\boxed{}}{18}$

$\dfrac{2}{20} = \dfrac{\boxed{}}{10}$ $\dfrac{2}{3} = \dfrac{\boxed{}}{12}$ $\dfrac{5}{100} = \dfrac{\boxed{}}{20}$

$\dfrac{11}{14} = \dfrac{\boxed{}}{28}$ $\dfrac{5}{6} = \dfrac{\boxed{}}{18}$ $\dfrac{2}{8} = \dfrac{\boxed{}}{4}$

$\dfrac{2}{12} = \dfrac{\boxed{}}{6}$ $\dfrac{9}{21} = \dfrac{\boxed{}}{7}$ $\dfrac{6}{20} = \dfrac{\boxed{}}{10}$

$\dfrac{7}{8} = \dfrac{28}{\boxed{}}$ $\dfrac{5}{20} = \dfrac{1}{\boxed{}}$ $\dfrac{5}{8} = \dfrac{10}{\boxed{}}$

$\dfrac{5}{25} = \dfrac{1}{\boxed{}}$ $\dfrac{25}{100} = \dfrac{5}{\boxed{}}$ $\dfrac{6}{30} = \dfrac{1}{\boxed{}}$

$\dfrac{5}{30} = \dfrac{1}{\boxed{}}$ $\dfrac{12}{14} = \dfrac{6}{\boxed{}}$ $\dfrac{1}{5} = \dfrac{2}{\boxed{}}$

$\dfrac{9}{18} = \dfrac{1}{\boxed{}}$ $\dfrac{40}{100} = \dfrac{2}{\boxed{}}$ $\dfrac{25}{30} = \dfrac{5}{\boxed{}}$

$\dfrac{3}{8} = \dfrac{9}{\boxed{}}$ $\dfrac{4}{100} = \dfrac{1}{\boxed{}}$ $\dfrac{1}{3} = \dfrac{5}{\boxed{}}$

$\dfrac{1}{12} = \dfrac{\boxed{}}{24} = \dfrac{3}{\boxed{}} = \dfrac{\boxed{}}{48} = \dfrac{\boxed{}}{60} = \dfrac{6}{\boxed{}}$

$\dfrac{20}{100} = \dfrac{\boxed{}}{25} = \dfrac{2}{\boxed{}} = \dfrac{1}{\boxed{}} = \dfrac{\boxed{}}{50} = \dfrac{\boxed{}}{200}$

$\dfrac{2}{5} = \dfrac{6}{\boxed{}} = \dfrac{\boxed{}}{20} = \dfrac{4}{\boxed{}} = \dfrac{\boxed{}}{50} = \dfrac{40}{\boxed{}}$

$\dfrac{1}{6} = \dfrac{\boxed{}}{12} = \dfrac{3}{\boxed{}} = \dfrac{4}{\boxed{}} = \dfrac{5}{\boxed{}} = \dfrac{6}{\boxed{}}$

$\dfrac{2}{3} = \dfrac{\boxed{}}{24} = \dfrac{\boxed{}}{36} = \dfrac{\boxed{}}{21} = \dfrac{6}{\boxed{}} = \dfrac{\boxed{}}{300}$

Properties of polygons

Circle the polygon that has two pairs of parallel sides.

Read the description and circle the polygon.

All the angles are right angles, but not all the sides are the same length.

Exactly three pairs of parallel sides.

Exactly one pair of sides is parallel.

All the sides are the same length, and all the angles are right angles.

All the sides are the same length, and all the angles are the same.

Naming polygons

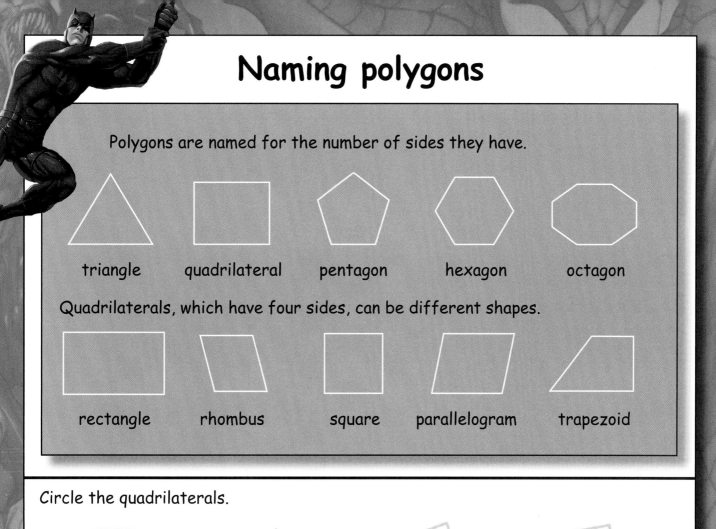

Polygons are named for the number of sides they have.

triangle   quadrilateral   pentagon   hexagon   octagon

Quadrilaterals, which have four sides, can be different shapes.

rectangle   rhombus   square   parallelogram   trapezoid

Circle the quadrilaterals.

Write the name of each polygon in the box.

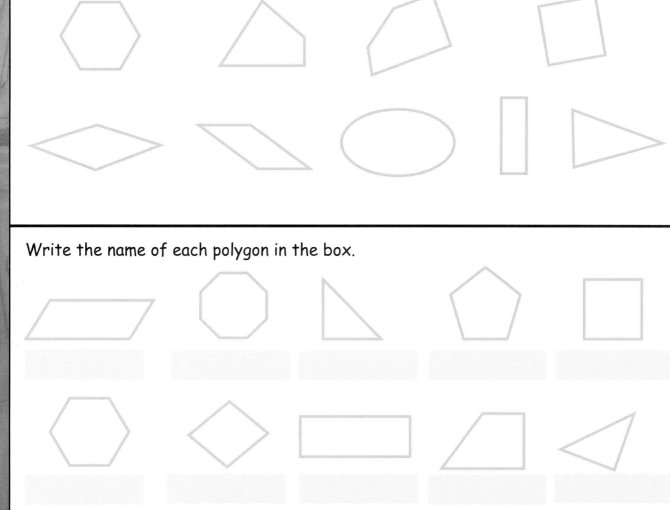

Adding decimals

Find each sum. Remember to regroup.

¹
$6.49
+ $2.36
$8.85

¹
3.18
+ 4.59
7.77

Can you see the point?

Find each sum. Don't forget to line up the decimals.

$4.34
+ $2.56

5.22
+ 3.49

$3.28
+ $9.22

8.21
+ 4.49

Find each sum.

6.58 m
+ 3.54 m

7.37 cm
+ 2.76 cm

2.77 km
+ 4.59 km

8.09 m
+ 4.96 m

Write each sum in the box.

$3.49 + $5.52 =

$6.37 + $5.09 =

$9.53 + $7.46 =

$8.22 + $1.19 =

5.77 km + 2.99 km =

5.24 m + 8.37 m =

Solve each problem.

Gambit throws two cards. One card hits a target 5.95 meters away. Another card hits a target 3.38 meters away. How far have the two cards traveled to hit their targets?

Next, Gambit throws two cards 9.70 meters and 6.44 meters. How far have these cards traveled?

Adding decimals

Find each sum. Remember to regroup.

$$\begin{array}{r} {}^{1} \\ \$5.96 \\ + \$2.83 \\ \hline \$8.79 \end{array}$$

$$\begin{array}{r} {}^{11} \\ 6.92 \text{ cm} \\ + 1.68 \text{ cm} \\ \hline 8.60 \text{ cm} \end{array}$$

It's not the end of the world...I should know!

Find each sum.

$9.57	$7.96	$5.73	$6.49
+ $9.99	+ $4.78	+ $9.97	+ $3.88

Find each sum.

9.98	7.34 cm	3.04 km	7.40 m
+ 8.09	+ 9.91 cm	+ 5.76 km	+ 4.19 m

Write each sum in the box.

6.49 + 5.03 =

$2.04 + $9.97 =

$9.58 + $8.32 =

2.04 m + 4.83 m =

$9.19 + $5.26 =

1.29 + 4.83 =

Solve each problem.

Daniel buys a Doom mask for $3.99 and a Galactus mask for $2.75. How much has he spent?

Daniel goes to another store. There he sees that Doom masks cost $2.49 each. If he bought two masks, how much would Daniel pay?

Subtracting decimals

Find the difference. Remember to regroup.

$$
\begin{array}{r}
\overset{7\ \ \overset{11}{\cancel{1}}\ 13}{8.2\cancel{3}} \\
-\ 4.78 \\
\hline
3.45
\end{array}
\qquad
\begin{array}{r}
\overset{1\ \ \overset{15}{\cancel{5}}\ 14}{2.6\cancel{4}} \\
-\ 1.77 \\
\hline
0.87
\end{array}
$$

Find the difference before I STRIKE.

Find each difference.

$7.26
- $3.48

$2.13
- $1.23

$9.47
-$4.79

$8.24
-$5.36

Find each difference.

5.21 m
- 2.99 m

3.64 km
- 1.99 km

9.12 cm
- 3.99 cm

6.63
- 4.79

Write each difference in the box.

7.71 - 1.99 =

3.55 km - 1.89 km =

$9.76 - $3.87 =

5.71 - 1.92 =

$2.22 - $1.63 =

8.14 - 3.25 =

Solve the problem.

Elektra's sword is 2.78 meters long, and Nightcrawler's sword is 1.62 meters long. How much longer is Elektra's sword than Nightcrawler's?

Subtracting decimals

Find each difference. Remember to regroup.

$$
\begin{array}{r}
\overset{6}{}\overset{\overset{11}{\cancel{1}}}{7}.\overset{13}{\cancel{2}}3 \\
- 1.94 \\
\hline
5.29
\end{array}
\qquad
\begin{array}{r}
\overset{5}{}\overset{\overset{11}{\cancel{1}}}{6}.\overset{13}{\cancel{2}}3 \\
- 2.84 \\
\hline
3.39
\end{array}
$$

The heat is turning up... get adding.

Find each difference.

$$
\begin{array}{r}
\$8.24 \\
- \$2.87 \\
\hline
\end{array}
\qquad
\begin{array}{r}
6.31 \\
- 2.89 \\
\hline
\end{array}
\qquad
\begin{array}{r}
\$4.23 \\
- \$2.24 \\
\hline
\end{array}
\qquad
\begin{array}{r}
8.91 \\
- 5.92 \\
\hline
\end{array}
$$

Find each difference.

$$
\begin{array}{r}
6.23 \\
- 2.24 \\
\hline
\end{array}
\qquad
\begin{array}{r}
7.48 \ \text{m} \\
- 3.49 \ \text{m} \\
\hline
\end{array}
\qquad
\begin{array}{r}
6.33 \ \text{km} \\
- 2.94 \ \text{km} \\
\hline
\end{array}
\qquad
\begin{array}{r}
9.11 \ \text{cm} \\
- 1.32 \ \text{cm} \\
\hline
\end{array}
$$

Write each difference in the box.

6.14 - 3.17 =

7.51 - 6.59 =

$7.14 - $3.46 =

7.42 - 4.57 =

$3.39 - $1.47 =

$6.23 - $5.34 =

Solve each problem.

Spider-Man shoots a web 7.95 meters onto a wall. He climbs up 3.62 meters. How far has he left to climb?

Spider-Man shoots a web 11.51 meters onto a wall. He climbs up 8.69 meters. How far has he left to climb?

Multiplying by one-digit numbers

Find each product. Remember to regroup.

$$\begin{array}{r} \overset{1\ 1}{465} \\ \times\ \ 3 \\ \hline \boxed{1{,}395} \end{array}$$

$$\begin{array}{r} \overset{3}{391} \\ \times\ \ 4 \\ \hline \boxed{1{,}564} \end{array}$$

$$\begin{array}{r} \overset{3\ 3}{178} \\ \times\ \ 4 \\ \hline \boxed{712} \end{array}$$

Under my hypnotic control, I guarantee you'll find each product.

Find each product.

$$\begin{array}{r} 573 \\ \times\ \ 3 \\ \hline \end{array}$$
$$\begin{array}{r} 920 \\ \times\ \ 2 \\ \hline \end{array}$$
$$\begin{array}{r} 438 \\ \times\ \ 3 \\ \hline \end{array}$$
$$\begin{array}{r} 813 \\ \times\ \ 2 \\ \hline \end{array}$$

$$\begin{array}{r} 582 \\ \times\ \ 4 \\ \hline \end{array}$$
$$\begin{array}{r} 832 \\ \times\ \ 3 \\ \hline \end{array}$$
$$\begin{array}{r} 405 \\ \times\ \ 5 \\ \hline \end{array}$$
$$\begin{array}{r} 396 \\ \times\ \ 6 \\ \hline \end{array}$$

Find each product.

$$\begin{array}{r} 317 \\ \times\ \ 3 \\ \hline \end{array}$$
$$\begin{array}{r} 224 \\ \times\ \ 3 \\ \hline \end{array}$$
$$\begin{array}{r} 543 \\ \times\ \ 4 \\ \hline \end{array}$$
$$\begin{array}{r} 218 \\ \times\ \ 3 \\ \hline \end{array}$$

$$\begin{array}{r} 128 \\ \times\ \ 4 \\ \hline \end{array}$$
$$\begin{array}{r} 276 \\ \times\ \ 5 \\ \hline \end{array}$$
$$\begin{array}{r} 798 \\ \times\ \ 6 \\ \hline \end{array}$$
$$\begin{array}{r} 365 \\ \times\ \ 6 \\ \hline \end{array}$$

$$\begin{array}{r} 100 \\ \times\ \ 5 \\ \hline \end{array}$$
$$\begin{array}{r} 373 \\ \times\ \ 4 \\ \hline \end{array}$$
$$\begin{array}{r} 882 \\ \times\ \ 4 \\ \hline \end{array}$$
$$\begin{array}{r} 954 \\ \times\ \ 3 \\ \hline \end{array}$$

Solve each problem.

Hightown middle school has 255 students. The high school has 6 times as many students. How many students are there at the high school?

A train can carry 375 passengers. How many can it carry on four trips?

six trips?

Multiplying by one-digit numbers

Find each product. Remember to regroup.

$$\begin{array}{r} \overset{33}{465} \\ \times \ \ 6 \\ \hline 2{,}790 \end{array}$$

$$\begin{array}{r} \overset{12}{823} \\ \times \ \ 8 \\ \hline 6{,}584 \end{array}$$

$$\begin{array}{r} \overset{44}{755} \\ \times \ \ 9 \\ \hline 6{,}795 \end{array}$$

Bigger and better!

Find each product.

$$\begin{array}{r} 395 \\ \times \ \ 7 \\ \hline \end{array}$$
$$\begin{array}{r} 734 \\ \times \ \ 8 \\ \hline \end{array}$$
$$\begin{array}{r} 826 \\ \times \ \ 8 \\ \hline \end{array}$$
$$\begin{array}{r} 943 \\ \times \ \ 9 \\ \hline \end{array}$$

$$\begin{array}{r} 643 \\ \times \ \ 7 \\ \hline \end{array}$$
$$\begin{array}{r} 199 \\ \times \ \ 6 \\ \hline \end{array}$$
$$\begin{array}{r} 823 \\ \times \ \ 7 \\ \hline \end{array}$$
$$\begin{array}{r} 546 \\ \times \ \ 8 \\ \hline \end{array}$$

Find each product.

$$\begin{array}{r} 502 \\ \times \ \ 7 \\ \hline \end{array}$$
$$\begin{array}{r} 377 \\ \times \ \ 8 \\ \hline \end{array}$$
$$\begin{array}{r} 845 \\ \times \ \ 8 \\ \hline \end{array}$$
$$\begin{array}{r} 222 \\ \times \ \ 9 \\ \hline \end{array}$$

$$\begin{array}{r} 473 \\ \times \ \ 9 \\ \hline \end{array}$$
$$\begin{array}{r} 224 \\ \times \ \ 8 \\ \hline \end{array}$$
$$\begin{array}{r} 606 \\ \times \ \ 6 \\ \hline \end{array}$$
$$\begin{array}{r} 514 \\ \times \ \ 7 \\ \hline \end{array}$$

$$\begin{array}{r} 500 \\ \times \ \ 9 \\ \hline \end{array}$$
$$\begin{array}{r} 800 \\ \times \ \ 9 \\ \hline \end{array}$$
$$\begin{array}{r} 900 \\ \times \ \ 9 \\ \hline \end{array}$$
$$\begin{array}{r} 200 \\ \times \ \ 9 \\ \hline \end{array}$$

Solve each problem.

A crate holds 230 oxygen cylinders. How many cylinders are there in 8 crates?

The Blackbird flies 4,570 miles a month on missions. How many miles does it fly in 6 months?

Division with remainders

Find each quotient.

```
     181 r 1        141 r 2          58 r 3
  2)363          3)425           4)235
    2              3               20
    16             12              35
    16             12              32
     3              5               3
     1              3
                    2
```

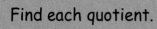

Tap into your cosmic powers to find the answers.

Find each quotient.

```
  3)572          3)200           4)203
```

```
  4)643          2)365           3)851
```

```
  4)737          4)951           2)413
```

Write the answer in the box.

What is 653 divided by 2?

What is 763 divided by 5?

What is 478 divided by 3?

What is 867 divided by 4?

Division with remainders

Find each quotient.

```
        62 r 5          84 r 4          66 r 3
     9)563           8)676           7)465
       54              64              42
       23              36              45
       18              32              42
        5               4               3
```

Get cracking!

Find each quotient.

```
7)503           8)654


6)777           7)121           6)431


9)404           8)589           6)199
```

Write the answer in the box.

What is 759 divided by 7? ▭   Divide 941 by 9. ▭

What is 463 divided by 8? ▭   Divide 232 by 6. ▭

85

Real-life problems

Elektra spent $4.68 at the store and had $4.77 left. How much did she start with?

$9.45

$$\begin{array}{r} \overset{1\ 1}{4.77} \\ +\ 4.68 \\ \hline 9.45 \end{array}$$

Jean Grey saves $30.00 a week. How much will she have if she saves all of it for 8 weeks?

$240

$$\begin{array}{r} 30.00 \\ \times\ \ \ \ 8 \\ \hline 240.00 \end{array}$$

Madripoor theater charges $4 for each matinee ticket. If it sells 560 tickets for a matinee performance, how much money does it take in?

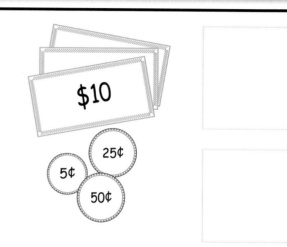

Peter Parker has saved $9.69. His friend has saved $3.24 less. How much does his friend have?

The cost for 9 children to see a Blade film is $54. How much does each child pay? If only 6 children go, what will the cost be?

Rogue has $12.95. Colossus gives her another $3.64, and she goes out and buys a coffee for $3.25. How much does she have left?

Wolverine has $60 in savings. He decides to spend $\frac{1}{4}$ of it. How much will he have left?

Real-life problems

The Fantastic Four have an hour to find their spaceship. They spend $\frac{1}{3}$ of the time checking satellite data. How many minutes is that?

20 minutes

1 hr = 60 min

$$\begin{array}{r} 20 \\ 3\overline{)60} \end{array}$$

While chasing a crook, Spider-Man uses two 2 long swings of 18.7 m and 21.9 m. How far does he swing altogether?

4.06 m

$$\begin{array}{r} 1\ 1 \\ 1.87 \\ +\ 2.19 \\ \hline 4.06 \end{array}$$

Captain America finds a vial of poison containing 400 ml. He takes out $\frac{1}{4}$ to test. How much is left?

Quicksilver runs 140 m in 7 seconds. At that speed, how far did he run in 1 second?

The S.H.I.E.L.D Helicarrier carries 2.25 tons of cargo. If 1.68 tons is left in the hold, how much has been dropped off?

She-Hulk's gamma-charger emits 25 pulses of gamma rays every 15 minutes. How many pulses are produced in 1 hour?

A computer in The Blackbird is 41.63 cm wide, and next to it is a printer that is 48.37 cm wide. How much space is left on the shelf for a scanner if the shelf is 1.5 m wide?

Perimeters of squares and rectangles

Find the perimeter of this rectangle.

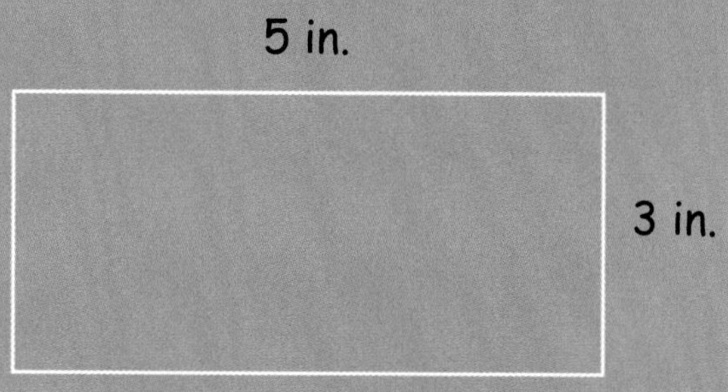

To find the perimeter of a rectangle or a square, add the lengths of the four sides.

5 in. + 5 in. + 3 in. + 3 in. = 16 in.

5 in.

3 in.

5 in.

Find the perimeters of these rectangles and squares.

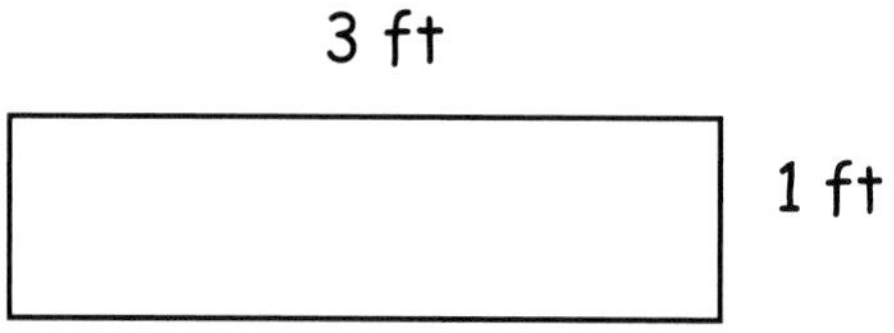

3 ft

3 ft

1 ft

in.

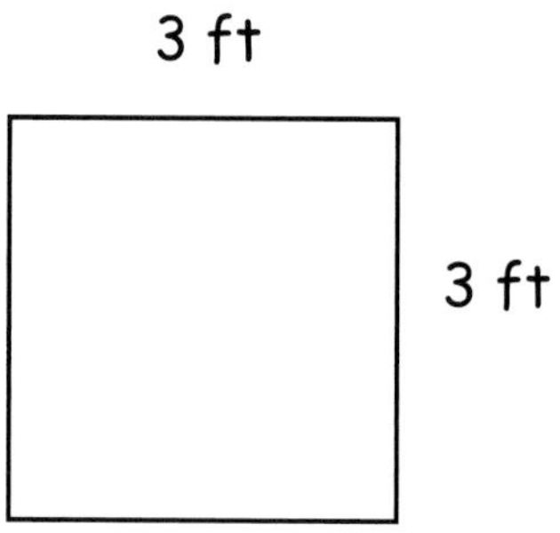

3 ft

3 ft

in.

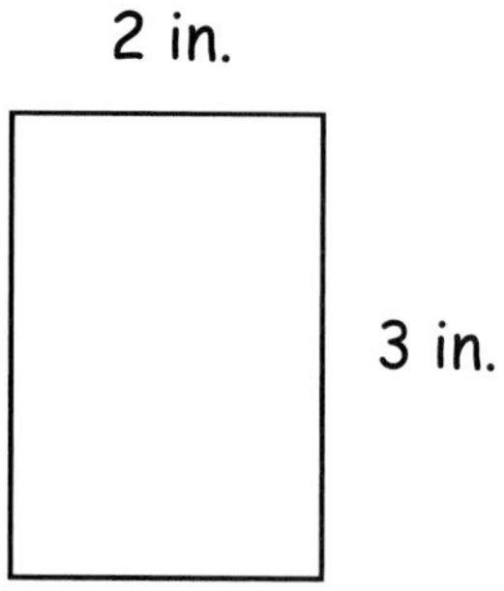

2 in.

3 in.

in.

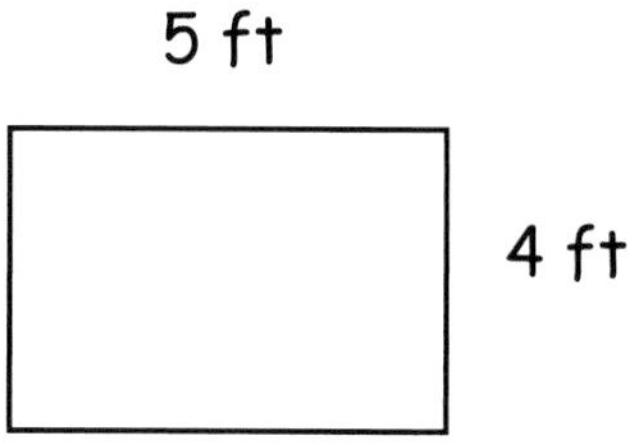

5 ft

4 ft

ft.

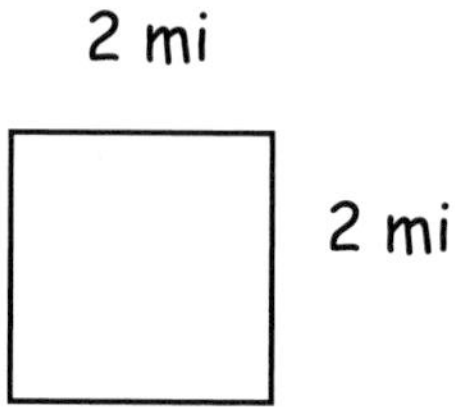

2 mi

2 mi

mi

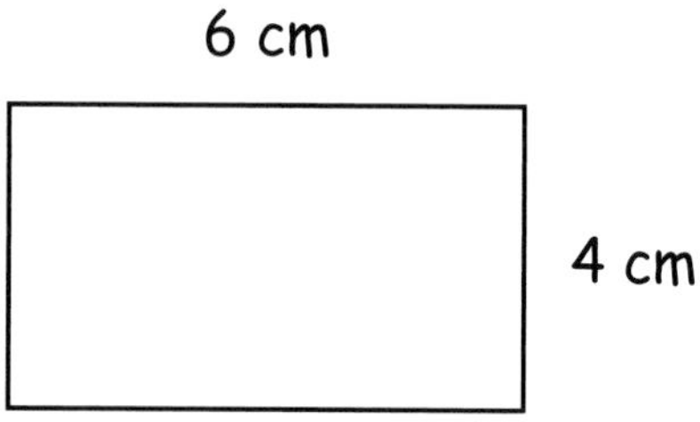

6 cm

4 cm

cm

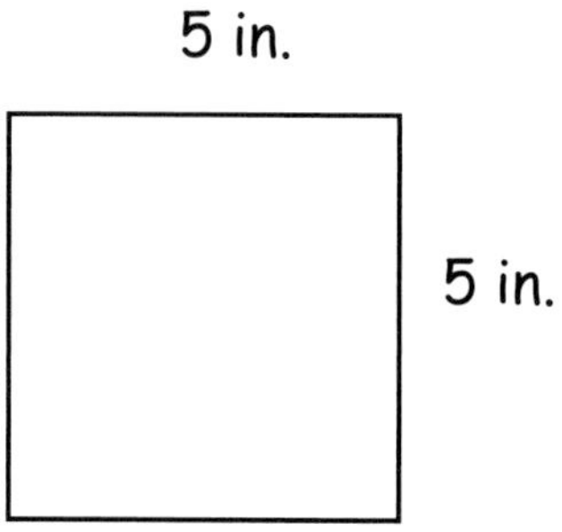

5 in.

5 in.

in.

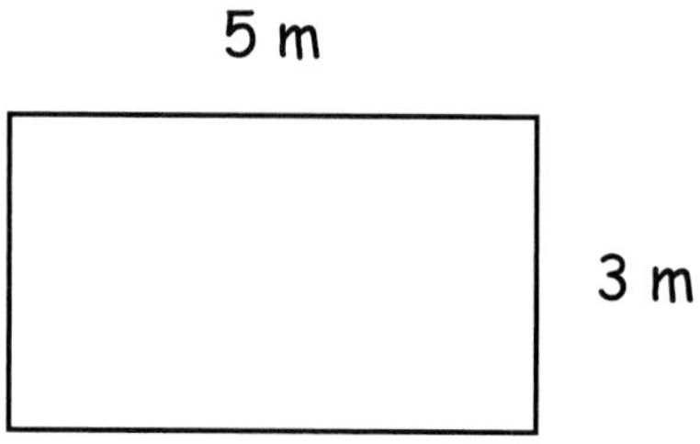

5 m

3 m

m

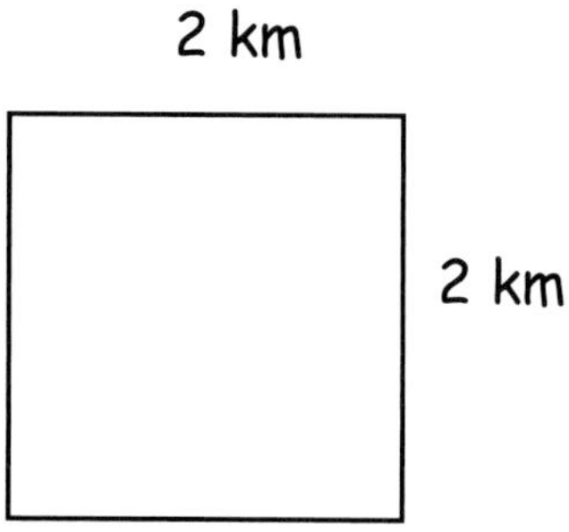

2 km

2 km

km

88

Problems involving time

The Beast spends 35 minutes studying genetics each day. How many minutes does he spend studying genetics from Monday through Friday?

175 minutes

$$\begin{array}{r} \overset{2}{35} \\ \times\ 5 \\ \hline 175 \end{array}$$

Colossus spends 175 minutes eating breakfast from Monday through Friday. How long does he spend eating breakfast each day?

35 minutes

$$5\overline{)175} = 35$$

Professor Xavier works in the Combat Operation Center from 9 A.M. to 5 P.M. He leaves for lunch from noon until 1 P.M. How many hours does he work in the center from Monday to Friday?

Patch walks by Madripoor Harbor for 15 minutes every morning and 10 minutes every evening. How many minutes does he walk in a 7-day week?

It takes 2 hours for one Avenger to file a report. If the report is divided equally between four Avengers, how long will it take to complete?

Mister Fantastic spent 7 days fixing the computers at Baxter Building. If he worked a total of 56 hours and he divided the work equally among the seven days, how long did he work each day?

It took Doctor Strange 45 hours to build a new computer circuit. If he spent 5 hours a day working on it, how many days did it take?

How many hours a day would he have worked to finish it in 5 days?

Using bar graphs

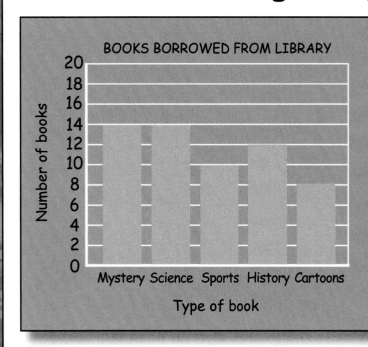

BOOKS BORROWED FROM LIBRARY

Number of books / Type of book

Mystery Science Sports History Cartoons

Use the graph to answer the questions.

How many cartoon books were borrowed?

8

How many more mystery books than history books were borrowed?

14 - 12 = 2

Use the graphs to answer the questions.

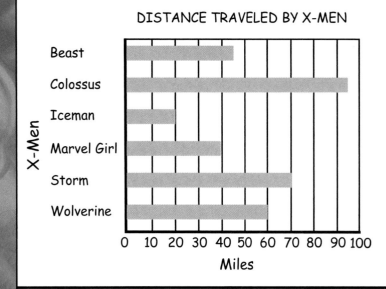

DISTANCE TRAVELED BY X-MEN

X-Men: Beast, Colossus, Iceman, Marvel Girl, Storm, Wolverine

Miles: 0 10 20 30 40 50 60 70 80 90 100

Who traveled the farthest?

How much farther did Storm travel than Wolverine?

Which X-Man traveled the shortest distance?

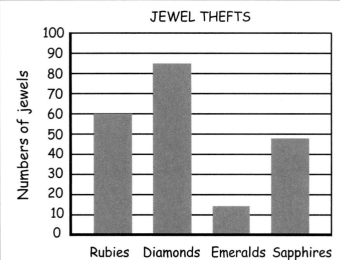

JEWEL THEFTS

Numbers of jewels / Jewels

Rubies Diamonds Emeralds Sapphires

About how many sapphires were stolen?

About how many more diamonds than rubies were stolen?

What jewel was most often stolen?

Congruency

Congruent triangles are triangles that are exactly the same shape and size. Triangles are congruent if the corresponding sides are the same and the three corresponding angles are the same.

Look at these triangles from a different angle!

a and c

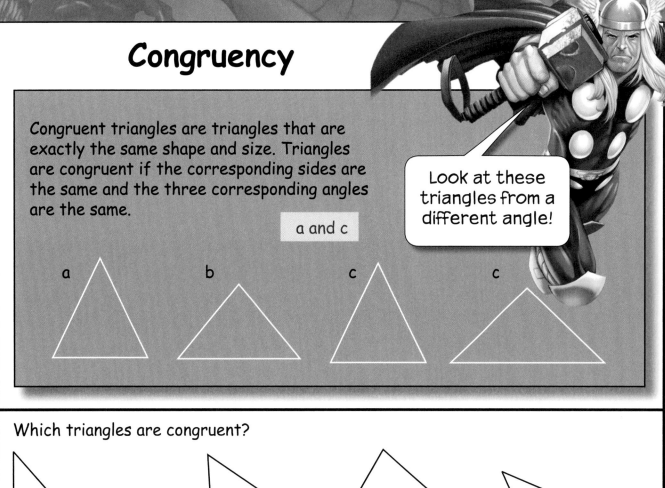

Which triangles are congruent?

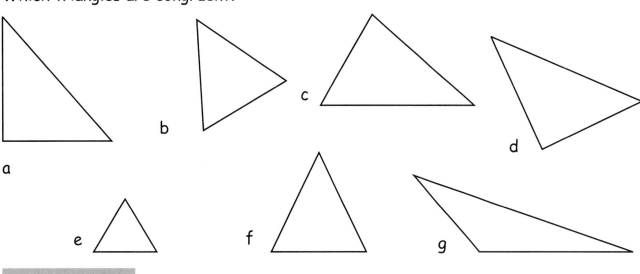

Which triangles are congruent?

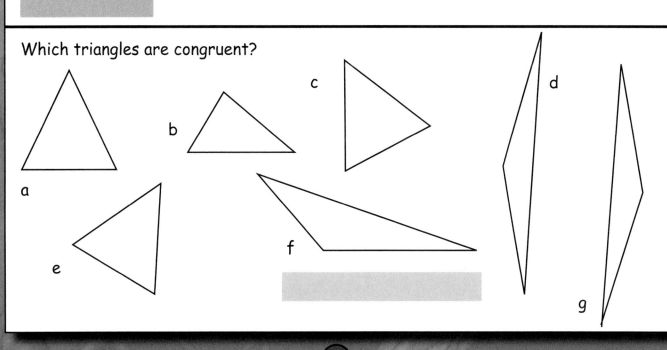

91

Lines of symmetry

How many lines of symmetry does this figure have?

6

Six lines can be drawn, each of which divides the figure in half.

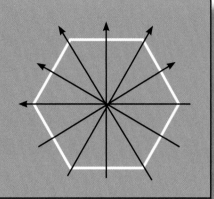

How many lines of symmetry do these figures have?

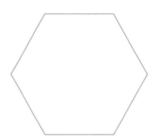

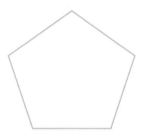

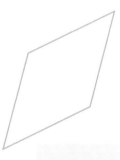

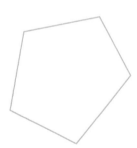

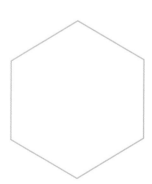

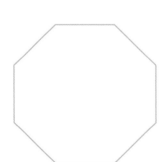

Writing equivalent number sentences

Write a multiplication sentence that goes with 30 ÷ 6 = 5.

6 x 5 = 30 or 5 x 6 = 30

Write a related subtraction sentence for 7 + 12 = 19.

19 - 7 = 12 or 19 - 12 = 7

However you add it up, I'm always formidable.

Write a related subtraction sentence for each sentence.

27 + 14 = 41

33 + 12 = 45

16 + 12 = 28

Write a related addition sentence for each sentence.

55 - 34 = 21

82 - 23 = 59

45 - 20 = 25

Write a related multiplication sentence for each sentence.

28 ÷ 7 = 4

45 ÷ 9 = 5

64 ÷ 2 = 32

Write a related division sentence for each sentence.

8 x 6 = 48

7 x 12 = 84

9 x 5 = 45

Multiplying and dividing

Write the answer in the box.

$26 \times 100 =$ [2,600] $400 \div 100 =$ [4]

Write the answer in the box.

$34 \times 10 =$ $41 \times 10 =$ $56 \times 10 =$

$95 \times 100 =$ $36 \times 100 =$ $75 \times 100 =$

$413 \times 10 =$ $204 \times 10 =$ $524 \times 10 =$

$787 \times 100 =$ $834 \times 100 =$ $254 \times 100 =$

Write the quotient in the box.

$120 \div 10 =$ $260 \div 10 =$ $480 \div 10 =$

$500 \div 100 =$ $800 \div 10 =$ $700 \div 100 =$

$20 \div 10 =$ $30 \div 10 =$ $60 \div 10 =$

$800 \div 100 =$ $100 \div 100 =$ $900 \div 100 =$

Write the number that has been multiplied by 100.

[ ] $\times 100 = 4,600$ [ ] $\times 100 = 72,300$

[ ] $\times 100 = 32,500$ [ ] $\times 100 = 25,000$

[ ] $\times 100 = 1,200$ [ ] $\times 100 = 45,600$

[ ] $\times 100 = 8,400$ [ ] $\times 100 = 62,300$

Write the number that has been divided by 100.

[ ] $\div 100 = 3$ [ ] $\div 100 = 7$

[ ] $\div 100 = 12$ [ ] $\div 100 = 18$

[ ] $\div 100 = 87$ [ ] $\div 100 = 23$

[ ] $\div 100 = 10$ [ ] $\div 100 = 64$

Go! Go! Go!

Ordering sets of measures

Write these amounts in order, from least to greatest.

75 cm	320 mm	3 km	6 m	340mm
320 mm	340 mm	75 cm	6 m	3 km

Write these amounts in order, from least to greatest.

600¢	$4.00	$5.50	350¢	640¢

10 qt	1 gal	12 pt	2 gal	3 qt

115 min	2 hr	210 min	¾ hr	1 hr

2,500 m	2 km	1,000 cm	20 m	1,000 m

$240	3,500¢	$125.00	4,600¢	$50.00

8 ft	1 yd	24 in.	72 in.	7 ft

6 qt	8 pt	3 gal	1 qt	4 pt

2 hr	65 min	1½ hr	100 min	150 min

44 mm	4 cm	4 m	4 km	40 cm

4 yd	36 in.	2 ft	29 in.	2 yd

6 pt	1 gal	9 qt	7 qt	10 pt

Decimal models

Fill in the grid to show the decimal.

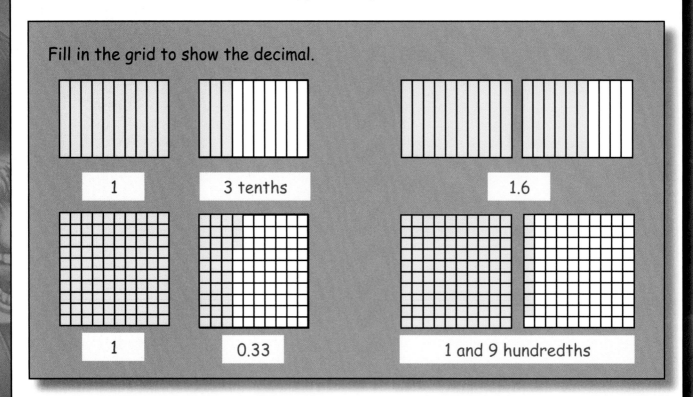

1   3 tenths   1.6

1   0.33   1 and 9 hundredths

Fill in the grid to show the decimal.

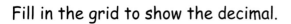

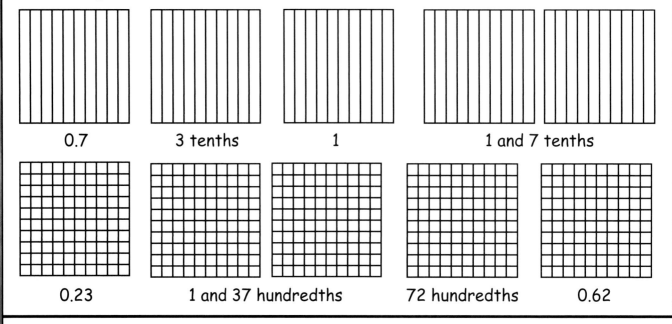

0.7   3 tenths   1   1 and 7 tenths

0.23   1 and 37 hundredths   72 hundredths   0.62

Write the decimal represented by the grid.

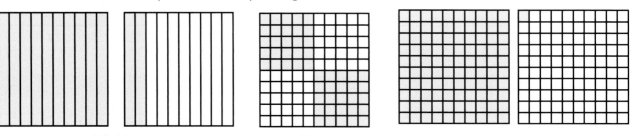

Identifying patterns

Continue each pattern.

Steps of 2:	$\frac{1}{2}$	$2\frac{1}{2}$	$4\frac{1}{2}$	$6\frac{1}{2}$	$8\frac{1}{2}$	$10\frac{1}{2}$
Steps of 5:	3.5	8.5	13.5	18.5	23.5	28.5

Continue each pattern.

$5\frac{1}{2}$	$10\frac{1}{2}$	$15\frac{1}{2}$		
$2\frac{1}{4}$	$4\frac{1}{4}$	$6\frac{1}{4}$		
$8\frac{1}{3}$	$9\frac{1}{3}$	$10\frac{1}{3}$	$12\frac{1}{3}$	
$65\frac{3}{4}$	$55\frac{3}{4}$	$45\frac{3}{4}$		
$44\frac{1}{2}$	$40\frac{1}{2}$	$36\frac{1}{2}$		$24\frac{1}{2}$
$4\frac{2}{3}$	$7\frac{2}{3}$	$10\frac{2}{3}$		
7.5	6.5	5.5		
29.3	26.3	23.3	17.3	
82.6	73.6	64.6		
6.4	10.4	14.4		
14.2	16.2	18.2		24.2
21.8	28.8	35.8		
$13\frac{3}{4}$	$19\frac{3}{4}$	$25\frac{3}{4}$		
57.5	48.5	39.5	21.5	
$11\frac{1}{2}$	$10\frac{1}{2}$	$9\frac{1}{2}$		$6\frac{1}{2}$
8.4	11.4	14.4		

I can't spot the pattern. Get me some help with these.

Products with odd and even numbers

Find the products of these numbers.

4 and 5   The product of 4 and 5 is 20.   6 and 7   The product of 6 and 7 is 42.

Find the products of these odd and even numbers.

3 and 4 _____   2 and 3 _____

7 and 4 _____   8 and 3 _____

6 and 3 _____   9 and 2 _____

10 and 3 _____   12 and 5 _____

What do you notice about your answers? _____
_____

Find the products of these odd numbers.

3 and 5 _____   3 and 9 _____

5 and 7 _____   7 and 3 _____

5 and 11 _____   9 and 7 _____

9 and 5 _____   1 and 5 _____

What do you notice about your answers? _____
_____

Find the products of these even numbers.

4 and 2 _____   4 and 6 _____

2 and 6 _____   4 and 8 _____

10 and 2 _____   4 and 10 _____

6 and 10 _____   2 and 8 _____

What do you notice about your answers? _____
_____

Squares of numbers

Find the square of 3.

$3 \times 3 = 9$

What is the area of this square?

3 in.

3 in.

$3 \times 3 = 9$

Area = 9 in.^{2}

Find the square of these numbers.

2

1

10

7

8

5

9

4

6

Now try these.

11

13

12

20

40

30

Find the areas of these squares.

4 in.

4 in.

in.^{2}

5 ft

5 ft

ft^2

6 cm

6 cm

cm^2

8 in.

8 in.

in.^{2}

9 ft

9 ft

ft^2

Square? Who says I'm square?

99

Factors of numbers from 66 to 100

The factors of 66 are: 1   2   3   6   11   22   33   66

Circle the factors of 94:   ①   ②   28   32   43   ㊼   71   86   ㉙④

Write the factors of each number in the box.

The factors of 70 are

The factors of 83 are

The factors of 63 are

The factors of 85 are

The factors of 75 are

The factors of 99 are

The factors of 69 are

The factors of 72 are

The factors of 96 are

> Consider all the factors when you're planning a crime caper.

Circle the factors.

Which numbers are factors of 68?

1   2   3   4   5   6   7   8   9   11   12   17   34   35   62   68

Which numbers are factors of 95?

1   2   3   4   5   15   16   17   19   24   59   85   90   95   96

Which numbers are factors of 88?

1   2   3   4   5   6   8   10   11   15   22   33   38   44   87   88

Which numbers are factors of 73?

1   2   3   4   6   8   9   10   12   13   14   15   37   42   73

A prime number has only two factors, 1 and itself. Write all the prime numbers between 66 and 100 in the box.

Renaming fractions

Rename these improper fractions as mixed numbers in simplest form.

$$\frac{19}{10} = \boxed{1\frac{9}{10}} \qquad \frac{26}{6} = \boxed{4\frac{1}{3}}$$

Rename this improper fraction as a mixed number in simplest form.

$$\frac{18}{10} = \boxed{1\frac{\overset{4}{\cancel{8}}}{\underset{5}{\cancel{10}}} = 1\frac{4}{5}}$$

Rename these improper fractions as mixed numbers in simplest form.

$\frac{17}{4} =$

$\frac{19}{12} =$

$\frac{19}{6} =$

$\frac{11}{4} =$

$\frac{9}{8} =$

$\frac{15}{8} =$

$\frac{16}{10} =$

$\frac{35}{10} =$

$\frac{26}{8} =$

$\frac{35}{15} =$

$\frac{28}{24} =$

$\frac{18}{12} =$

$\frac{14}{10} =$

$\frac{22}{10} =$

$\frac{24}{5} =$

$\frac{19}{2} =$

$\frac{11}{6} =$

$\frac{43}{4} =$

$\frac{36}{8} =$

$\frac{22}{6} =$

$\frac{20}{8} =$

$\frac{22}{4} =$

$\frac{32}{6} =$

$\frac{50}{4} =$

$\frac{27}{5} =$

$\frac{17}{6} =$

$\frac{13}{3} =$

$\frac{14}{9} =$

$\frac{15}{7} =$

$\frac{11}{5} =$

$\frac{18}{8} =$

$\frac{24}{20} =$

$\frac{16}{12} =$

There's nothing improper here!

Ordering sets of decimals

Write these decimals in order, from least to greatest.

0.54	0.27	2.11	1.45	3.72	2.17
0.27	0.54	1.45	2.11	2.17	3.72

Write these decimals in order, from least to greatest.

6.63	2.14	5.6	3.91	1.25

0.95	0.79	8.25	7.63	7.49

1.05	2.36	1.09	2.41	7.94

3.92	5.63	2.29	4.62	5.36

27.71	21.87	27.28	21.78	27.09

Write these decimals in order, from least to greatest.

110.75 km	65.99 km	94.36 km	76.91 km	87.05 km

$65.25	$32.40	$11.36	$32.04	$65.99

19.51 m	16.15 m	15.53 m	12.65 m	24.24 m

4.291	8.921	8.291	10.651	7.351

1.34 cm	0.98 cm	0.89 cm	1.43 cm	1.09 cm

Symmetry

One optical blast will see straight through these.

How many lines of symmetry does each figure have?

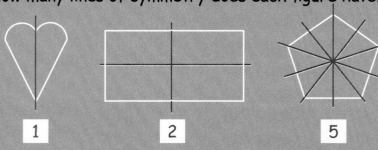

| 1 | 2 | 5 | 0 |

Is the dashed line a line of symmetry? Write yes or no.

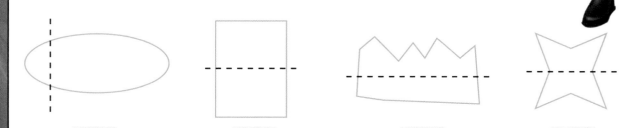

Draw the lines of symmetry. Write how many there are.

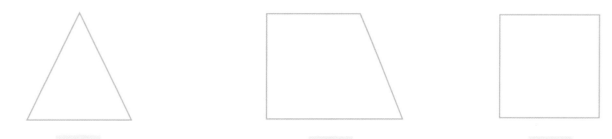

Draw the lines of symmetry. Write how many there are.

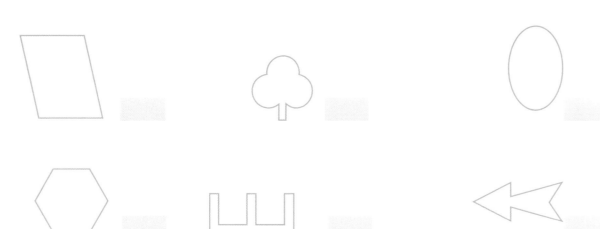

103

Comparing areas

Write how many units are in each figure.

18 units

16 units

Which figure has the greater area?

The figure on the left has the greater area.

Write how many units are in each figure.
Then circle the figure with the greatest area in each group.

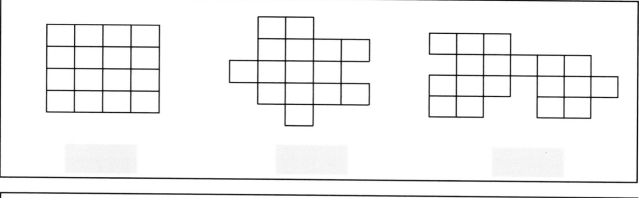

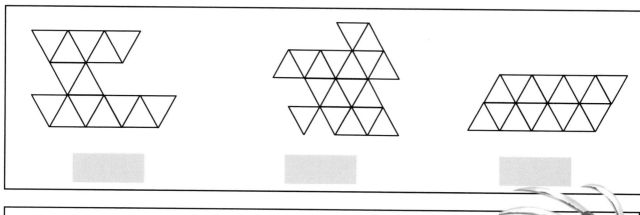

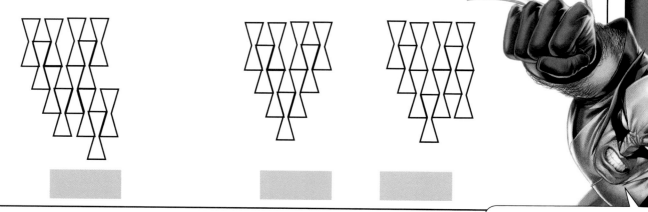

Gggggrrrrr!!!

104

Probability

Use the table to answer the questions.

PROFESSOR X's TIES

Color	Number of ties
Red	4
Blue	4
Green	5
Yellow	6
Black	3

If Professor X picks a tie without looking, which color is he most likely to pick?

yellow

Which color is Professor X as likely to pick as red?

blue

Use the table to answer the questions.

ROGUE'S SKIRTS

Yellow	Blue	Red	Green
IIII IIII III	IIII II	IIII IIII	IIII IIII IIII IIII

If Rogue picks a skirt without looking, is she more likely to choose a yellow skirt or a green skirt?

Which color is she least likely to pick?

Use the graph to answer the questions.

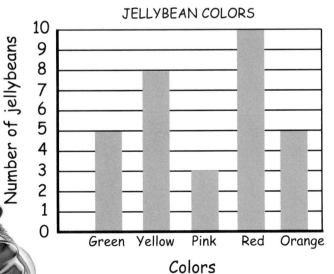

JELLYBEAN COLORS

Number of jellybeans

Colors: Green, Yellow, Pink, Red, Orange

If you pick a jellybean without looking, which color will you most probably pick?

Are you more likely to pick a pink jellybean or a yellow jellybean?

Which color jellybean are you as likely to pick as on orange one?

Column addition

Find these sums.
Regroup if needed.

$$
\begin{array}{r}
{\scriptstyle 1\ 21} \\
4,612 \text{ km} \\
1,096 \text{ km} \\
2,363 \text{ km} \\
+\ 1,374 \text{ km} \\
\hline
9,445 \text{ km}
\end{array}
\qquad
\begin{array}{r}
{\scriptstyle 1\ 1} \\
\$455 \\
\$644 \\
\$327 \\
+\ \$923 \\
\hline
\$2,349
\end{array}
$$

Find these sums.

8,010 mi	3,852 mi	2,112 mi	4,352 mi
7,793 mi	4,534 mi	6,231 mi	3,920 mi
1,641 mi	1,512 mi	1,573 mi	8,439 mi
+ 7,684 mi	+ 3,756 mi	+ 3,141 mi	+ 1,348 mi

$4,721	$3,654	$8,171	$4,563
$8,342	$5,932	$1,475	$2,395
$1,711	$6,841	$7,760	$1,486
+ $2,365	+ $4,736	+ $8,102	+ $6,374

8,690 m	6,329 m	5,245 m	6,431 m
5,243 m	3,251 m	2,845 m	7,453 m
6,137 m	2,642 m	1,937 m	4,650 m
+ 5,843 m	+ 4,823 m	+ 5,610 m	+ 3,782 m

539 yd	206 yd	481 yd	735 yd
965 yd	812 yd	604 yd	234 yd
774 yd	619 yd	274 yd	391 yd
+ 347 yd	+ 832 yd	+ 976 yd	+ 863 yd

763 lb	944 lb	817 lb	746 lb
861 lb	835 lb	591 lb	201 lb
608 lb	391 lb	685 lb	432 lb
+ 671 lb	+ 105 lb	+ 245 lb	+ 309 lb

Column addition

Find these sums.
Regroup if needed.

```
  1 11            1 1 1
 $3,614          2,534
 $4,159          3,120
 $3,522          7,459
 $2,100          6,102
+$3,461        + 8,352
 $16,856         27,567
```

Everything adds up!

Find these sums.

```
  3,846 km       2,510 km       3,144 km       1,475 km
  1,769 km       1,734 km       2,345 km       2,653 km
  6,837 km       5,421 km       8,479 km       2,765 km
  1,593 km       3,205 km       1,004 km       3,742 km
+ 3,276 km     + 2,365 km     + 6,310 km     + 5,905 km
_____     _____     _____     _____
```

```
  $4,468         $3,823         $7,525         $8,618
  $3,533         $9,275         $7,875         $3,453
  $6,400         $3,669         $4,256         $4,404
  $8,675         $2,998         $5,752         $4,361
+ $2,901       + $7,564       + $2,594       + $5,641
_____     _____     _____     _____
```

```
  1,480 m        4,527 m        3,063 m        8,741 m
  6,366 m        8,309 m        8,460 m        6,334 m
  1,313 m        6,235 m        2,712 m        3,231 m
  3,389 m        4,487 m        3,756 m        6,063 m
+ 4,592 m      + 4,065 m      + 5,650 m      + 4,096 m
_____     _____     _____     _____
```

```
  3,742 mi       2,739 mi       8,463 mi       8,596 mi
  2,785 mi       6,517 mi       5,641 mi       5,430 mi
  7,326 mi       6,014 mi       9,430 mi       8,379 mi
  1,652 mi       7,115 mi       8,204 mi       2,943 mi
+ 5,753 mi     + 2,704 mi     + 6,326 mi     + 1,081 mi
_____     _____     _____     _____
```

Adding fractions

Write the sum in simplest form.

$$\frac{1}{8} + \frac{5}{8} = \frac{6}{8} = \frac{3}{4} \qquad \frac{3}{5} + \frac{3}{5} = \frac{6}{5} = 1\frac{1}{5}$$

Write the sum in simplest form.

$\frac{2}{3} + \frac{2}{3} = \square \quad \square$

$\frac{1}{4} + \frac{1}{4} = \square$

$\frac{3}{7} + \frac{5}{7} = \square = \square$

$\frac{7}{13} + \frac{7}{13} = \square = \square$

$\frac{9}{10} + \frac{7}{10} = \square = \square = \square$

$\frac{3}{8} + \frac{5}{8} = \square$

$\frac{5}{16} + \frac{7}{16} = \square = \square$

$\frac{8}{9} + \frac{7}{9} = \square = \square = \square$

$\frac{4}{11} + \frac{5}{11} = \square$

$\frac{5}{6} + \frac{5}{6} = \square = \square = \square$

$\frac{2}{5} + \frac{4}{5} = \square = \square$

$\frac{5}{12} + \frac{5}{12} = \square = \square$

$\frac{8}{14} + \frac{5}{14} = \square$

$\frac{1}{7} + \frac{4}{7} = \square$

$\frac{1}{8} + \frac{5}{8} = \square = \square$

$\frac{5}{7} + \frac{1}{7} = \square$

$\frac{1}{12} + \frac{3}{12} = \square = \square$

$\frac{5}{11} + \frac{9}{11} = \square = \square = \square$

$\frac{5}{18} + \frac{4}{18} = \square = \square$

$\frac{5}{9} + \frac{5}{9} = \square = \square = \square$

$\frac{4}{15} + \frac{7}{15} = \square$

$\frac{2}{5} + \frac{1}{5} = \square$

$\frac{1}{8} + \frac{5}{8} = \square = \square$

$\frac{3}{4} + \frac{3}{4} = \square = \square = \square$

$\frac{4}{15} + \frac{7}{15} = \square$

$\frac{7}{12} + \frac{11}{12} = \square = \square = \square = \square$

$\frac{9}{14} + \frac{9}{14} = \square = \square = \square$

$\frac{1}{7} + \frac{5}{7} = \square$

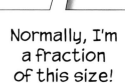

Normally, I'm a fraction of this size!

Adding fractions

Write the sum in simplest form.

$$\frac{1}{12} + \frac{3}{4} = \frac{1}{12} + \frac{9}{12} = \frac{10}{12} = \frac{5}{6}$$

$$\frac{3}{5} + \frac{7}{10} = \frac{6}{10} + \frac{7}{10} = \frac{13}{10} = 1\frac{3}{10}$$

Write the sum in simplest form.

$$\frac{1}{6} + \frac{2}{3} = \frac{}{} + \frac{}{} = \frac{}{}$$

$$\frac{1}{10} + \frac{1}{2} = \frac{}{} + \frac{}{} = \frac{}{} = \frac{}{}$$

$$\frac{8}{12} + \frac{5}{24} = \frac{}{} + \frac{}{} = \frac{}{} = \frac{}{}$$

$$\frac{6}{10} + \frac{7}{30} = \frac{}{} + \frac{}{} = \frac{}{} = \frac{}{}$$

$$\frac{5}{6} + \frac{9}{12} = \frac{}{} + \frac{}{} = \frac{}{} = \square\frac{}{}$$

$$\frac{7}{12} + \frac{7}{36} = \frac{}{} + \frac{}{} = \frac{}{} = \frac{}{}$$

$$\frac{5}{7} + \frac{7}{14} = \frac{}{} + \frac{}{} = \frac{}{} = \square\frac{}{}$$

$$\frac{7}{12} + \frac{5}{6} = \frac{}{} + \frac{}{} = \frac{}{} = \square\frac{}{}$$

$$\frac{4}{9} + \frac{2}{3} = \frac{}{} + \frac{}{} = \frac{}{} = \square\frac{}{}$$

$$\frac{19}{25} + \frac{2}{5} = \frac{}{} + \frac{}{} = \frac{}{} = \square\frac{}{}$$

$$\frac{5}{8} + \frac{5}{24} = \frac{}{} + \frac{}{} = \frac{}{} = \frac{}{}$$

$$\frac{2}{3} + \frac{7}{15} = \frac{}{} + \frac{}{} = \frac{}{} = \square\frac{}{}$$

$$\frac{4}{5} + \frac{3}{10} = \frac{}{} + \frac{}{} = \frac{}{} = \square\frac{}{}$$

$$\frac{7}{8} + \frac{1}{2} = \frac{}{} + \frac{}{} = \frac{}{} = \square\frac{}{}$$

$$\frac{11}{14} + \frac{9}{28} = \frac{}{} + \frac{}{} = \frac{}{} = \square\frac{}{}$$

$$\frac{7}{8} + \frac{3}{16} = \frac{}{} + \frac{}{} = \frac{}{} = \square\frac{}{}$$

$$\frac{3}{10} + \frac{7}{20} = \frac{}{} + \frac{}{} = \frac{}{}$$

$$\frac{25}{33} + \frac{5}{11} = \frac{}{} + \frac{}{} = \frac{}{} = \square\frac{}{}$$

Give me a hand with these sums.

Subtracting fractions

Write the answer in simplest form.

$$\frac{5}{6} - \frac{4}{6} = \boxed{\frac{1}{6}}$$

$$\frac{5}{8} - \frac{3}{8} = \boxed{\frac{\cancel{2}}{\cancel{8}}_{4}^{1}} = \boxed{\frac{1}{4}}$$

Write the answer in simplest form.

$$\frac{1}{4} - \frac{1}{4} = \boxed{}$$

$$\frac{2}{3} - \frac{1}{3} = \boxed{\frac{}{}}$$

$$\frac{11}{12} - \frac{1}{12} = \boxed{\frac{}{}} = \boxed{\frac{}{}}$$

$$\frac{6}{7} - \frac{5}{7} = \boxed{\frac{}{}}$$

$$\frac{18}{30} - \frac{12}{30} = \boxed{\frac{}{}} = \boxed{\frac{}{}}$$

$$\frac{5}{6} - \frac{1}{6} = \boxed{\frac{}{}} = \boxed{\frac{}{}}$$

$$\frac{11}{16} - \frac{7}{16} = \boxed{\frac{}{}} = \boxed{\frac{}{}}$$

$$\frac{9}{13} - \frac{5}{13} = \boxed{\frac{}{}}$$

$$\frac{12}{13} - \frac{8}{13} = \boxed{\frac{}{}}$$

$$\frac{9}{10} - \frac{7}{10} = \boxed{\frac{}{}} = \boxed{\frac{}{}}$$

$$\frac{5}{16} - \frac{2}{16} = \boxed{\frac{}{}}$$

$$\frac{7}{11} - \frac{3}{11} = \boxed{\frac{}{}}$$

$$\frac{7}{8} - \frac{3}{8} = \boxed{\frac{}{}} = \boxed{\frac{}{}}$$

$$\frac{19}{20} - \frac{7}{20} = \boxed{\frac{}{}} = \boxed{\frac{}{}}$$

$$\frac{7}{16} - \frac{4}{16} = \boxed{\frac{}{}}$$

$$\frac{8}{14} - \frac{5}{14} = \boxed{\frac{}{}}$$

$$\frac{11}{18} - \frac{8}{18} = \boxed{\frac{}{}} = \boxed{\frac{}{}}$$

$$\frac{4}{5} - \frac{1}{5} = \boxed{\frac{}{}}$$

$$\frac{5}{6} - \frac{1}{6} = \boxed{\frac{}{}} = \boxed{\frac{}{}}$$

$$\frac{14}{15} - \frac{4}{15} = \boxed{\frac{}{}} = \boxed{\frac{}{}}$$

$$\frac{5}{9} - \frac{2}{9} = \boxed{\frac{}{}} = \boxed{\frac{}{}}$$

$$\frac{5}{11} - \frac{3}{11} = \boxed{\frac{}{}}$$

$$\frac{7}{8} - \frac{1}{8} = \boxed{\frac{}{}} = \boxed{\frac{}{}}$$

$$\frac{9}{12} - \frac{5}{12} = \boxed{\frac{}{}} = \boxed{\frac{}{}}$$

$$\frac{7}{9} - \frac{4}{9} = \boxed{\frac{}{}} = \boxed{\frac{}{}}$$

$$\frac{5}{7} - \frac{1}{4} = \boxed{\frac{}{}}$$

Keep it simple for a smooth ride.

Subtracting fractions

Write the answer in simplest form.

$$\frac{1}{4} - \frac{1}{12} = \frac{3}{12} - \frac{1}{12} = \frac{2}{12} = \frac{1}{6}$$

$$\frac{3}{5} - \frac{4}{10} = \frac{6}{10} - \frac{4}{10} = \frac{2}{10} = \frac{1}{5}$$

Write the answer in simplest form.

$$\frac{8}{21} - \frac{2}{7} = \underline{\quad} - \underline{\quad} = \underline{\quad}$$

$$\frac{7}{8} - \frac{1}{2} = \underline{\quad} - \underline{\quad} = \underline{\quad}$$

$$\frac{3}{4} - \frac{3}{20} = \underline{\quad} - \underline{\quad} = \underline{\quad} = \underline{\quad}$$

$$\frac{8}{12} - \frac{3}{24} = \underline{\quad} - \underline{\quad} = \underline{\quad}$$

$$\frac{5}{7} - \frac{1}{21} = \underline{\quad} - \underline{\quad} = \underline{\quad} = \underline{\quad}$$

$$\frac{7}{9} - \frac{7}{36} = \underline{\quad} - \underline{\quad} = \underline{\quad} = \underline{\quad}$$

$$\frac{1}{2} - \frac{5}{12} = \underline{\quad} - \underline{\quad} = \underline{\quad}$$

$$\frac{6}{14} - \frac{9}{28} = \underline{\quad} - \underline{\quad} = \underline{\quad}$$

$$\frac{6}{16} - \frac{1}{4} = \underline{\quad} - \underline{\quad} = \underline{\quad} = \underline{\quad}$$

$$\frac{7}{8} - \frac{6}{16} = \underline{\quad} - \underline{\quad} = \underline{\quad} = \underline{\quad}$$

$$\frac{4}{6} - \frac{8}{12} = \underline{\quad} - \underline{\quad} = \underline{\quad}$$

$$\frac{6}{7} - \frac{5}{21} = \underline{\quad} - \underline{\quad} = \underline{\quad}$$

$$\frac{8}{9} - \frac{2}{3} = \underline{\quad} - \underline{\quad} = \underline{\quad}$$

$$\frac{17}{18} - \frac{7}{9} = \underline{\quad} - \underline{\quad} = \underline{\quad} = \underline{\quad}$$

$$\frac{2}{3} - \frac{2}{6} = \underline{\quad} - \underline{\quad} = \underline{\quad} = \underline{\quad}$$

$$\frac{6}{10} - \frac{7}{30} = \underline{\quad} - \underline{\quad} = \underline{\quad}$$

$$\frac{3}{5} - \frac{8}{15} = \underline{\quad} - \underline{\quad} = \underline{\quad}$$

$$\frac{3}{10} - \frac{3}{20} = \underline{\quad} - \underline{\quad} = \underline{\quad}$$

$$\frac{14}{18} - \frac{5}{9} = \underline{\quad} - \underline{\quad} = \underline{\quad} = \underline{\quad}$$

$$\frac{7}{12} - \frac{2}{6} = \underline{\quad} - \underline{\quad} = \underline{\quad} = \underline{\quad}$$

$$\frac{6}{10} - \frac{7}{30} = \underline{\quad} - \underline{\quad} = \underline{\quad}$$

$$\frac{10}{15} - \frac{5}{30} = \underline{\quad} - \underline{\quad} = \underline{\quad} = \underline{\quad}$$

Multiplying by two-digit numbers

Write the product for each problem.

```
    1           2
    1           1
   56          45
 x  32       x  43
 ─────       ─────
  112         135
1,680       1,800
─────       ─────
1,792       1,935
```

Can you figure out the answers to these problems?

Write the product for each problem.

84 x 22	47 x 25	23 x 24	56 x 23
75 x 24	64 x 33	51 x 32	45 x 34

Write the product for each problem.

65 x 54	72 x 68	84 x 61	85 x 79
94 x 63	58 x 57	37 x 92	75 x 26

Multiplying by two-digit numbers

Write the product for each problem.

```
      6              7
      6              6
     38             68
   x 88           x 98
    304            544
  3,040          6,120
  3,344          6,664
```

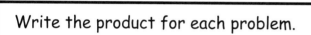

Write the product for each problem.

```
     86             76             94             99
   x 98           x 78           x 69           x 65
_____        _____        _____        _____
_____        _____        _____        _____


     74             67             94             87
   x 33           x 76           x 79           x 49
_____        _____        _____        _____
_____        _____        _____        _____
```

Write the product for each problem.

```
     46             84             87             58
   x 67           x 71           x 79           x 63
_____        _____        _____        _____
_____        _____        _____        _____


     73             79             96             48
   x 98           x 87           x 78           x 27
_____        _____        _____        _____
_____        _____        _____        _____
```

Dividing by one-digit numbers

Find the quotient. Estimate your answer first.

3 x 100 = 300, so the quotient will be less than 100.
3 x 80 = 240 and 3 x 90 = 270, so the quotient will be between 80 and 90.

$$\begin{array}{r} 89\ \text{r}\ 1 \\ 3\overline{)268} \\ 24 \\ \hline 28 \\ 27 \\ \hline 1 \end{array}$$

Find the quotients. Remember to estimate your answers first.

$2\overline{)467}$　　　　$4\overline{)823}$　　　　$3\overline{)605}$

Make a good guess then check it out...QUICKLY!

$2\overline{)147}$　　　　$3\overline{)259}$　　　　$5\overline{)812}$

$3\overline{)739}$　　　　$4\overline{)406}$　　　　$2\overline{)593}$

114

Dividing by one-digit numbers

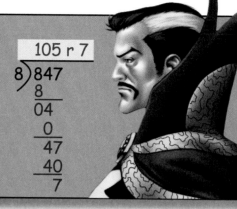

Find the quotients. Remember to estimate your answers first.

6)733

7)465

8)941

8)532

7)566

7)499

9)184

6)598

7)635

I just love dividing up the spoils of battle!

115

Real-life problems

Find the answer to each problem.

Jean spends $42.99 on new shoes. Scott spends $76.54 on gifts. How much more does he spend than Jean?

```
        14
      5 4 14
    7̶6̶.̶5̶4̶
   -  42.99
      33.55
```
$33.55

Professor X buys some new equipment. He spends $99 a day for 16 days. How much does he spend?

```
       99
    ×  16
      594
      990
    1,584
```
$1,584

Black Cat has $5,762 in stocks and $3,247 in her bank. How much does she have altogether?

A shop in Chicago takes in $9,651 on a Saturday. It is burgled by Black Cat, who steals $3,247. How much does the Chicago shop have left?

117 S.H.I.E.L.D. agents claim $2 each for their expenses, and 251 agents claim $3 each, how much did the agents claim altogether?

Jean Grey has $50. She spends $2.50 on candies, $5.75 on flowers, and $24.25 on new shoes. How much money does she have left?

Agent Zero earns $1,200 a day as a mercenary. How much will he earn in 5 days?

Real-life problems

Find the answer to each problem.

The Human Torch flies around
a building 8 times. If he flies
a total of 944 yards, what
is the perimeter of the building?

118 yd

```
      118
   ┌──────
 8 ) 944
      8
      14
      8
      64
      64
      0
```

Professor X's study is 5.75 m long
and his dining room is 4.37 m long.
If he knocks out the wall between
the two rooms to make one room,
how long will it be?

10.12 m

```
   5.75
 + 4.37
  10.12
```

The Ghost Rider took 5 hours to reach his
destination. If he traveled 600 miles each
hour, how far did he travel altogether?

Two Marvel heroes weigh 218 lb and 173 lb. What
is the difference between their weights?

A school raises money for charity. If 127 children
brought in $2 each, and 261 children brought in $3
each, how much did the school raise altogether?

An electrician uses 560 yd of wire in the Baxter Building's
7 offices. If he uses the same amount of wire in each
office, how much wire did he use per office?

One of Thor's hammers weighs 36 oz. How much will
8 hammers weigh?

Quicksilver runs 1,432 m in 40 seconds. Wolverine
runs 227.22 m in the same time. How much farther
does Quicksilver run than Wolverine?

Problems involving time

Find the answer to each problem.

A yard sale began at 1 P.M. and ended at 4:35 P.M. How long did it last?

1:00 -> 4:00 = 3 h

4:00 -> 4:35 = 35 min

Total = 3 h 35 min

3 h 35 min

Find the answer to this problem.

Professor X's watch says 2:27. What time will it say in 1 h 26 min?

2:27 + 1 h = 3:27

3:27 + 26 min = 3:53

3:53

Wolverine's mission takes 2 hours 25 minutes to complete. If he began the mission at 1:35 P.M., at what time was Wolverine finished ?

It takes 1 hour 10 minutes to test The Blackbird's engines and another 55 minutes to check its avionics. What is the total time needed to get The Blackbird ready to fly?

Moira MacTaggert has to be at the Mutant Research Center by 7:50 A.M. If she takes 1 hour 15 minutes to get ready, and the trip takes 50 minutes, at what time does she need to get up?

Looking at graphs

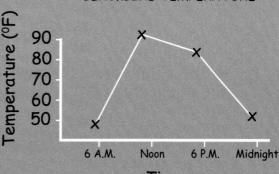

I need a graph to plot a plan...

Forge recorded the temperature in The Blackbird during one day. At what time was the temperature at its highest?

noon

By how much did the temperature fall between 6 P.M. and midnight?

35°F

BLACKBIRD TEMPERATURE

Temperature (°F)

90
80
70
60
50

6 A.M.   Noon   6 P.M.   Midnight

Time

Professor X keeps a score of X-Men missions.

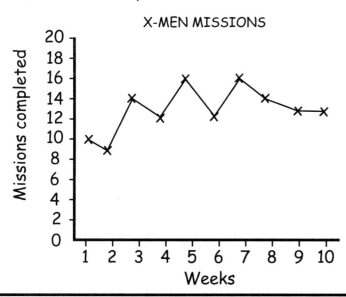

X-MEN MISSIONS

Missions completed

20
18
16
14
12
10
8
6
4
2
0

1 2 3 4 5 6 7 8 9 10

Weeks

How many missions were there in week 3?

In which 2 consecutive weeks were the same number of missions run?

What was the highest total of missions in a week?

The graph shows the maximum temperatures in Madripoor.

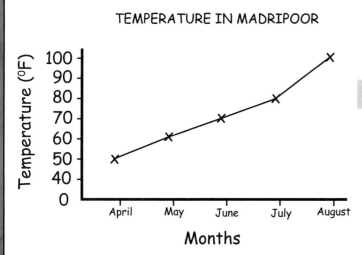

TEMPERATURE IN MADRIPOOR

Temperature (°F)

100
90
80
70
60
50
40
0

April   May   June   July   August

Months

What was the maximum temperature in July?

How much did the temperature rise between April and August?

Place value for whole numbers

Write the value of 6 in 563 in standard form and word form.

60   sixty

What happens to the value of 247 if you change the 2 to a 3?

The value of the number increases by 100.

Everyone should know their place ... and value.

Write the value of 7 in these numbers in standard and number form.

27	172	37,904	12,712

Circle the numbers that have a 5 with a value of fifty.

457,682   53   570,234   372,985

154   23,451   4,950   16,757

Write what happens to the value of each number.

Change the 6 in 3,586 to 3.

Change the 9 in 1,921 to 8.

Change the 7 in 7,246 to 9.

Change the 5 in 50,247 to 1.

Change the 2 in 90,205 to 9.

Change the 4 in 4,601 to 1.

Place value for decimals

Write the value of 5 in 7.53 in standard form and word form.

0.5	5 tenths

What happens to the value of 3.48 if you change the 8 to 1?

The value of the number decreases by 0.07.

Write the value of the 8 in these numbers in standard and written form.

2.8	0.18	875.04	8.12

0.98	581.65	18.95	3.86

Write what happens to the value of each number.

Change the 6 in 12,586 to 3.

Change the 2 in 1.02 to 6.

Change the 3 in 3,460 to 9.

Change the 3 in 328.45 to 1.

Circle the numbers that have a 5 with the value of 5 hundredths.

555.52   99.95   16.53   5.35   52.59

Circle the numbers that have an 8 with a value of 8 tenths.

557.68   2.8   75.82   8.09   557.86

Circle the numbers that have a 3 with the value of 3 tenths.

3,603.3   0.93   32.45   5.33   23.53

121

Reading tally charts

Use the chart to answer the questions.

PET PREFERENCES

Pet	Number
Dog	IIII IIII IIII
Cat	IIII IIII IIII I
Fish	IIII III

What is the most popular pet for X-Men?

cats

How many more prefer dogs than fish?

14 - 8 = 6

Use the chart to answer the question.

APPEARANCES IN MARVEL

Wolverine	Lizard	Rogue	Spider-Man
IIII IIII IIII IIII	IIII III	IIII IIII I	IIII IIII IIII IIII

Which characters appeared more than 12 times?

How many times did Rogue appear?

How many more times did Wolverine appear than Rogue?

I will NOT let Spider-Man win!

Use the chart to answer the questions.

SNACKS CHOSEN BY S.H.I.E.L.D AGENTS

Carrots	Fries	Cookies	Pretzels
IIII	IIII IIII III	IIII IIII IIII II	IIII IIII IIII IIII II

What snack did fewer than 12 agents choose?

How many chose the most popular snack?

What is the total number of agents who chose fries and cookies?

Volumes of cubes

This cube is 1 cm long, 1 cm high, and 1 cm wide. We say it has a volume of 1 cubic centimeter (1 cm³). If we put 4 of these cubes together, the new shape has a volume of 4 cm³.

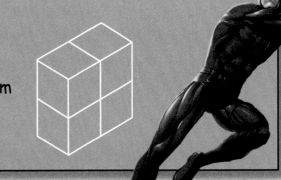

These shapes are made of 1 cm³ cubes. What are their volumes?

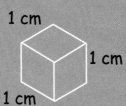

cm³

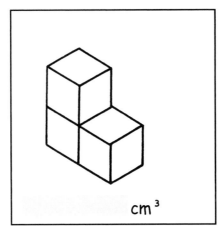

cm³

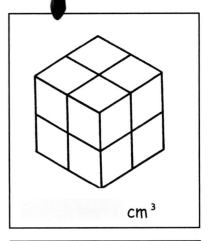

cm³

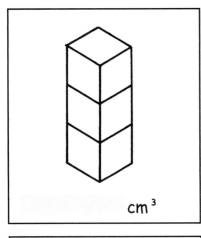

cm³

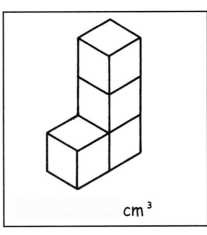

cm³

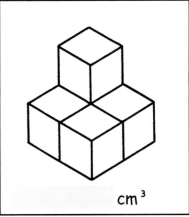

cm³

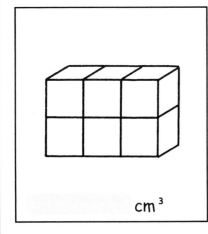

cm³

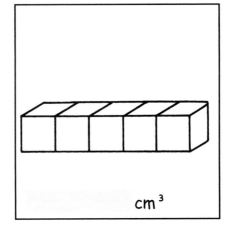

cm³

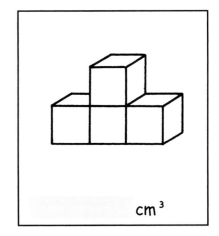

cm³

Acute and obtuse angles

A right angle forms a square corner.

An obtuse angle is greater than a right angle.

An acute angle is less than a right angle.

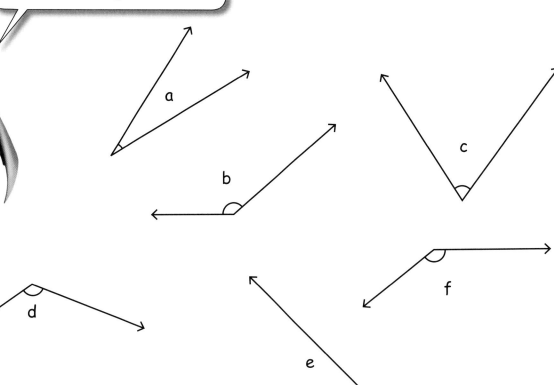

I don't like tight corners.

Which of the angles are acute?

Which of the angles are obtuse?

Acute and obtuse angles

This angle measures 45°.

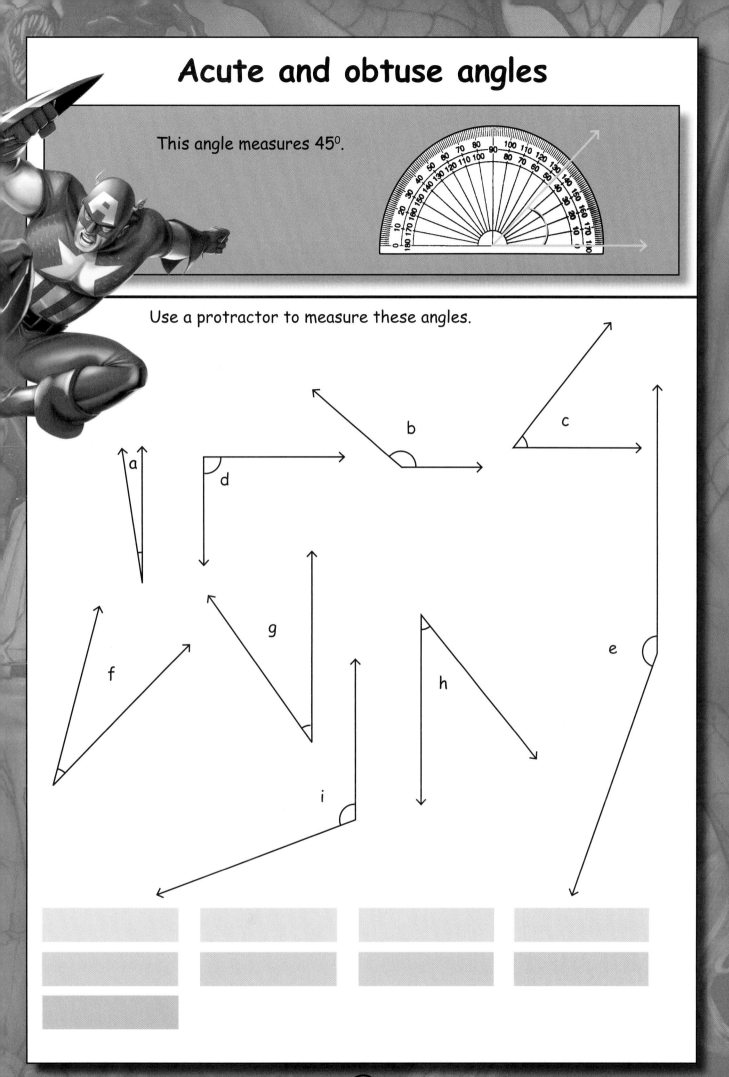

Use a protractor to measure these angles.

Addition fact families

Circle the number sentence that is in the same fact family as the first pair.

| 24 - 10 = 12
12 + 10 = 24 | 12 - 6 = 6 | (10 + 12 = 24) | 12 + 12 = 24 |
| 10 - 8 = 2
8 + 2 = 10 | 8 + 10 = 18 | (10 - 2 = 8) | 18 - 10 = 8 |

Circle the number sentence that is in the same fact family as the first pair.

7 + 8 = 15 8 + 7 = 15	8 - 7 = 1	15 - 8 = 7	7 + 5 = 12
15 - 6 = 9 9 + 6 = 15	15 - 9 = 6	15 + 6 = 21	21 - 15 = 6
14 - 5 = 9 14 - 9 = 5	9 - 3 = 6	14 + 9 = 23	5 + 9 = 14
7 + 9 = 16 9 + 7 = 16	16 - 9 = 7	16 + 9 = 25	7 + 16 = 23
19 - 9 = 10 19 - 10 = 9	9 + 3 = 12	9 + 10 = 19	18 - 8 = 10
6 + 7 = 13 13 - 7 = 6	13 + 6 = 19	13 - 6 = 7	7 + 13 = 20

Me and my alien costume make a great pair.

Write the fact family for every group of numbers.

| 7, 12, 5 | 6, 10, 4 | 5, 13, 8 |

Odds and evens

Everything evens out in the end.

Write the answer in the box.

5 + 5 = [10]   6 + 5 = [11]   7 + 3 = [10]   2 + 6 = [8]

Add the even numbers to the even numbers.

6 + 8 =   12 + 8 =   10 + 6 =   20 + 40 =

18 + 14 =   14 + 12 =   16 + 10 =   30 + 20 =

14 + 16 =   18 + 6 =   22 + 8 =   8 + 14 =

What do you notice about each answer? _____

Add the odd numbers to the odd numbers.

3 + 5 =   5 + 7 =   11 + 5 =   13 + 15 =

7 + 7 =   9 + 3 =   15 + 5 =   13 + 7 =

11 + 3 =   17 + 9 =   15 + 9 =   9 + 5 =

What do you notice about each answer? _____

Add the odd numbers to the even numbers.

3 + 8 =   13 + 30 =   5 + 18 =   7 + 14 =

13 + 4 =   13 + 10 =   15 + 6 =   21 + 4 =

7 + 20 =   9 + 12 =   11 + 16 =   17 + 8 =

What do you notice about each answer? _____

Add the even numbers to the odd numbers.

8 + 7 =   8 + 5 =   8 + 13 =   2 + 17 =

12 + 29 =   14 + 3 =   16 + 9 =   12 + 5 =

What do you notice about each answer? _____

Word problems

Write the answer in the box.

I multiply a number by 6 and the answer is 24.

What number did I begin with?   4

Do it NOW!

Write the answer in the box.

A number multiplied by 7 equals 35. What is the number?

I divide a number by 10 and the answer is 4. What number did I divide?

I multiply a number by 4 and the answer is 20. What is the number
I multiplied?

After dividing a piece of wood into four equal sections, each section
is 4 in. long. How long was the piece of wood I started with?

A number multiplied by 5 gives the answer 25. What is the number?

Some money is divided into five equal amounts. Each amount is 10
cents. How much money was there before it was divided?

I multiply a number by 7 and the result is 42. What number
was multiplied?

A number divided by 6 is 4. What number was divided?

Three children share 21 peanuts equally among themselves.
How many peanuts does each child receive?

A number divided by 4 is 9. What is the number?

I multiply a number by 6 and the answer is 30. What is the number?

Four sets of a number equal 20. What is the number?

A child divides a number by 8 and gets 2. What was the number?

Three groups of a number equal 27. What is the number?

Word problems

Write the answer in the box.

Phoenix is given ten dimes. How much money does she have altogether?

$1

Write the answer in the box.

Four helicopters carry a total of 100 spies. How many spies are in each helicopter?

The Beast has a box containing 6 computer disks. How many boxes would he need to buy to have 18 disks?

Peter Parker is given three bags of candy. There are 20 pieces of candy in each bag. How many pieces of candy does Peter have in total?

There are 210 planets in a solar system and the Silver Surfer visits 60. How many has he not visited in the system?

Rogue, Daredevil, and Dazzler win the lottery and share $900 equally among themselves. How much does each receive?

A truck contains 50 barrels of oil. It delivers 27 barrels to Kingpin. How many barrels are left on the truck?

Gambit has a collection of 150 cards. He gives 35 of them to a friend. How many cards does he have left?

When Storm multiplies her apartment number by 4, the result is 76. What is her apartment number?

One Marvel comic costs $1.80. How much will three comics cost?

The Hulk transforms 20 times on Monday, 30 times on Tuesday, and 40 times on Wednesday. How many times has he transformed altogether in these three days?

Rogue's car trip is supposed to be 70 miles long but her car breaks down half-way. How far has she traveled?

Blade battles with 32 vampires. Only 13 vampires escape. How many vampires has Blade defeated?

Multiples

Circle the multiples of 3.

4   7   (9)   14   20   (24)

Circle the multiples of 3.

8	11	16	18	24	27	31	35
10	20	30	40	50	60	70	80
1	3	5	7	9	11	13	15
2	5	8	11	14	17	20	23
4	11	15	19	26	30	34	41
0	3	9	12	15	21	24	30
11	19	30	41	49	60	71	79
5	10	16	20	26	31	40	47
2	7	13	17	21	25	33	60

Circle the multiples of 4.

2	7	11	15	19	23	28	31
2	4	6	8	10	12	14	16
1	3	5	7	9	11	13	15
5	10	15	20	25	30	35	40
8	16	22	30	34	40	48	54
3	6	9	12	15	18	21	24
9	11	12	15	16	18		
11	13	15	17	19	20		
18	24	30	36	42	48		

Factors

Write the factors of each number.

| 6 | 1, 2, 3, 6 | 8 | 1, 2, 4, 8 |

You've only got one chance.

Write the factors of each number.

9		10		12	
4		3		14	
5		15		17	
7		20		19	
13		24		11	
2		30		16	

Write the factors of each number.

1		4		16	
25		36		49	
64		81		100	

Do you notice anything about the number of factors each of the numbers has?
_____
Do you know the name for these special numbers? _____

Write the factors of each number.

7		3		13	
2		11		5	
29		19		37	
17		31		23	

Do you notice anything about the number of factors each of the numbers has?
_____
Do you know the name for these special numbers? _____

Fractions

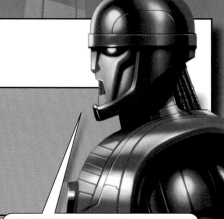

Write the answer in the box.

$$1 \frac{1}{2} + \frac{1}{4} = \boxed{1 \frac{3}{4}} \qquad 2 \frac{1}{4} + 3 \frac{1}{2} = \boxed{5 \frac{3}{4}}$$

Every piece counts!

Write the answer in the box.

$$3 \frac{1}{4} + 2 \frac{1}{4} = \qquad\qquad 2 \frac{1}{2} + 3 \frac{1}{2} = \qquad\qquad 1 \frac{1}{4} + 4 \frac{1}{2} =$$

$$3 \frac{1}{2} + 1 = \qquad\qquad 2 \frac{1}{4} + 4 = \qquad\qquad 2 \frac{1}{2} + 3 \frac{1}{4} =$$

$$1 \frac{1}{4} + 4 \frac{1}{2} = \qquad\qquad 5 + 1 \frac{1}{2} = \qquad\qquad 2 \frac{1}{2} + 1 \frac{1}{2} =$$

$$3 \frac{1}{4} + 1 \frac{1}{2} = \qquad\qquad 2 + 3 \frac{1}{2} = \qquad\qquad 8 \frac{1}{4} + 1 \frac{1}{2} =$$

$$4 + \frac{1}{4} = \qquad\qquad 5 \frac{1}{4} + \frac{1}{2} = \qquad\qquad 2 \frac{1}{2} + 7 \frac{1}{4} =$$

Write the answer in the box.

$$1 \frac{1}{3} + 2 \frac{2}{3} = \qquad\qquad 3 \frac{1}{3} + 4 \frac{2}{3} = \qquad\qquad 1 \frac{2}{3} + 5 =$$

$$1 \frac{2}{3} + 2 = \qquad\qquad 4 \frac{1}{3} + 1 \frac{2}{3} = \qquad\qquad 3 \frac{1}{3} + 1 \frac{2}{3} =$$

$$3 \frac{2}{3} + 1 \frac{2}{3} = \qquad\qquad 2 \frac{1}{3} + 4 \frac{1}{3} = \qquad\qquad 3 + 2 \frac{1}{3} =$$

$$5 \frac{2}{3} + 2 \frac{2}{3} = \qquad\qquad 3 \frac{1}{3} + 1 \frac{1}{3} = \qquad\qquad 2 \frac{2}{3} + 2 \frac{2}{3} =$$

$$6 \frac{1}{3} + 2 \frac{1}{3} = \qquad\qquad 4 \frac{2}{3} + 2 \frac{2}{3} = \qquad\qquad 1 \frac{2}{3} + 4 =$$

Write the answer in the box.

$$3 \frac{2}{5} + \frac{2}{5} = \qquad\qquad \frac{3}{5} + \frac{3}{5} = \qquad\qquad 1 \frac{4}{5} + 6 =$$

$$3 \frac{2}{5} + \frac{4}{5} = \qquad\qquad 5 \frac{3}{5} + 1 \frac{1}{5} = \qquad\qquad 3 \frac{1}{5} + 3 \frac{2}{5} =$$

Fractions and decimals

Write each fraction as a decimal.

$5\frac{1}{2}$ = $9\frac{1}{2}$ = $4\frac{6}{10}$ = $11\frac{1}{2}$ =

$2\frac{1}{10}$ = $2\frac{4}{10}$ = $8\frac{1}{10}$ = $5\frac{1}{2}$ =

$7\frac{8}{10}$ = $2\frac{3}{10}$ = $6\frac{1}{2}$ = $8\frac{4}{10}$ =

$7\frac{4}{10}$ = $3\frac{1}{10}$ = $6\frac{7}{10}$ = $1\frac{1}{2}$ =

Write each decimal as a fraction.

3.2 =   4.5 =   17.5 =   1.2 =

6.5 =   2.7 =   13.2 =   5.5 =

7.2 =   8.5 =   9.7 =   10.2 =

11.5 =   12.7 =   5.2 =   14.5 =

14.7 =   16.2 =   1.7 =   18.7 =

Write each fraction as a decimal.

$1\frac{1}{2}$ = $2\frac{2}{10}$ = $3\frac{3}{10}$ =

Write each decimal as a fraction.

2.5 =   1.2 =   3.7 =

133

Real-life problems

Write the answer in the box.

A number multiplied by 8 is 56.
What is the number? `7`

I divide a number by 8 and the result is 6.
What is the number? `48`

Write the answer in the box.

A number multiplied by 7 is 42.
What is the number?

I divide a number by 7 and
the result is 4. What number
did I begin with?

I divide a number by 9 and
the result is 6. What number
did I begin with?

A number multiplied by itself
gives the answer 36. What is
the number?

I divide a number by 7 and
the answer is 7. What number
did I begin with?

When I multiply a number by 7
I end up with 56. What number
did I begin with?

Seven times a number is 63.
What is the number?

What do I have to multiply
8 by to get the result 72?

Six times a number is 42.
What is the number?

Nine times a number is 81.
What is the number?

A number divided by 8 gives
the answer 10. What was the
starting number?

When 6 is multiplied by a number
the result is 42. What number
was 6 multiplied by?

I multiply a number by 9 and
end up with 45. What number
did I multiply?

I multiply a number by 9 and
the result is 81. What number
did I begin with?

SAVE YOURSELF!
Do these as
quickly as
you can.

Symmetry

The dotted line is a mirror line. Complete each shape.

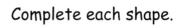

Complete each shape.

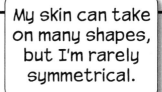

My skin can take on many shapes, but I'm rarely symmetrical.

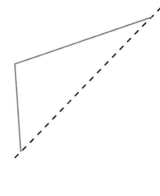

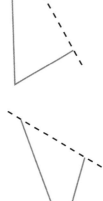

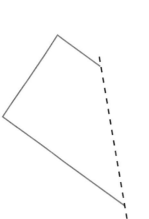

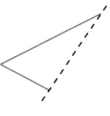

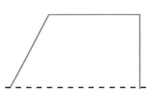

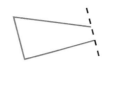

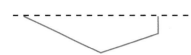

Fractions and decimals

Write each fraction as a decimal.

$\frac{1}{10}$ $\frac{1}{2}$ $\frac{3}{10}$ $\frac{2}{5}$

$\frac{2}{10}$ $\frac{9}{10}$ $\frac{1}{10}$ $\frac{9}{10}$

$\frac{4}{10}$ $\frac{3}{10}$ $\frac{8}{10}$ $\frac{5}{10}$

$\frac{6}{10}$ $\frac{7}{10}$ $\frac{5}{10}$ $\frac{1}{2}$

Write each decimal as a fraction.

0.25 =   0.4 =   0.5 =   0.9 =

0.8 =   0.6 =   0.2 =   0.8 =

0.1 =   0.7 =   0.3 =   0.4 =

0.2 =   0.5 =   0.6 =   0.75 =

Write the answer in the box.

Which two of the fractions above are the same as 0.5?

Which two of the fractions above are the same as 0.4?

Which two of the fractions above are the same as 0.6?

Which two of the fractions above are the same as 0.2?

Fractions of shapes

Shade $\frac{3}{5}$ of each shape.

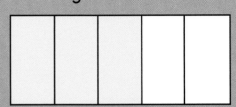

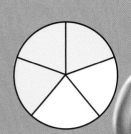

Can you see the whole picture?

Shade $\frac{4}{5}$ of each shape.

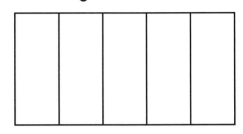

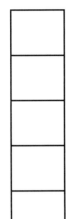

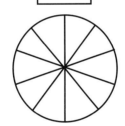

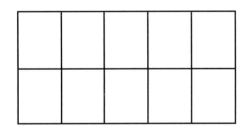

Shade the fraction shown of each shape.

$\frac{3}{10}$

$\frac{8}{10}$

$\frac{3}{10}$

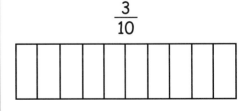

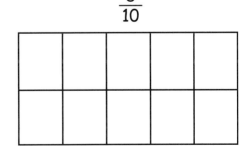

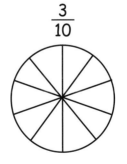

$\frac{7}{10}$

$\frac{6}{10}$

$\frac{9}{10}$

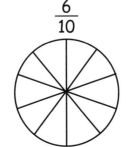

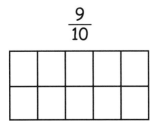

Fractions

Color $\frac{3}{4}$ of each shape.

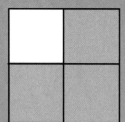
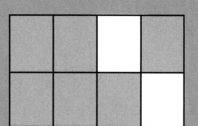

Color $\frac{2}{3}$ of each shape.

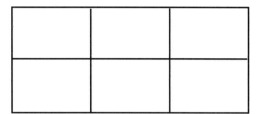
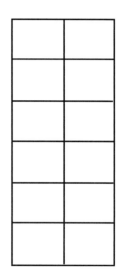

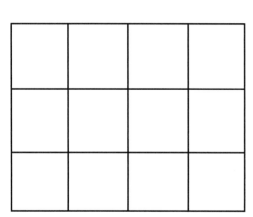
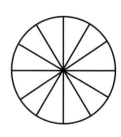

Color $\frac{3}{4}$ of each shape.

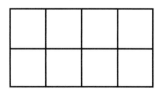
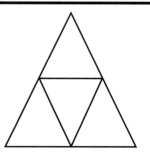
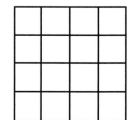
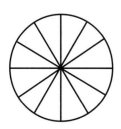
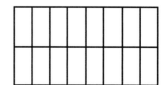

Reading timetables

	Harbor	Hightown	Barker Plaza	Princess St.
Redline bus	8:10	8:15	8:25	8:35
Blueline tram	8:15	no stop	no stop	8:30
City taxi	8:30	8:35	8:45	8:55
Greenline trolley	8:16	no stop	8:21	8:24

The timetable shows the times it takes to travel between different places in Madripoor, using different transport companies.

Write the answer in the box.

How long does the Redline bus take to travel from the Harbor to Princess Street?

When does the City taxi arrive at Barker Plaza?

Where is the Greenline trolley at 8:21?

Where does the trolley not stop?

Does the tram stop at Barker Plaza?

How long does the tram take to travel between the Harbor and Princess Street?

Which is the fastest trip between the Harbor and Princess Street?

Which service arrives at Princess Street at 8:30?

How long does the City taxi take to get from Hightown to Barker Plaza?

Where is the City taxi at 8:35?

Averages

Write the mean average of this row in the box.

| 5 | 3 | 3 | 3 | 7 | 4 | 3 |

The mean average is **4**

Write the mean average of each row in the box.

3	4	8	5	3	8	3	6	
1	2	6	3	1	6	1	4	
5	3	5	3	5	2	4	5	
5	7	7	9	2	4	8	6	
4	3	4	3	4	7	4	3	
1	4	2	7	3	2	8	5	
7	5	8	3	6	3	8	8	

Write the mean average of each row in the box.

6	4	8	6	3	9	6	6	
5	5	9	2	6	9	1	3	
5	6	3	8	6	1	5	6	
6	3	8	6	7	5	9	4	
4	1	8	3	4	2	6	4	
7	9	5	8	7	4	7	9	
1	3	2	3	1	2	2	2	
6	3	7	4	5	8	2	5	

Multiplying larger numbers by ones

Write the product for each problem.

Time to run!

$$\begin{array}{r} {\scriptstyle 1\ 3} \\ 529 \\ \times\ \ \ 4 \\ \hline 2,116 \end{array} \qquad \begin{array}{r} {\scriptstyle 1\ 3\ 1} \\ 1,273 \\ \times\ \ \ 5 \\ \hline 6,365 \end{array}$$

Write the product for each problem.

$$\begin{array}{r} 724 \\ \times\ \ 2 \\ \hline \end{array} \qquad \begin{array}{r} 831 \\ \times\ \ 3 \\ \hline \end{array} \qquad \begin{array}{r} 126 \\ \times\ \ 3 \\ \hline \end{array} \qquad \begin{array}{r} 455 \\ \times\ \ 4 \\ \hline \end{array}$$

$$\begin{array}{r} 261 \\ \times\ \ 4 \\ \hline \end{array} \qquad \begin{array}{r} 182 \\ \times\ \ 5 \\ \hline \end{array} \qquad \begin{array}{r} 449 \\ \times\ \ 5 \\ \hline \end{array} \qquad \begin{array}{r} 253 \\ \times\ \ 6 \\ \hline \end{array}$$

$$\begin{array}{r} 328 \\ \times\ \ 6 \\ \hline \end{array} \qquad \begin{array}{r} 465 \\ \times\ \ 6 \\ \hline \end{array} \qquad \begin{array}{r} 105 \\ \times\ \ 4 \\ \hline \end{array} \qquad \begin{array}{r} 562 \\ \times\ \ 4 \\ \hline \end{array}$$

Write the product for each problem.

$$\begin{array}{r} 4,268 \\ \times\ \ \ 3 \\ \hline \end{array} \qquad \begin{array}{r} 1,582 \\ \times\ \ \ 3 \\ \hline \end{array} \qquad \begin{array}{r} 3,612 \\ \times\ \ \ 4 \\ \hline \end{array} \qquad \begin{array}{r} 4,284 \\ \times\ \ \ 4 \\ \hline \end{array}$$

$$\begin{array}{r} 4,907 \\ \times\ \ \ 5 \\ \hline \end{array} \qquad \begin{array}{r} 1,263 \\ \times\ \ \ 5 \\ \hline \end{array} \qquad \begin{array}{r} 1,303 \\ \times\ \ \ 6 \\ \hline \end{array} \qquad \begin{array}{r} 1,467 \\ \times\ \ \ 6 \\ \hline \end{array}$$

$$\begin{array}{r} 5,521 \\ \times\ \ \ 6 \\ \hline \end{array} \qquad \begin{array}{r} 8,436 \\ \times\ \ \ 6 \\ \hline \end{array} \qquad \begin{array}{r} 1,599 \\ \times\ \ \ 6 \\ \hline \end{array} \qquad \begin{array}{r} 3,761 \\ \times\ \ \ 6 \\ \hline \end{array}$$

$$\begin{array}{r} 6,837 \\ \times\ \ \ 4 \\ \hline \end{array} \qquad \begin{array}{r} 6,394 \\ \times\ \ \ 5 \\ \hline \end{array} \qquad \begin{array}{r} 8,124 \\ \times\ \ \ 6 \\ \hline \end{array} \qquad \begin{array}{r} 3,914 \\ \times\ \ \ 6 \\ \hline \end{array}$$

Multiplying larger numbers by ones

Write the product for each problem.

$$
\begin{array}{r}
{\scriptstyle 1\,4}\\
417\\
\times\ \ 7\\
\hline
2,919\\
\end{array}
\qquad
\begin{array}{r}
{\scriptstyle 1\ 7\,4}\\
2,185\\
\times\ \ \ \ 9\\
\hline
19,665\\
\end{array}
$$

Smash through these sums!

Write the answer to each problem.

$$
\begin{array}{r}
604\\
\times\ \ 7\\
\hline
\end{array}
\qquad
\begin{array}{r}
413\\
\times\ \ 7\\
\hline
\end{array}
\qquad
\begin{array}{r}
682\\
\times\ \ 8\\
\hline
\end{array}
\qquad
\begin{array}{r}
327\\
\times\ \ 7\\
\hline
\end{array}
$$

$$
\begin{array}{r}
436\\
\times\ \ 8\\
\hline
\end{array}
\qquad
\begin{array}{r}
171\\
\times\ \ 9\\
\hline
\end{array}
\qquad
\begin{array}{r}
715\\
\times\ \ 8\\
\hline
\end{array}
\qquad
\begin{array}{r}
254\\
\times\ \ 8\\
\hline
\end{array}
$$

$$
\begin{array}{r}
235\\
\times\ \ 8\\
\hline
\end{array}
\qquad
\begin{array}{r}
319\\
\times\ \ 9\\
\hline
\end{array}
\qquad
\begin{array}{r}
581\\
\times\ \ 9\\
\hline
\end{array}
\qquad
\begin{array}{r}
999\\
\times\ \ 9\\
\hline
\end{array}
$$

Work out the answer to each problem.

$$
\begin{array}{r}
2,816\\
\times\ \ \ \ 7\\
\hline
\end{array}
\qquad
\begin{array}{r}
4,331\\
\times\ \ \ \ 7\\
\hline
\end{array}
\qquad
\begin{array}{r}
2,617\\
\times\ \ \ \ 8\\
\hline
\end{array}
\qquad
\begin{array}{r}
1,439\\
\times\ \ \ \ 8\\
\hline
\end{array}
$$

$$
\begin{array}{r}
4,022\\
\times\ \ \ \ 8\\
\hline
\end{array}
\qquad
\begin{array}{r}
3,104\\
\times\ \ \ \ 8\\
\hline
\end{array}
\qquad
\begin{array}{r}
2,591\\
\times\ \ \ \ 9\\
\hline
\end{array}
\qquad
\begin{array}{r}
4,361\\
\times\ \ \ \ 9\\
\hline
\end{array}
$$

$$
\begin{array}{r}
4,361\\
\times\ \ \ \ 9\\
\hline
\end{array}
\qquad
\begin{array}{r}
3,002\\
\times\ \ \ \ 8\\
\hline
\end{array}
\qquad
\begin{array}{r}
2,567\\
\times\ \ \ \ 7\\
\hline
\end{array}
\qquad
\begin{array}{r}
1,514\\
\times\ \ \ \ 8\\
\hline
\end{array}
$$

$$
\begin{array}{r}
4,624\\
\times\ \ \ \ 7\\
\hline
\end{array}
\qquad
\begin{array}{r}
3,894\\
\times\ \ \ \ 8\\
\hline
\end{array}
\qquad
\begin{array}{r}
2,993\\
\times\ \ \ \ 8\\
\hline
\end{array}
\qquad
\begin{array}{r}
1,710\\
\times\ \ \ \ 9\\
\hline
\end{array}
$$

Real-life multiplication problems

There are 157 gamma-chargers in each box.
How many will there be in three boxes?

471 gamma-chargers

$$\begin{array}{r} \overset{1\,2}{157} \\ \times\quad 3 \\ \hline 471 \end{array}$$

Each of Doctor Strange's disk holders can hold 660 disks.
If he has 5 holders, how many will they hold altogether?

A train that runs across District X can take 425 passengers.
How many can it take on five trips?

Bullseye puts $278 into the bank every
month. How much will he have put in
after 6 months?

Hightown theater can seat 4,536 people. If a play runs for 7
days, what is the maximum number of people who will be able
to see the play?

Punisher's motorcycle costs $35,956.
How much will it cost the X-Men to buy
4 new motorcycles?

The Blackbird flies at a steady speed
of 1,550 mph. How far will the plane
travel in 6 hours?

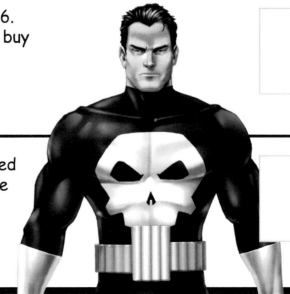

Area of rectangles and squares

Find the area of the tan rectangle.

To find the area of a rectangle or square, we multiply length (l) by width (w).

Area = 800 in.²

(w)

(l)

25 in.

32 in.

$$\begin{array}{r} \overset{1}{3}2 \\ \times\ 25 \\ \hline 160 \\ +\ 640 \\ \hline 800 \text{ in.}^2 \end{array}$$

Find the area of these rectangles and squares. You may need to do your work on a separate sheet.

There's no limit to the area my storms cover.

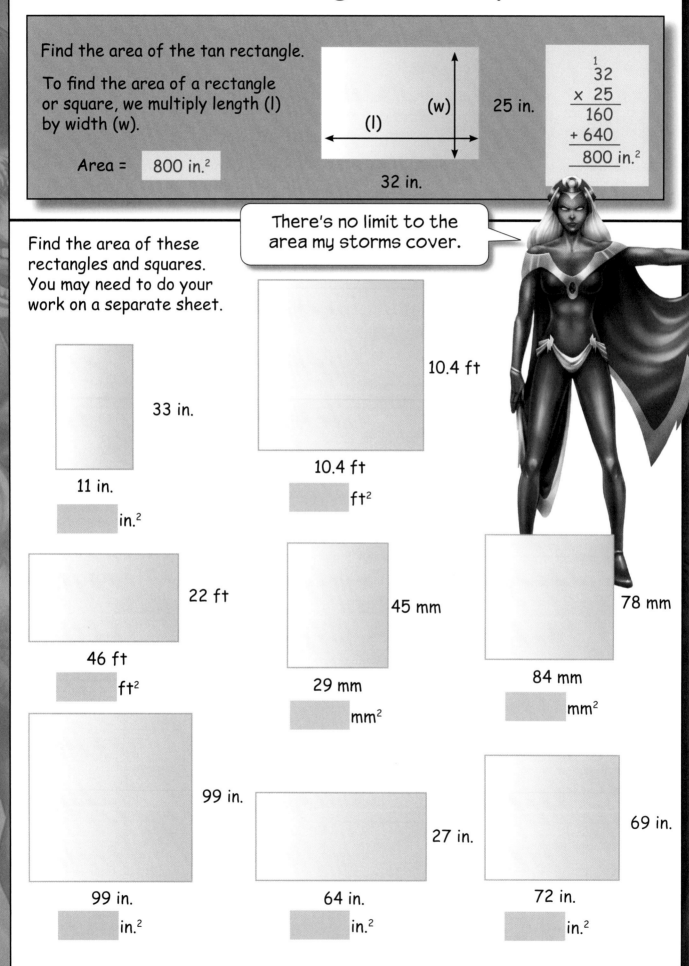

33 in.

11 in.

in.²

10.4 ft

10.4 ft

ft²

22 ft

46 ft

ft²

45 mm

29 mm

mm²

78 mm

84 mm

mm²

99 in.

99 in.

in.²

27 in.

64 in.

in.²

69 in.

72 in.

in.²

Perimeter of shapes

Find the perimeter of this brown rectangle. To find the perimeter of a rectangle or square, we add the two lengths and the two widths together.

13.3 in.

25.4 in.

```
  1 1
 13.3
 13.3
 25.4
+25.4
 77.4 in.
```

77.4 in.

Find the perimeter of these rectangles and squares. You may need to do your work on an extra sheet.

20.6 ft

20.6 ft

_____ ft

28.9 ft

48.3 ft

_____ ft

134 mm

134 mm

_____ mm

25 mm

55 mm

_____ mm

35.6 ft

18.2 ft

_____ ft

50.5 ft

50.5 ft

_____ ft

17 in.

35 in.

_____ in.

35 mm

19 mm

_____ mm

145

Adding fractions

Work out the answer to the problem.

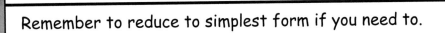

$$\frac{1}{5} + \frac{3}{5} = \boxed{\frac{4}{5}} \qquad \frac{4}{9} + \frac{2}{9} = \frac{6 \div 2}{9 \div 3} = \boxed{\frac{2}{3}}$$

Add the numerators but keep the denominators when they are the same.

Remember to reduce to simplest form if you need to.

$\dfrac{2}{9} + \dfrac{5}{9} = \dfrac{}{9}$ $\qquad$ $\dfrac{2}{7} + \dfrac{3}{7} = \dfrac{}{7}$ $\qquad$ $\dfrac{1}{3} + \dfrac{1}{3} = \dfrac{}{3}$

$\dfrac{2}{9} + \dfrac{3}{9} = \dfrac{}{}$ $\qquad$ $\dfrac{2}{8} + \dfrac{1}{8} = \dfrac{}{}$ $\qquad$ $\dfrac{3}{10} + \dfrac{6}{10} = \dfrac{}{}$

$\dfrac{4}{20} + \dfrac{5}{20} = \dfrac{}{}$ $\qquad$ $\dfrac{1}{100} + \dfrac{16}{100} = \dfrac{}{}$ $\qquad$ $\dfrac{7}{10} + \dfrac{2}{10} = \dfrac{}{}$

$\dfrac{2}{5} + \dfrac{1}{5} = \dfrac{}{}$ $\qquad$ $\dfrac{1}{7} + \dfrac{3}{7} = \dfrac{}{}$ $\qquad$ $\dfrac{4}{9} + \dfrac{1}{9} = \dfrac{}{}$

$\dfrac{1}{6} + \dfrac{2}{6} = \dfrac{}{} = \dfrac{}{}$ $\qquad$ $\dfrac{19}{100} + \dfrac{31}{100} = \dfrac{}{} = \dfrac{}{}$ $\qquad$ $\dfrac{5}{20} + \dfrac{10}{20} = \dfrac{}{} = \dfrac{}{}$

$\dfrac{4}{10} + \dfrac{4}{10} = \dfrac{}{} = \dfrac{}{}$ $\qquad$ $\dfrac{3}{12} + \dfrac{6}{12} = \dfrac{}{} = \dfrac{}{}$ $\qquad$ $\dfrac{2}{6} + \dfrac{2}{6} = \dfrac{}{} = \dfrac{}{}$

$\dfrac{3}{8} + \dfrac{3}{8} = \dfrac{}{} = \dfrac{}{}$ $\qquad$ $\dfrac{1}{8} + \dfrac{3}{8} = \dfrac{}{} = \dfrac{}{}$ $\qquad$ $\dfrac{5}{12} + \dfrac{1}{12} = \dfrac{}{} = \dfrac{}{}$

$\dfrac{1}{4} + \dfrac{1}{4} = \dfrac{}{} = \dfrac{}{}$ $\qquad$ $\dfrac{4}{20} + \dfrac{1}{20} = \dfrac{}{} = \dfrac{}{}$ $\qquad$ $\dfrac{1}{6} + \dfrac{3}{6} = \dfrac{}{} = \dfrac{}{}$

$\dfrac{3}{7} + \dfrac{3}{7} = \dfrac{}{}$ $\qquad$ $\dfrac{2}{9} + \dfrac{2}{9} = \dfrac{}{}$ $\qquad$ $\dfrac{13}{20} + \dfrac{5}{20} = \dfrac{}{} = \dfrac{}{}$

$\dfrac{81}{100} + \dfrac{9}{100} = \dfrac{}{} = \dfrac{}{}$ $\qquad$ $\dfrac{5}{20} + \dfrac{8}{20} = \dfrac{}{}$ $\qquad$ $\dfrac{2}{8} + \dfrac{3}{8} = \dfrac{}{}$

$\dfrac{6}{10} + \dfrac{2}{10} = \dfrac{}{} = \dfrac{}{}$ $\qquad$ $\dfrac{28}{100} + \dfrac{47}{100} = \dfrac{}{} = \dfrac{}{}$ $\qquad$ $\dfrac{72}{100} + \dfrac{18}{100} = \dfrac{}{} = \dfrac{}{}$

Adding fractions

Write the answer to each problem.

$$\frac{3}{8} + \frac{5}{8} = \boxed{\frac{8}{8}} = \boxed{1} \qquad\qquad \frac{3}{4} + \frac{3}{4} = \boxed{\frac{6 \div 2}{4 \div 2}} = \boxed{\frac{3}{2}} = \boxed{1}\ \boxed{\frac{1}{2}}$$

Make these answers visible!

Write the answer to each problem.

$$\frac{7}{10} + \frac{6}{10} = \frac{}{10} = 1\ \frac{}{10} \qquad\qquad \frac{7}{10} + \frac{6}{10} = \frac{}{10} = 1\ \frac{}{10}$$

$$\frac{6}{10} + \frac{5}{10} = \frac{}{} = \frac{}{} \qquad \frac{6}{13} + \frac{7}{13} = \frac{}{} = \qquad \frac{4}{8} + \frac{11}{8} = \frac{}{} = \frac{}{}$$

$$\frac{3}{8} + \frac{7}{8} = \frac{}{} = \frac{}{} = \frac{}{} \qquad \frac{2}{5} + \frac{3}{5} = \frac{}{} = \qquad \frac{5}{8} + \frac{7}{8} = \frac{}{} = \frac{}{} = \frac{}{}$$

$$\frac{10}{20} + \frac{15}{20} = \frac{}{} = \frac{}{} = \frac{}{} \qquad \frac{5}{12} + \frac{8}{12} = \frac{}{} = \frac{}{} \qquad \frac{9}{10} + \frac{5}{10} = \frac{}{} = \frac{}{} = \frac{}{}$$

$$\frac{10}{20} + \frac{12}{20} = \frac{}{} = \frac{}{} = \frac{}{} \qquad \frac{7}{10} + \frac{3}{10} = \frac{}{} = \qquad \frac{75}{100} + \frac{75}{100} = \frac{}{} = \frac{}{} = \frac{}{}$$

$$\frac{5}{6} + \frac{3}{6} = \frac{}{} = \frac{}{} = \frac{}{} \qquad \frac{2}{3} + \frac{1}{3} = \frac{}{} = \qquad \frac{5}{6} + \frac{5}{6} = \frac{}{} = \frac{}{} = \frac{}{}$$

$$\frac{10}{20} + \frac{16}{20} = \frac{}{} = \frac{}{} = \frac{}{} \qquad \frac{4}{5} + \frac{4}{5} = \frac{}{} = \frac{}{} \qquad \frac{11}{21} + \frac{17}{21} = \frac{}{} = \frac{}{} = \frac{}{}$$

Subtracting fractions

Write the answer to each problem.

$$\frac{4}{5} - \frac{2}{5} = \boxed{\frac{2}{5}}$$

$$\frac{8}{9} - \frac{5}{9} = \boxed{\frac{3 \div 3}{9 \div 3}} = \boxed{\frac{1}{3}}$$

Subtract the numerators but keep the denominators when they are the same.

Find the difference of each problem.

$$\frac{4}{5} - \frac{1}{5} = \boxed{}{5}$$
$$\frac{5}{7} - \frac{2}{7} = \boxed{}{7}$$

No one takes anything from me.

$$\frac{5}{10} - \frac{4}{10} = \boxed{\frac{}{}}$$
$$\frac{6}{9} - \frac{2}{9} = \frac{}{}$$

$$\frac{7}{8} - \frac{3}{8} = \frac{}{} = \frac{}{}$$
$$\frac{14}{20} - \frac{8}{20} = \frac{}{} = \frac{}{}$$
$$\frac{4}{6} - \frac{1}{6} = \frac{}{} = \frac{}{}$$

$$\frac{11}{12} - \frac{7}{12} = \frac{}{} = \frac{}{}$$
$$\frac{17}{20} - \frac{12}{20} = \frac{}{} = \frac{}{}$$
$$\frac{8}{12} - \frac{2}{12} = \frac{}{} = \frac{}{}$$

$$\frac{8}{9} - \frac{2}{9} = \frac{}{} = \frac{}{}$$
$$\frac{12}{12} - \frac{2}{12} = \frac{}{} = \frac{}{}$$
$$\frac{8}{10} - \frac{3}{10} = \frac{}{} = \frac{}{}$$

$$\frac{6}{10} - \frac{4}{10} = \frac{}{} = \frac{}{}$$
$$\frac{6}{8} - \frac{4}{8} = \frac{}{} = \frac{}{}$$
$$\frac{9}{12} - \frac{5}{12} = \frac{}{} = \frac{}{}$$

$$\frac{3}{4} - \frac{2}{4} = \frac{}{}$$
$$\frac{6}{8} - \frac{1}{8} = \frac{}{}$$
$$\frac{18}{20} - \frac{4}{20} = \frac{}{} = \frac{}{}$$

$$\frac{4}{6} - \frac{2}{6} = \frac{}{} = \frac{}{}$$
$$\frac{7}{12} - \frac{6}{12} = \frac{}{}$$
$$\frac{5}{8} - \frac{2}{8} = \frac{}{}$$

$$\frac{5}{7} - \frac{1}{7} = \frac{}{}$$
$$\frac{5}{16} - \frac{1}{16} = \frac{}{} = \frac{}{}$$
$$\frac{70}{100} - \frac{60}{100} = \frac{}{} = \frac{}{}$$

Showing decimals

Write the decimals on the number line.

0.4, 0.5, 0.6, 0.8, 0.9, 0.25, 0.45, 0.63

```
0         0.25      0.45      0.65                1
←→————•——•——•——•——•——•——•——•——•——•——•——•——•——•——←→
         0.1  0.2  0.3  0.4  0.5  0.6  0.7  0.8  0.9
```

Write the decimals on the number line.

0.1, 0.2, 0.45, 0.6, 0.85, 0.95

```
0          0.25        0.5        0.75         1
←→——•——•——•——•———————•——•——•——•——————•——•——•——←→
   ▭  ▭        ▭     ▭      ▭  ▭
```

Write the decimals on the number line.

1.2, 1.3, 1.4, 1.7, 1.8, 1.95

```
1          1.25        1.5        1.75         2
←→——•——•——•——•——•——————————•——•——•——————•——•——←→
    ▭   ▭   ▭           ▭   ▭   ▭
```

Write the decimals on the number line.

2.2, 2.35, 2.6, 2.8, 2.85, 3.15

```
2                    2.5                3
←→——•——•——•——————•——•——————•—•————•——•——←→
    ▭    ▭       ▭       ▭  ▭      ▭
```

Conversions: length

Units of length

12 inches	1 foot
3 feet	1 yard
5,280 feet	1 mile
1,760 yards	1 mile

This conversion table shows how to convert inches, feet, yards, and miles.

Daredevil's stunt rope is 3 yards long. How many inches is that?

3 x 3 = 9
9 x 12 = 108

9 feet long
108 inches

Mister Fantastic stretches 120 inches. How many feet is that?

120 ÷ 12 = 10

10 feet long

Convert each measurement to feet.

36 inches	12 inches	48 inches

Convert each measurement to yards.

6 feet	12 feet	27 feet	36 feet

Convert each measurement to inches.

4 feet	12 feet	8 feet	5 feet

Convert each measurement.

4 yards	5 yards	4 miles	1 mile
feet	inches	feet	inches

15,840 feet	31,680 feet	1,760 yards	3,520 yards
miles	miles	miles	miles

Conversions: capacity

Units of capacity	
8 fluid ounces	1 cup
2 cups	1 pint
2 pints	1 quart
4 quarts	1 gallon

This conversion table shows how to convert ounces, cups, pints, quarts, and gallons.

Wolverine's water bottle holds 6 cups. How many pints does it hold?

| 6 ÷ 2 = 3 | 3 pints |

Beast's water bottle holds 8 pints. How many cups does it hold?

| 8 x 2 = 16 | 16 cups |

Inventors have to know measures.

Convert each measurement to cups.

32 fluid ounces	16 fluid ounces	96 fluid ounces

Convert each measurement to pints.

6 cups	12 cups	30 quarts	6 quarts

Convert each measurement to gallons.

16 quarts	32 quarts	100 quarts	20 quarts

Convert each measurement.

3 gallons	5 quarts	36 cups	72 pints
pints	cups	quarts	gallons

1 quart	240 fluid ounces	7 quarts	11 gallons
fluid ounces	pints	cups	pints

Rounding money

Round to the nearest dollar. If 5 or more, round up.

$2.70 rounds to $1.75 rounds to

$9.65 rounds to $6.95 rounds to

$4.15 rounds to $3.39 rounds to $7.14 rounds to

$7.75 rounds to $4.30 rounds to $2.53 rounds to

Round to the nearest ten dollars.

$38.35 rounds to $32.75 rounds to $85.05 rounds to

$22.75 rounds to $66.70 rounds to $24.55 rounds to

$56.85 rounds to $14.95 rounds to $15.00 rounds to

Round to the nearest hundred dollars.

$407.25 rounds to $357.85 rounds to $115.99 rounds to

$870.45 rounds to $524.45 rounds to $650.15 rounds to

$849.75 rounds to $728.55 rounds to $467.25 rounds to

Estimating sums of money

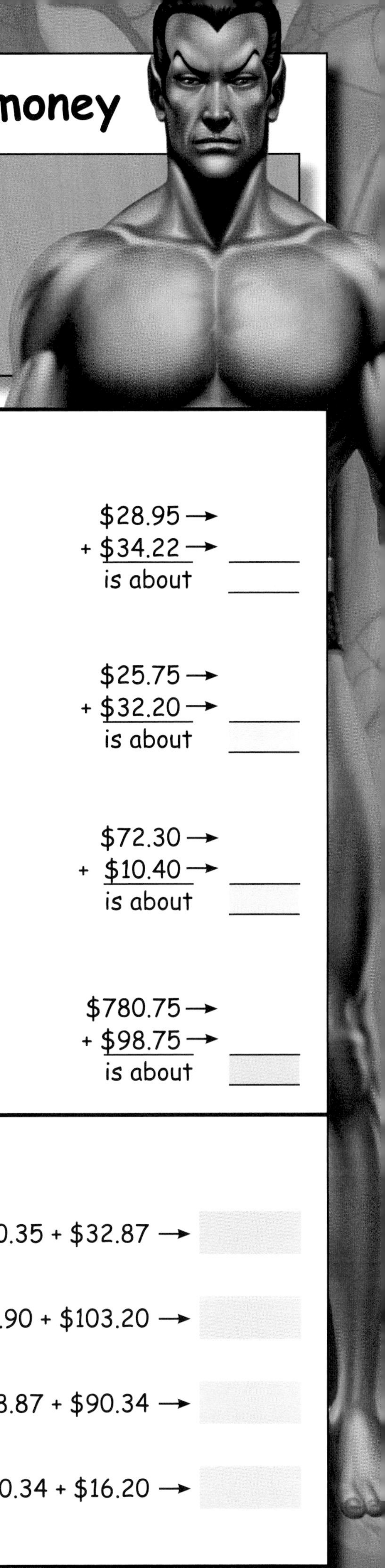

Round to the leading digit. Estimate the sum.

$3.26 → $3
+ $4.82 → + $5
is about $8

$68.53 → $70
+ $34.60 → + $30
is about $100

Round to the leading digit. Estimate the sum.

$53.64 → _____
+ $28.40 → _____
is about _____

$18.45 → _____
+ $23.05 → _____
is about _____

$28.95 → _____
+ $34.22 → _____
is about _____

$35.95 → _____
+ $12.70 → _____
is about _____

$63.40 → _____
+ $47.80 → _____
is about _____

$25.75 → _____
+ $32.20 → _____
is about _____

$47.30 → _____
+ $23.85 → _____
is about _____

$28.73 → _____
+ $32.60 → _____
is about _____

$72.30 → _____
+ $10.40 → _____
is about _____

$560.70 → _____
+ $332.40 → _____
is about _____

$382.60 → _____
+ $238.50 → _____
is about _____

$780.75 → _____
+ $98.75 → _____
is about _____

Round to the leading digit. Estimate the sum.

$17.95 + $75.95 →

$20.35 + $32.87 →

$51.19 + $39.50 →

$875.90 + $103.20 →

$517.75 + $291.50 →

$48.87 + $90.34 →

$83.40 + $12.30 →

$90.34 + $16.20 →

Estimating differences of money

Round the numbers to the leading digit.
Estimate the differences.

$8.75 →	$9		$63.20 →	$60
- $4.83 →	- $5		- $48.35 →	- $50
is about	$4		is about	$10

Round the numbers to the leading digit. Estimate the differences.

$27.80 →
- $11.90 → ____
is about [ ]

$48.35 →
- $32.25 → ____
is about [ ]

$89.20 →
- $22.40 → ____
is about [ ]

$37.40 →
- $31.20 → ____
is about [ ]

$58.20 →
- $17.30 → ____
is about [ ]

$326.30 →
- $178.90 → ____
is about [ ]

$54.10 →
- $33.80 → ____
is about [ ]

$87.40 →
- $8.75 → ____
is about [ ]

$783.90 →
- $417.60 → ____
is about [ ]

Round the numbers to the leading digit. Estimate the differences.

$8.12 - $3.78

→   = [ ]

$49.60 - $21.80

→   = [ ]

$7.70 - $3.20

→   = [ ]

$84.20 - $39.80

→   = [ ]

$5.95 - $4.60

→   = [ ]

$675.80 - $267.50

→   = [ ]

$32.85 - $21.90

→   = [ ]

$829.90 - $516.20

→   = [ ]

$56.78 - $38.90

→   = [ ]

$679.20 - $211.10

→   = [ ]

Estimating sums and differences

Round the numbers to the leading digit. Estimate the sum or difference.

$$
\begin{array}{rcl}
3{,}762 & \rightarrow & 4{,}000 \\
+\ 1{,}204 & \rightarrow & +\ 1{,}000 \\
\hline
\text{is about} & & \boxed{5{,}000}
\end{array}
\qquad
\begin{array}{rcl}
287{,}257 & \rightarrow & 300{,}000 \\
-\ \ 98{,}592 & \rightarrow & -\ 100{,}000 \\
\hline
\text{is about} & & \boxed{200{,}000}
\end{array}
$$

Round the numbers to the leading digit. Estimate the sum or difference.

$587 \rightarrow$ ____	$22{,}945 \rightarrow$ ____	$8{,}265 \rightarrow$ ____
$+\ \ 496 \rightarrow$ ____	$-\ 12{,}352 \rightarrow$ ____	$+\ 2{,}156 \rightarrow$ ____
is about ____	is about ____	is about ____

$685{,}271 \rightarrow$ ____	$57{,}998 \rightarrow$ ____	$492{,}076 \rightarrow$ ____
$+\ 213{,}876 \rightarrow$ ____	$-\ 22{,}135 \rightarrow$ ____	$+\ 237{,}631 \rightarrow$ ____
is about ____	is about ____	is about ____

$23{,}957 \rightarrow$ ____	$8{,}752 \rightarrow$ ____	$62{,}973 \rightarrow$ ____
$+\ 14{,}702 \rightarrow$ ____	$-\ 2{,}398 \rightarrow$ ____	$+\ 21{,}482 \rightarrow$ ____
is about ____	is about ____	is about ____

$5{,}294 \rightarrow$ ____	$736 \rightarrow$ ____	$33{,}729 \rightarrow$ ____
$+\ 3{,}813 \rightarrow$ ____	$+\ 829 \rightarrow$ ____	$-\ 19{,}372 \rightarrow$ ____
is about ____	is about ____	is about ____

Write > or < for each problem.

I'm greater than all of these!

$567 + 295$ ____ 800	
$467 - 307$ ____ 100	$11{,}987 - 5{,}424$ ____ 6,000
$41{,}925 - 12{,}354$ ____ 40,000	$8{,}183 - 6{,}875$ ____ 1,000
$19{,}885 + 12{,}681$ ____ 30,000	$645{,}900 + 183{,}650$ ____ 800,000
$753 - 347$ ____ 400	$913{,}312 - 432{,}667$ ____ 500,000

Conversion tables

Draw a table to convert dollars to cents.

$	Cents
1	100
2	200
3	300

Weeks	Days
1	7
2	
10	70

Complete the conversion table.

I don't need any help!

If there are 60 minutes in 1 hour, make a conversion chart for up to 10 hours.

Time's ticking away!

Hours	Minutes

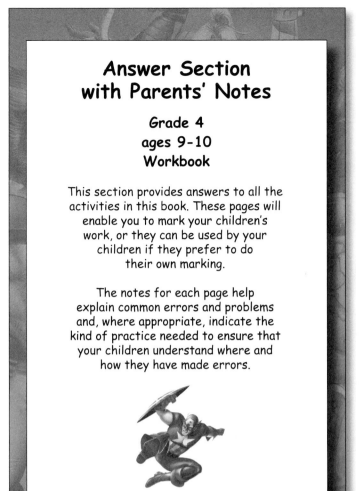

Answer Section with Parents' Notes

Grade 4
ages 9-10
Workbook

This section provides answers to all the activities in this book. These pages will enable you to mark your children's work, or they can be used by your children if they prefer to do their own marking.

The notes for each page help explain common errors and problems and, where appropriate, indicate the kind of practice needed to ensure that your children understand where and how they have made errors.

2

Reading and writing numbers

Help me out!

Write each of these numbers in words.

146,289 in words is | One hundred forty-six thousand, two hundred eighty-nine

Two million, three hundred ten thousand, five hundred sixty is | 2,310,560

Write each of these numbers in words.

146,209	One hundred forty-six thousand, two hundred nine
407,543	Four hundred seven thousand, five hundred forty-three
245,107	Two hundred forty-five thousand, one hundred seven

Write each of these in numbers.

Four hundred fifteen thousand, thirty-two	415,032
Six hundred ninety-four thousand, seven hundred eleven	694,711
Seven hundred nine thousand, two hundred three	709,203

Write each of these numbers in words.

9,307,012	Nine million, three hundred seven thousand, twelve
2,024,390	Two million, twenty-four thousand, three hundred ninety
8,908,434	Eight million, nine hundred eight thousand, four hundred thirty-four

Write each of these numbers in words.

Try these!

One million, two hundred fifty-one	1,000,251
Three million, forty thousand, four hundred four	3,040,404
Nine million, three hundred two thousand, one hundred one	9,302,101

Children may use zeros incorrectly in numbers. In word form, zeros are omitted, but children should take care to include them when writing numbers in standard form.

3

Multiplying and dividing by 10

Write the answer in the box.

22 x 10 = | 220

50 ÷ 10 = | 5

How fast are you?

Write the product in the box.

26 x 10 =	260	43 x 10 =	430	55 x 10 =	550
66 x 10 =	660	33 x 10 =	330	47 x 10 =	470
137 x 10 =	1,370	936 x 10 =	9,360	284 x 10 =	2,840
634 x 10 =	6,340	821 x 10 =	8,210	473 x 10 =	4,730

Write the quotient in the box.

40 ÷ 10 =	4	20 ÷ 10 =	2	50 ÷ 10 =	5
60 ÷ 10 =	6	70 ÷ 10 =	7	580 ÷ 10 =	58
130 ÷ 10 =	13	270 ÷ 10 =	27	100 ÷ 10 =	10
540 ÷ 10 =	54	980 ÷ 10 =	98	710 ÷ 10 =	71

Write the number that has been multiplied by 10 in the box.

47 x 10 = 470	64 x 10 = 640	74 x 10 = 740
79 x 10 = 790	10 x 10 = 100	83 x 10 = 830
714 x 10 = 7,140	306 x 10 = 3,060	529 x 10 = 5,290

Write the quotient in the box.

30 ÷ 10 =	3	20 ÷ 10 =	2	90 ÷ 10 =	9
70 ÷ 10 =	7	50 ÷ 10 =	5	580 ÷ 10 =	58
310 ÷ 10 =	31	270 ÷ 10 =	27	100 ÷ 10 =	10

Again, make sure that children understand the use of zeros in numbers.

4

Ordering sets of large numbers

Write these numbers in order, from least to greatest.

| 3,322 | 526 | 304 | 42 | 2,240 | 440 |
| 42 | 304 | 440 | 526 | 2,240 | 3,322 |

I'm the greatest!

Write the numbers in each row in order, from least to greatest.

320	195	945	402	910	986
195	320	402	910	945	986
308	640	380	805	364	910
308	364	380	640	805	910
259	349	25	1,000	619	100
25	100	259	349	619	1,000
20,501	36,821	2,501	45,601	40,561	25,001
2,501	20,501	25,001	36,821	40,561	45,601

Write the numbers in each row in order, from least to greatest.

984,000	8,840,000	8,900	98,240	7,560	75,600
7,560	8,900	75,600	98,240	984,000	8,840,000
301,550	6,405,000	6,450,000	64,500	31,500	3,150
3,150	31,500	64,500	301,550	6,405,000	6,450,000
7,000,100	70,100	7,100,000	710	710,000	7,100
710	7,100	70,100	710,000	7,000,100	7,100,000

| CLAIRTON Population 85,440 | DISTRICT X Population 8,440 | SAPIEN TOWN Population 8,404,420 | WESTCHESTER COUNTY Population 8,440,042 |

Which town has:

| The second-smallest population? | Clairton |

| The smallest population? | District X | The second-largest population? | Sapien Town |

Children should realize that multiplying by 10 means adding a zero to a number. The ones become tens and the tens become hundreds, leaving a blank space—the zero—in the ones column.

5

Rounding numbers

Round each number.

46 to the nearest ten: **50**

224 to the nearest hundred: **200**

5,360 to the nearest thousand: **5,000**

Remember: If a number is halfway between, round it up.

Some of these numbers are BIG!

Round each number to the nearest ten.

14	10	81	80	45	50	63	60
57	60	58	60	49	50	35	40
82	80	47	50	22	20	62	60
46	50	26	30	85	90	99	100
33	30	51	50	68	70	29	30

Round each number to the nearest hundred.

286	300	224	200	825	800	460	500
539	500	329	300	378	400	937	900
772	800	255	300	449	400	612	600
116	100	750	800	618	600	990	1,000

Round each number to the nearest thousand.

4,240	4,000	3,500	4,000	9,940	10,000	1,051	1,000
8,945	9,000	5,050	5,000	5,530	6,000	4,850	5,000
6,200	6,000	7,250	7,000	6,499	6,000	8,450	8,000
12,501	13,000	8,762	9,000	6,500	7,000	4,292	4,000

Children may have difficulty with numbers that have final digits of 5 or greater—for example, if rounding to the nearest 100, they might round 449 to 500 rather than 400. Make sure children understand which digit determines how to round the number.

6

Identifying patterns

Continue each pattern.

Steps of 8:	6	14	22	30	38
Steps of 14:	20	34	48	62	76

I'm BIG on patterns. Can you do these?

Continue each pattern.

4	34	64	94	124	154	184	214
10	61	112	163	214	265	316	367
48	100	152	204	256	308	360	412
20	37	54	71	88	105	122	139
25	100	175	250	325	400	475	550
25	45	65	85	105	125	145	165
8	107	206	305	404	503	602	701
7	25	43	61	79	97	115	133
22	72	122	172	222	272	322	372
60	165	270	375	480	585	690	795
13	37	61	85	109	133	157	181
11	30	49	68	87	106	125	144
32	48	64	80	96	112	128	144
36	126	216	306	396	486	576	666
32	54	76	98	120	142	164	186
26	127	228	329	430	531	632	733
12	72	132	192	252	312	372	432
32	50	68	86	104	122	140	158

Children should determine what number to add to the first number to make the second number, and double check that adding the same number turns the second number into the third. They can then repeat the operation to continue the pattern.

7

Recognizing multiples of 6, 7, and 8

Circle the multiples of 6. For example, 6 x 2 = 12, so circle 12.

8 **(12)** 15 **(18)** 20 **(24)**

Circle the multiples of 6.

20	32	62	(6)	(42)	34
(24)	10	38	(72)	16	(60)
14	22	44	8	(30)	(18)
66	64	52	25	(54)	28

Try to work through these at lightning speed.

Circle the multiples of 7.

27	34	(49)	36	47	(35)
(21)	60	58	19	(56)	26
(28)	73	40	46	23	(63)
18	25	(14)	37	69	27

Circle the multiples of 8.

50	(32)	62	12	(16)	25
(56)	18	38	28	60	(24)
34	(72)	(48)	44	82	14
22	54	70	(40)	(64)	(80)

Circle the number that is a multiple of 6 and 7.

24   35   (42)   62   70   72

Circle the numbers that are multiples of both 6 and 8.

16   (24)   28   (48)   54   60

Success on this page will basically depend on a knowledge of multiplication tables. Where children experience difficulty, multiplication table practice should be encouraged.

8

Factors of numbers from 1 to 30

Factors are numbers that divide evenly into a larger number.

Circle the factors of 4   (1)   (2)   3   (4)

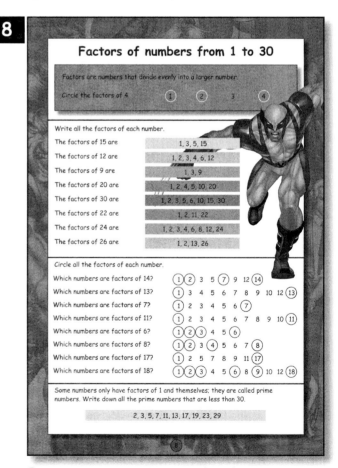

Write all the factors of each number.

The factors of 15 are   1, 3, 5, 15

The factors of 12 are   1, 2, 3, 4, 6, 12

The factors of 9 are   1, 3, 9

The factors of 20 are   1, 2, 4, 5, 10, 20

The factors of 30 are   1, 2, 3, 5, 6, 10, 15, 30

The factors of 22 are   1, 2, 11, 22

The factors of 24 are   1, 2, 3, 4, 6, 8, 12, 24

The factors of 26 are   1, 2, 13, 26

Circle all the factors of each number.

Which numbers are factors of 14?   (1) (2) 3 5 (7) 9 12 (14)

Which numbers are factors of 13?   (1) 3 4 5 6 7 8 9 10 12 (13)

Which numbers are factors of 7?   (1) 2 3 4 5 6 (7)

Which numbers are factors of 11?   (1) 2 3 4 5 6 7 8 9 10 (11)

Which numbers are factors of 6?   (1)(2)(3) 4 5 (6)

Which numbers are factors of 8?   (1)(2) 3 (4) 5 6 7 (8)

Which numbers are factors of 17?   (1) 2 5 7 8 9 11 (17)

Which numbers are factors of 18?   (1)(2)(3) 4 5 (6) 8 (9) 10 12 (18)

Some numbers only have factors of 1 and themselves; they are called prime numbers. Write down all the prime numbers that are less than 30.

2, 3, 5, 7, 11, 13, 17, 19, 23, 29

Encourage a systematic approach such as starting at 1 and working toward the number that is half of the number in question. Children often forget that 1 and the number itself are factors. You may need to point out that 1 is not a prime number.

Recognizing equivalent fractions

Make each pair of fractions equal by writing a number in the box.

Can you help me with these?

$$\frac{1}{2} = \frac{2}{4} \qquad \frac{1}{3} = \frac{3}{9}$$

Make each pair of fractions equal by writing a number in the box.

$\frac{1}{5} = \frac{4}{20}$	$\frac{3}{4} = \frac{12}{16}$	$\frac{1}{3} = \frac{4}{12}$
$\frac{2}{3} = \frac{6}{9}$	$\frac{6}{12} = \frac{4}{8}$	$\frac{4}{8} = \frac{1}{2}$
$\frac{1}{2} = \frac{2}{4}$	$\frac{4}{12} = \frac{2}{6}$	$\frac{3}{5} = \frac{6}{10}$
$\frac{1}{4} = \frac{2}{8}$	$\frac{6}{18} = \frac{3}{9}$	$\frac{4}{16} = \frac{1}{4}$
$\frac{3}{9} = \frac{9}{27}$	$\frac{4}{10} = \frac{2}{5}$	$\frac{3}{4} = \frac{15}{20}$
$\frac{4}{16} = \frac{2}{8}$	$\frac{9}{12} = \frac{3}{4}$	$\frac{6}{12} = \frac{2}{4}$
$\frac{3}{5} = \frac{6}{10}$	$\frac{2}{12} = \frac{1}{3}$	$\frac{9}{12} = \frac{3}{4}$

Make each pair of fractions equal by writing a number in the box.

$$\frac{1}{2} = \frac{2}{4} = \frac{3}{6} = \frac{4}{8} = \frac{5}{10} = \frac{6}{12}$$

$$\frac{1}{4} = \frac{2}{8} = \frac{3}{12} = \frac{4}{16} = \frac{5}{20} = \frac{6}{24}$$

$$\frac{3}{4} = \frac{6}{8} = \frac{9}{12} = \frac{12}{16} = \frac{15}{20} = \frac{18}{24}$$

$$\frac{1}{3} = \frac{2}{6} = \frac{3}{9} = \frac{4}{12} = \frac{5}{15} = \frac{6}{18}$$

$$\frac{1}{5} = \frac{2}{10} = \frac{3}{15} = \frac{4}{20} = \frac{5}{25} = \frac{6}{30}$$

$$\frac{2}{3} = \frac{4}{6} = \frac{6}{9} = \frac{8}{12} = \frac{10}{15} = \frac{12}{18}$$

If children have problems with this page, point out that fractions remain the same as long as you multiply the numerator and the denominator by the same number, or divide the numerator and denominator by the same number.

10

Ordering sets of numbers

Write the numbers in order, from least to greatest.

$$2 \qquad 1\frac{1}{4} \qquad \frac{3}{4} \qquad \frac{1}{4} \qquad \frac{1}{2}$$

$$\frac{1}{4} \qquad \frac{1}{2} \qquad \frac{3}{4} \qquad 1\frac{1}{4} \qquad 2$$

Write the numbers in order, from least to greatest.

2	$1\frac{1}{4}$	$3\frac{1}{2}$	$1\frac{1}{2}$	$2\frac{1}{2}$	$1\frac{1}{4}$	$1\frac{1}{2}$	2	$2\frac{1}{2}$	$3\frac{1}{2}$
2	$1\frac{1}{2}$	1	$2\frac{1}{4}$	3	1	$1\frac{1}{2}$	2	$2\frac{1}{4}$	3
4	$2\frac{1}{2}$	$1\frac{3}{4}$	$1\frac{1}{4}$	$3\frac{1}{2}$	$1\frac{1}{4}$	$1\frac{3}{4}$	$2\frac{1}{2}$	$3\frac{1}{2}$	4
$6\frac{1}{2}$	$4\frac{1}{4}$	$1\frac{1}{2}$	$1\frac{1}{4}$	$2\frac{3}{4}$	$1\frac{1}{4}$	$1\frac{1}{2}$	$2\frac{3}{4}$	$4\frac{1}{4}$	$6\frac{1}{2}$
$4\frac{1}{4}$	$3\frac{1}{2}$	$2\frac{3}{4}$	$2\frac{1}{2}$	$3\frac{1}{4}$	$2\frac{1}{2}$	$2\frac{3}{4}$	$3\frac{1}{4}$	$3\frac{1}{2}$	$4\frac{1}{4}$
$3\frac{2}{3}$	$3\frac{1}{2}$	$3\frac{3}{4}$	$3\frac{1}{4}$	$4\frac{1}{4}$	$3\frac{1}{4}$	$3\frac{1}{2}$	$3\frac{2}{3}$	$3\frac{3}{4}$	$4\frac{1}{4}$
$3\frac{3}{4}$	$3\frac{1}{3}$	$4\frac{1}{4}$	$3\frac{2}{3}$	$3\frac{1}{2}$	$3\frac{1}{3}$	$3\frac{1}{2}$	$3\frac{2}{3}$	$3\frac{3}{4}$	$4\frac{1}{4}$
$6\frac{1}{2}$	$5\frac{3}{4}$	$6\frac{3}{4}$	$6\frac{1}{4}$	$5\frac{1}{2}$	$5\frac{1}{2}$	$5\frac{3}{4}$	$6\frac{1}{4}$	$6\frac{1}{2}$	$6\frac{3}{4}$
$13\frac{1}{2}$	$14\frac{3}{4}$	$14\frac{1}{2}$	$13\frac{3}{4}$	$12\frac{3}{4}$	$12\frac{3}{4}$	$13\frac{1}{2}$	$13\frac{3}{4}$	$14\frac{1}{2}$	$14\frac{3}{4}$
$10\frac{1}{5}$	$9\frac{3}{4}$	$10\frac{1}{2}$	$9\frac{1}{5}$	$9\frac{1}{2}$	$9\frac{1}{5}$	$9\frac{1}{2}$	$9\frac{3}{4}$	$10\frac{1}{5}$	$10\frac{1}{2}$
$7\frac{1}{3}$	$9\frac{3}{4}$	$10\frac{1}{2}$	$9\frac{1}{5}$	$9\frac{1}{2}$	$7\frac{1}{3}$	$9\frac{1}{5}$	$9\frac{1}{2}$	$9\frac{3}{4}$	$10\frac{1}{2}$

The most likely area of difficulty will be ordering fractions such as $3/4$ and $2/3$. If children experience difficulty, refer them to the previous page or use two index cards, cut into quarters and into thirds, to allow comparison.

Rounding decimals

Round each decimal to the nearest whole number.

If the whole number has 5 after it, round to the next greatest whole number.

3.4	3
5.7	6
4.5	5

Get these done now!

Round each decimal to the nearest whole number.

1.1	1	6.2	6	7.3	7	4.8	5
2.8	3	5.8	6	8.6	9	3.7	4
1.3	1	3.2	3	8.5	9	6.4	6
6.5	7	4.7	5	0.9	1	2.1	2

Round each decimal to the nearest whole number.

22.2	22	14.8	15	27.5	28	33.8	34
56.2	56	37.8	38	48.2	48	56.7	57
75.4	75	81.8	82	66.5	67	71.6	72
98.3	98	42.1	42	19.9	20	36.4	36

Round each decimal to the nearest whole number.

110.4	110	126.3	126	107.1	107	111.9	112
275.3	275	352.7	353	444.4	444	398.7	399
359.8	360	276.8	277	348.3	348	599.8	600
673.4	673	785.6	786	543.2	543	987.4	987
867.2	867	686.8	687	743.2	743	845.5	846

If children experience difficulty, you might want to use a number line showing tenths. Errors often occur when a number with 9 in the ones column is rounded up. Children also often neglect to alter the tens digit in a number such as 19.9.

Adding two numbers

Find each sum.

211	482
+ 214	+ 573
425	1,055

I KNOW you can work it out!

Remember to regroup if you have to.

Find each sum.

224	452	612
+ 365	+ 227	+ 345
589	679	957

485	563	535
+ 606	+ 147	+ 187
1,091	710	722

Write the answer in the box.

$$313 + 237 = 550 \qquad 635 + 267 = 902$$

Write the missing number in the box.

362	266	701	739
+ 419	+ 581	+ 264	+ 240
781	847	965	979

Find each sum.

Blade destroys 107 vampires in one night and 103 vampires the following night. How many vampires has he destroyed altogether? — 210

Daredevil rounds up 134 criminals in one week. The next week, he rounds up 241. How many criminals has he rounded up during those two weeks? — 375

The questions on this page involve straightfoward addition work. If children have difficulty with the horizontal sums, suggest that they rewrite them in vertical form. Some errors may result from neglecting to regroup.

13

Adding two numbers

Find each sum.

1,234	3,794
+ 5,642	+ 5,125
6,876	8,919

Remember to regroup if you need to.

Find each sum.

2,552	5,325	2,471
+ 3,214	+ 2,653	+ 4,238
5,766	7,978	6,709

3,749	4,675	8,482
+ 2,471	+ 3,916	+ 1,349
6,220	8,591	9,831

Help me crack this case!

Write the answer in the box.

2,431 + 4,621 = 7,052   1,342 + 3,264 = 4,606

1,738 + 4,261 = 5,999   2,013 + 3,642 = 5,655

Write the missing number in the box.

3,741	1,652	3,642
+ 2,943	+ 3,274	+ 4,831
6,684	4,926	8,473

Find each sum.

On Monday, Phoenix helped 2,521 people to safety, and the Colossus helped 2,443 people. How many people did they help on Monday? **4,964**

On Saturday, Nightcrawler rescued 4,476 people, and Wolverine rescued 3,478 people on Sunday. How many people did they rescue that weekend? **7,954**

This page is similar to the previous page, with larger numbers. If children have difficulty with the section on missing numbers, have them try various digits until they find the correct one.

14

Subtracting three-digit numbers

Write the difference between the lines. Regroup if needed.

644	471 cm
- 223	- 252 cm
421	219 cm

Do you know the difference?

Write the difference between the lines.

363	578	745	693
- 151	- 334	- 524	- 481
212	244	221	212

480 ft	559 ft	750 ft	472 ft
- 130 ft	- 218 ft	- 640 ft	- 362 ft
350 ft	341 ft	110 ft	110 ft

Write the difference in the box.

364 - 122 = 242   799 - 354 = 445

$776 - $515 = $261 $840 - $730 = $110

$684 - $574 = $110 $220 - $120 = $100

Write the difference between the lines.

463	584	661	494
- 145	- 237	- 342	- 185
318	347	319	309

325	837	468	852
- 116	- 719	- 209	- 329
209	118	259	523

Find the answer to each problem.

Spider-Man shoots 234 webs, but 127 are destroyed. How many webs are left? **107**

Spider-Man has 860 web cartridges. 420 are stolen. How many cartridges remain? **440**

In some of these problems, children may incorrectly subtract the smaller digit from the larger one, when they should be subtracting the larger digit from the smaller one. In such cases, point out that children should regroup.

15

Subtracting three-digit numbers

Write the difference between the lines.

715	711 m
- 152	- 292 m
563	419 m

Write the difference between the lines.

624 m	419 m	747 m
- 263 m	- 137 m	- 456 m
361 m	282 m	291 m

614	826	521	815 m
- 407	- 727	- 355	- 193 m
207	99	166	622 m

Write the difference in the box.

516 - 308 = 208   748 - 339 = 409

631 - 542 = 89   477 - 198 = 279

Write the difference between the lines.

535	715	312	924
- 247	- 518	- 113	- 528
288	197	199	396

Write the missing numbers in the box.

723	662	416	532
- 128	- 317	- 317	- 185
595	345	99	347

Find the answer to each problem.

Mister Fantastic gets $137 million to fund his starship project. The project costs $260 million. How much more funding does he need? **$123**

There are 664 people involved in the starship project. 276 are building computers. How many are taking part in other activities? **388**

Some children may have difficulty with the section on missing numbers. Have them use trial and error until they find the correct number, or encourage them to use addition and subtraction fact families to find the number.

16

Adding decimals

Write the answer between the lines. Line up the decimal points. Write zeros as needed.

$6.25	3.35 m
+ $2.60	+ 3.50 m
$8.85	6.85 m

Write the answer between the lines.

$3.25	$6.50	$3.35
+ $4.50	+ $2.25	+ $1.50
$7.75	$8.75	$4.85

$6.55	$4.15	$3.50
+ $2.45	+ $4.75	+ $3.95
$9.00	$8.90	$7.45

You have to be good at math to time travel.

4.50 m	3.60 m	7.30 m
+ 2.35 m	+ 4.15 m	+ 1.65 m
6.85 m	7.75 m	8.95 m

7.15 m	3.30 m	5.20 m
+ 2.20 m	+ 6.55 m	+ 1.75 m
9.35 m	9.85 m	6.95 m

Write the sum in the box.

$6.25 + $3.30 = $9.55 $7.15 + $2.50 = $9.65 $6.35 + $2.30 = $8.65

$6.20 + $2.65 = $8.85 $3.45 + $6.10 = $9.55 $7.45 + $1.50 = $8.95

Find the answer to each problem.

On Monday Doctor Strange travels forward in time by 1.90 days. On Tuesday he fast forwards another 4.75 days. How many days ahead is he now? **6.65 days**

Doctor Strange travels another 2.13 days forward. How many days ahead is he now? **8.78 days**

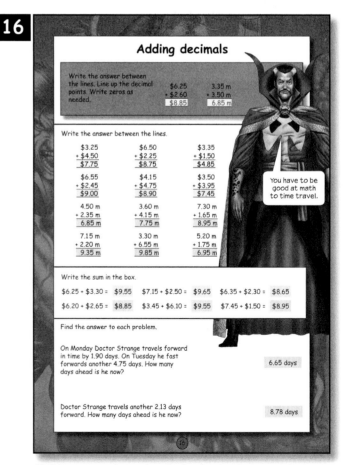

Children may place the decimal point incorrectly in problems that are presented horizontally. Have them rewrite the problems in vertical form, lining up the decimal points. You may also need to remind children to regroup when necessary.

17

Adding decimals

Write the answer between the lines. Line up the decimal points. Write zeros as needed.

$3.35 + $5.55 $8.90	4.45 m + 1.25 m 5.70 m

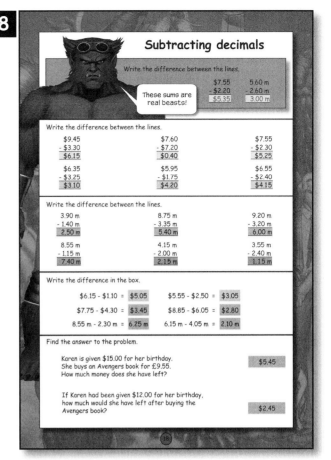

ROOOAR! I need your help to figure out these sums!

Write the sum between the lines.

$3.35 + $5.55 $8.90	$7.60 + $3.25 $10.85	$4.45 + $1.50 $5.95
$4.55 + $4.35 $8.90	$7.15 + $2.75 $9.90	$3.50 + $2.95 $6.45
4.50 m + 2.35 m 6.85 m	5.60 m + 2.05 m 7.65 m	3.30 m + 1.55 m 4.85 m
7.25 m + 2.20 m 9.45 m	4.40 m + 6.55 m 10.95 m	6.30 m + 1.75 m 8.05 m

Write the sum in the box.

$4.75 + $3.30 = $8.05 $1.50 + $4.15 = $5.65 $5.45 + $2.30 = $7.75

$3.20 + $2.55 = $5.75 $6.10 + $2.45 = $8.55 $8.35 + $1.40 = $9.75

Work out the answer for each problem.

Max buys two Marvel comics that cost $3.55 and $2.95. How much does he spend? $6.50

5¢ 25¢ $5

Max buys two different comics that cost $3.25 and $2.75. How much does he spend altogether? $6.00

You may wish to discuss with children that when the final decimal place of a sum is zero, it can be written, but it can also be omitted—unless the sum is an amount of dollars.

18

Subtracting decimals

Write the difference between the lines.

These sums are real beasts!

$7.55 - $2.20 $5.35	5.60 m - 2.60 m 3.00 m

Write the difference between the lines.

$9.45 - $3.30 $6.15	$7.60 - $7.20 $0.40	$7.55 - $2.30 $5.25
$6.35 - $3.25 $3.10	$5.95 - $1.75 $4.20	$6.55 - $2.40 $4.15

Write the difference between the lines.

3.90 m - 1.40 m 2.50 m	8.75 m - 3.35 m 5.40 m	9.20 m - 3.20 m 6.00 m
8.55 m - 1.15 m 7.40 m	4.15 m - 2.00 m 2.15 m	3.55 m - 2.40 m 1.15 m

Write the difference in the box.

$6.15 - $1.10 = $5.05 $5.55 - $2.50 = $3.05

$7.75 - $4.30 = $3.45 $8.85 - $6.05 = $2.80

8.55 m - 2.30 m = 6.25 m   6.15 m - 4.05 m = 2.10 m

Find the answer to the problem.

Karen is given $15.00 for her birthday. She buys an Avengers book for £9.55. How much money does she have left? $5.45

If Karen had been given $12.00 for her birthday, how much would she have left after buying the Avengers book? $2.45

Some children are confused about subtracting decimals. Show them that once they line up the decimal points, they can simply subtract the digits, lining up the decimal point in the answer as well.

19

Subtracting decimals

Write the difference between the lines. Line up the decimal points. Write zeros as needed.

$6.35 + $2.40 $3.95	7.25 m + 1.65 m 5.60 m

I can handle whatever you throw at me!

Write the difference between the lines.

$5.65 - $2.75 $2.90	$7.45 - $3.65 $3.80	$6.85 - $4.75 $2.10
$3.15 - $1.25 $1.90	$7.50 - $2.90 $4.60	$4.15 - $1.75 $2.40

Write the difference between the lines.

4.35 m - 2.55 m 1.80 m	7.25 m - 2.55 m 4.70 m	4.85 m - 2.95 m 1.90 m
5.45 m - 2.65 m 2.80 m	8.25 m - 2.30 m 5.95 m	7.30 m - 3.50 m 3.80 m

Write the difference in the box.

$6.25 - $3.50 = $2.75 $4.35 - $2.55 = $1.80

$8.20 - $3.30 = $4.90 $7.40 - $3.80 = $3.60

6.45 m - 2.55 m = 3.90 m   7.35 m - 3.55 m = 3.80 m

Find the answer to the problem.

Blade's sword is 3.55 meters long. He breaks off a piece 0.75 meters long. How long is his sword now?

2.80 m

I'm gonna make you pay for breaking my sword....

This page follows from the previous page, but the subtraction involves more regrouping. You may need to remind children that they can regroup across a decimal point in the same way as they would if the decimal point were not there.

Multiplying by one-digit numbers

Find each product. Multiply the ones. Regroup if needed, then multiply the tens.

22 x 2 44	26 x 3 78	44 x 4 176

I've got a favor to ask! Help me find each product.

Find each product.

37 x 2 74	19 x 2 38	16 x 4 64	32 x 3 96
21 x 3 63	25 x 4 100	16 x 6 96	33 x 5 165
39 x 2 78	24 x 2 48	41 x 2 82	36 x 3 108
29 x 3 87	35 x 2 70	28 x 3 78	26 x 6 156
10 x 6 60	30 x 2 60	20 x 4 80	50 x 3 150

Find the answer to each problem.

Magneto flies through the air at 150 miles per hour. Storm can fly at twice that speed. How fast can Storm travel?   300 mph

Magneto's helmet is 30 cm tall. How tall will a pile of 4 helmets be?   120 cm

Errors made on this page generally highlight gaps in children's knowledge of the 2, 3, 4, 5, and 6 multiplication tables. Other errors can result from neglecting to regroup.

21

Multiplying by one-digit numbers

Find each product.
Multiply the ones.
Regroup if needed,
then multiply the tens.

43	76	35
× 3	× 6	× 7
129	456	245

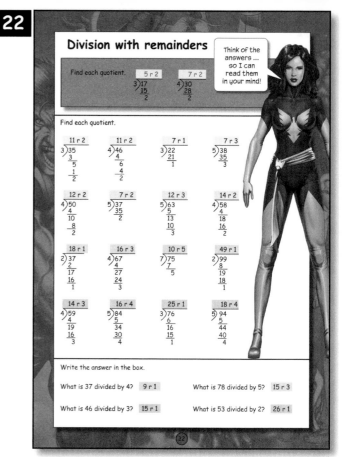

Get me the products NOW!

Find each product.

46	48	40	32	36
× 8	× 5	× 7	× 6	× 9
368	240	280	192	324

54	55	58	96	42
× 4	× 6	× 7	× 3	× 9
216	330	406	288	378

82	24	81	64	52
× 3	× 9	× 7	× 4	× 6
246	216	567	256	312

37	40	50	30	20
× 7	× 8	× 3	× 7	× 9
259	320	150	210	180

27	36	21	42	57
× 5	× 4	× 6	× 9	× 2
135	144	126	378	114

Find the answer to the problem.

Colossus can wreck 48 cars an hour.
How many cars can he wreck in 6 hours?   288 cars

A canister belt can hold 7 gas
canisters. How many canisters
can 28 belts hold?   196

Errors made on this page generally highlight gaps in children's knowledge of the 6, 7, 8, and 9 times tables. As on the previous page, errors may result from neglecting to regroup.

22

Division with remainders

Find each quotient.

```
      5 r 2        7 r 2
  3)17         4)30
    15           28
     2            2
```

Think of the answers ... so I can read them in your mind!

Find each quotient.

```
   11 r 2      11 r 2       7 r 1        7 r 3
 3)35        4)46        3)22         5)38
   3            4           21           35
    5            6            1            3
    1            4
    2            2
```

```
   12 r 2       7 r 2      12 r 3       14 r 2
 4)50        5)37        5)63         4)58
   4            35          5            4
   10            2          13           18
    8                       10           16
    2                        3            2
```

```
   18 r 1      16 r 3      10 r 5       49 r 1
 2)37        4)67        7)75         2)99
   2            4           7            8
   17           27           5           19
   16           24                       18
    1            3                        1
```

```
   14 r 3      16 r 4      25 r 1       18 r 4
 4)59        5)84        3)76         5)94
   4            5           6            5
   19           34          16           44
   16           30          15           40
    3            4           1            4
```

Write the answer in the box.

What is 37 divided by 4?   9 r 1   What is 78 divided by 5?   15 r 3

What is 46 divided by 3?   15 r 1   What is 53 divided by 2?   26 r 1

Children may have difficulty finding quotients with remainders. Have them perform long division until the remaining value to be divided is less than the divisor. That value is the remainder.

23

Division with remainders

Find each quotient.

```
      5 r 3        7 r 2
  6)33         7)51
    30           49
     3            2
```

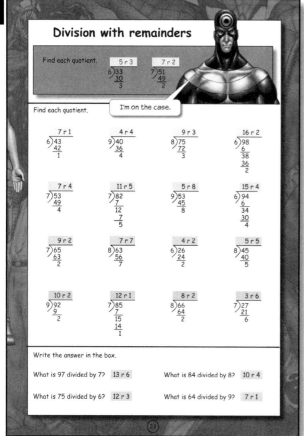

I'm on the case.

Find each quotient.

```
    7 r 1        4 r 4        9 r 3       16 r 2
 6)43        9)40        8)75         6)98
   42           36          72           6
    1            4           3           38
                                         36
                                          2
```

```
    7 r 4       11 r 5        5 r 8       15 r 4
 7)53        7)82        9)53         6)94
   49           7           45           6
    4           12           8           34
                 7                       30
                 5                        4
```

```
    9 r 2        7 r 7        4 r 2        5 r 5
 7)65        8)63        6)26         8)45
   63           56          24           40
    2            7           2            5
```

```
   10 r 2       12 r 1        8 r 2        3 r 6
 9)92        7)85        8)66         7)27
   9            7           64           21
   2           15            2            6
               14
                1
```

Write the answer in the box.

What is 97 divided by 7?   13 r 6   What is 84 divided by 8?   10 r 4

What is 75 divided by 6?   12 r 3   What is 64 divided by 9?   7 r 1

24

Real-life problems

Write the answers in the box.

Wolverine has $4.50 and he is given another
$3.20. How much money does he have? $7.70

```
   4.50
 + 3.20
   7.70
```

Longshot has 120 cards. He divides
them equally among five people.
How many cards does each person get?   24

```
     24
 5)120
   10
   20
   20
    0
```

Write the answers in the box.

Daredevil buys a mask for
$5.50 and a belt for $6.65.
How much does he spend? $12.15

How much does he have left
from $20? $7.85

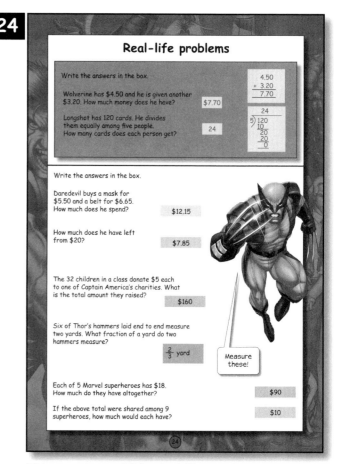

The 32 children in a class donate $5 each
to one of Captain America's charities. What
is the total amount they raised? $160

Six of Thor's hammers laid end to end measure
two yards. What fraction of a yard do two
hammers measure? $\frac{2}{3}$ yard

Measure these!

Each of 5 Marvel superheroes has $18.
How much do they have altogether? $90

If the above total were shared among 9
superheroes, how much would each have? $10

This page tests children's ability to choose operations required to solve real-life problems, mostly involving money. Discussing whether the answer will be larger or smaller than the question will help children decide what operation to use.

25

Real-life problems

The Goblin's glider is 16 in. wide. How wide will six gliders side by side be?

96 in.

$$\begin{array}{r} 16 \\ \times\ 6 \\ \hline 96 \end{array}$$

Rogue is 1.20 m tall. Her friend is 1.55 m tall. How much taller than Rogue is her friend?

0.35 m

$$\begin{array}{r} 1.55 \\ -\ 1.20 \\ \hline 0.35 \end{array}$$

Black Cat has a container of poison that contains 800 ml. She pours 320 ml into a glass, how much is left in the container?

480 ml

$$\begin{array}{r} ^{7\ 10} \\ 800 \\ -\ 320 \\ \hline 480 \end{array}$$

One of Maggot's slugs weighs 280 g. Another weighs 130 g. How much heavier is the first slug than the smaller slug?

150 g

$$\begin{array}{r} 280 \\ -\ 130 \\ \hline 150 \end{array}$$

There are 7 shelves of Marvel comics. 5 shelves are 1.2 m long. 2 shelves are 1.5 m long. What is the total length of the 7 shelves?

9 m

$$\begin{array}{cc} 1.2 & 1.5 \\ \times\ 5 & \times\ 2 \\ \hline 6.0 & 3.0 \end{array}$$
$$6 + 3 = 9$$

Storm has read 5 pages of a 20-page comic book. If it has taken her 9 minutes, how long is it likely to take her to read the whole comic book?

36 minutes

$$\begin{array}{r} 1.8 \\ 5\overline{)9.0} \\ 5 \\ \hline 40 \\ 40 \end{array}$$
$$\begin{array}{r} 20 \\ \times\ 1.8 \\ \hline 160 \\ +\ 200 \\ \hline 36.0 \end{array}$$

If you want to get a move on, get a glider!

The Green Goblin is flying around the city. He circles the city 36 times in a minute. How many times does he fly around the city in 30 seconds?

18 times

$$\begin{array}{r} 18 \\ 2\overline{)36} \\ 2 \\ \hline 16 \\ -\ 16 \end{array}$$

This page continues with real-life problems, but with units other than money. To solve the third problem children must perform three operations.

26

Areas of rectangles and squares

Find the area of this rectangle.

24 ft²

6 ft

4 ft

To find the area of a rectangle or square, multiply length (l) by width (w).
Area = l × w = 6 ft × 4 ft = 24 ft²

Find the area of these squares and rectangles.

Be careful! I'm here to check your answers.

3 in.
9 in.
27 in.²

4 yd
4 yd
16 yd²

2 ft
2 ft
4 ft²

8 cm
2 cm
16 cm²

4 in.
12 in.
48 in.²

5 mi
4 mi
20 mi²

3 yd
3 yd
9 yd²

Children should understand that area is measured in square units, such as cm². They will reach incorrect answers if they add sides instead of multiplying them, or try to find the area of a square by doubling the length of one side.

Problems involving time

Find the answer to this problem.

The Ghost Rider leaves town at 7:30 A.M. and arrives at the next town at 10:45 A.M. How long did his journey take?

7:30 → 10:30 = 3 h
10:30 → 10:45 = 15 min
Total = 3 h 15 min

Find the answer to each problem.

An X-Men film starts at 7:00 P.M. and finishes at 8:45 P.M. How long is the film?

1 hour 45 minutes

7:00 → 8:00 = 1 h
8:00 → 8:45 = 45 min
Total = 1 h 45 min

It takes Moira MacTaggert 1 hour 10 minutes to find a cure for a deadly virus. If she begins work at 10:35 A.M., at what time will she find the cure?

11:45 A.M.

10:35 + 1 h = 11:35
11:35 + 10 min = 11:45

It takes Magneto 2 hours 25 minutes to change Earth's magnetic field. If he starts the operation at 1:25 P.M., at what time will he finish?

3:50 P.M.

1:25 + 2 h = 3:25
3:25 + 25 min = 3:50

Gambit takes his helicopter in for repair at 7:00 A.M. It is finished at 1:50 P.M. How long did the repair take?

6 hours 50 minutes

7:00 → 1:00 = 6 h
1:00 → 1:50 = 50 min
Total = 6 h 50 min

Professor X has to be at a meeting by 8:50 A.M. If he takes 1 hour 30 minutes to get ready, and the trip takes 35 minutes, at what time does he need to get up?

6:45 A.M.

8:50 – 1 h = 7:50
7:50 – 30 min = 7:20
7:20 – 35 min = 6:45

Children can reach the correct answers using a variety of methods. Sample methods are provided in the answers, but any method that children use to reach a correct answer is acceptable.

Bar graphs

Use this bar graph to answer each question.

SUPERHERO MASKS
(Number of masks / Colors: Red, Black, Green, Blue)

What color mask was sold the most?

black

How many more green masks were sold than blue masks?

15

Use the bar graphs to answer the questions.

CRIMINALS CAUGHT BY PHOENIX
(Number of criminals caught / Date: May 1, May 2, May 3, May 4)

How many criminals did Phoenix catch on May 4?

100

How many more did she catch on May 3 than on May 2?

20

On which date were 90 criminals caught?

May 1

Can you read these graphs?

DISTANCE RUN BY MARVEL HEROES
(Marvel heroes: Beast, Cable, Rogue, Storm / Miles: 0 5 10 15 20 25 30 35 40 45 50)

Who ran 40 miles?

Storm

Who ran the same distance as Beast?

Rogue

How much farther did Cable run than Rogue?

15 miles

This page requires children to read information, to look for specific information, and to manipulate the information they read on a bar graph. They may need to be reassured that horizontal bar graphs can be read in much the same way as vertical graphs.

Probability

Mark each event on the probability line.

impossible — poor chance — even chance — good chance — certain

a) It will get dark tonight.
b) When I toss a coin, it will land showing heads.
c) Wolverine will come for lunch.

Mark each event on the probability line.

d   a   c   e   b
impossible — poor chance — even chance — good chance — certain

a) Snow will fall in July.
b) The sun will come up tomorrow.
c) A new baby will be a girl.
d) Iron Man will visit my school.
e) I will watch some television tonight.

> Is anything certain in this world?

Mark each event on the probability line.

d   a   e   b   c
impossible — poor chance — even chance — good chance — certain

a) Magneto rolls a 6 on a number cube.
b) Magneto does not roll a 6 on a number cube.
c) Magneto rolls a number between 1 and 6.
d) Magneto rolls a 7 on a number cube.
e) Magneto rolls a 1, 2, or 3 on a number cube.

Mark each event on the probability line.

d   c   b   e   a
impossible — poor chance — even chance — good chance — certain

a) I will drink something today.
b) If I drop my book, it will fall face down.
c) The next book I read will have exactly 96 pages.
d) I will see Spider-Man today.
e) I will see a black car today.

In the first section, children should be able to identify events categorically. As the second section is based on mathematical probability, the answers are not subjective. There may be some discussion of answers for the third section.

30

Triangles

> Hammer these triangles into shape!

Look at these different triangles.

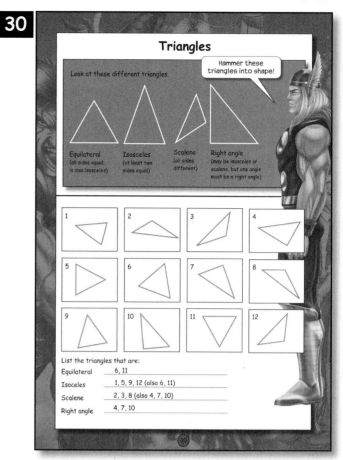

Equilateral (all sides equal; is also isosceles)
Isosceles (at least two sides equal)
Scalene (all sides different)
Right angle (may be isosceles or scalene, but one angle must be a right angle)

1   2   3   4
5   6   7   8
9   10   11   12

List the triangles that are:

Equilateral   6, 11
Isoceles   1, 5, 9, 12 (also 6, 11)
Scalene   2, 3, 8 (also 4, 7, 10)
Right angle   4, 7, 10

This page will highlight any gaps in children's ability to recognize and name triangles. Make sure that children can identify triangles that have been rotated.

31

Expanded form

What is the value of 3 in 3,208?   3,000

Write 7,143 in expanded form.   (7 x 1,000) + (1 x 100) + (4 x 10) + (3 x 1)

7,000 + 100 + 40 + 3

What is the value of 3 in these numbers?

| 139 | 30 | 3,526 | 3,000 | 1,003 | 3 |
| 37 | 30 | 37,641 | 30,000 | 399 | 300 |

What is the value of 7 in these numbers?

| 927 | 7 | 7,423 | 7,000 | 278 | 70 |
| 3,279 | 70 | 17,444 | 7,000 | 765 | 700 |

What is the value of 5 in these numbers?

| 2,500 | 500 | 885 | 5 | 51 | 50 |

Circle each number in which 6 has the value of 60.

6,782   926   (860)   (362)
(161)   676   (865)   60,000

Write these numbers in expanded form.

3,897	3,000 + 800 + 90 + 7
24,098	20,000 + 4,000 + 90 + 8
6,098	6,000 + 90 + 8
8,945	8,000 + 900 + 40 + 5

Errors may occur when children write numbers that include zeros in expanded form. When they work out the problems, they need not write 0 x 100 for a number such as 6,098. However, for a number such as 60,000, they should write 60 x 1,000.

Speed trials

> Let's fire our way through these!

Write the answers as fast as you can, but get them right!

4 x 10 = 40   8 x 2 = 16

Write the answers as fast as you can, but get them right!

3 x 2 =	6	1 x 5 =	5	4 x 10 =	40	1 x 3 =	3
2 x 2 =	4	10 x 5 =	50	8 x 10 =	80	2 x 3 =	6
5 x 2 =	10	0 x 5 =	0	6 x 10 =	60	10 x 3 =	30
1 x 2 =	2	3 x 5 =	15	1 x 10 =	10	8 x 3 =	24
6 x 2 =	12	4 x 5 =	20	5 x 10 =	50	6 x 3 =	18
4 x 2 =	8	8 x 5 =	40	3 x 10 =	30	4 x 3 =	12
7 x 2 =	14	6 x 5 =	30	7 x 10 =	70	7 x 3 =	21
9 x 2 =	18	7 x 5 =	35	0 x 10 =	0	0 x 3 =	0
10 x 2 =	20	9 x 5 =	45	2 x 10 =	20	5 x 3 =	15
8 x 2 =	16	5 x 5 =	25	9 x 10 =	90	3 x 3 =	9
0 x 2 =	0	3 x 5 =	15	10 x 10 =	100	8 x 4 =	32
2 x 7 =	14	5 x 3 =	15	10 x 1 =	10	7 x 4 =	28
2 x 1 =	2	5 x 8 =	40	10 x 7 =	70	6 x 4 =	24
2 x 4 =	8	5 x 9 =	45	10 x 4 =	40	3 x 4 =	12
3 x 7 =	21	5 x 7 =	35	10 x 3 =	30	10 x 4 =	40
2 x 5 =	10	5 x 4 =	20	10 x 5 =	50	0 x 4 =	0
2 x 9 =	18	5 x 1 =	5	10 x 8 =	80	3 x 4 =	12
2 x 6 =	12	4 x 7 =	28	10 x 6 =	60	9 x 4 =	36
2 x 8 =	16	5 x 10 =	50	10 x 2 =	20	5 x 4 =	20
2 x 3 =	6	5 x 2 =	10	10 x 9 =	90	2 x 4 =	8

All the 3s

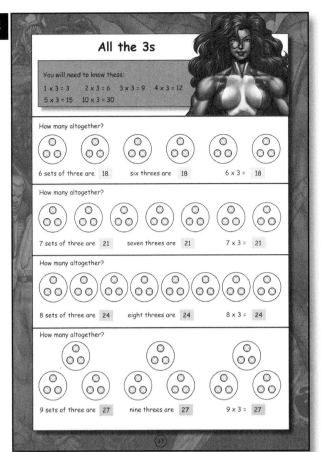

You will need to know these:

1 × 3 = 3   2 × 3 = 6   3 × 3 = 9   4 × 3 = 12
5 × 3 = 15   10 × 3 = 30

How many altogether?

6 sets of three are 18   six threes are 18   6 × 3 = 18

How many altogether?

7 sets of three are 21   seven threes are 21   7 × 3 = 21

How many altogether?

8 sets of three are 24   eight threes are 24   8 × 3 = 24

How many altogether?

9 sets of three are 27   nine threes are 27   9 × 3 = 27

34

All the 3s again

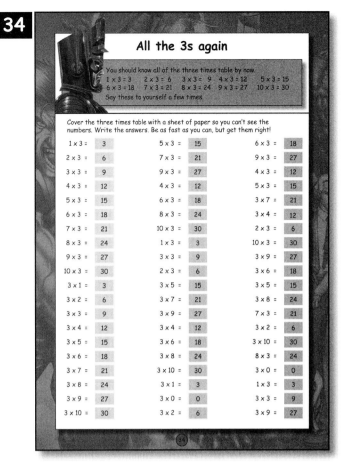

You should know all of the three times table by now.
1 × 3 = 3   2 × 3 = 6   3 × 3 = 9   4 × 3 = 12   5 × 3 = 15
6 × 3 = 18   7 × 3 = 21   8 × 3 = 24   9 × 3 = 27   10 × 3 = 30
Say these to yourself a few times.

Cover the three times table with a sheet of paper so you can't see the numbers. Write the answers. Be as fast as you can, but get them right!

1 × 3 =	3	5 × 3 =	15	6 × 3 =	18
2 × 3 =	6	7 × 3 =	21	9 × 3 =	27
3 × 3 =	9	9 × 3 =	27	4 × 3 =	12
4 × 3 =	12	4 × 3 =	12	5 × 3 =	15
5 × 3 =	15	6 × 3 =	18	3 × 7 =	21
6 × 3 =	18	8 × 3 =	24	3 × 4 =	12
7 × 3 =	21	10 × 3 =	30	2 × 3 =	6
8 × 3 =	24	1 × 3 =	3	10 × 3 =	30
9 × 3 =	27	3 × 3 =	9	3 × 9 =	27
10 × 3 =	30	2 × 3 =	6	3 × 6 =	18
3 × 1 =	3	3 × 5 =	15	3 × 5 =	15
3 × 2 =	6	3 × 7 =	21	3 × 8 =	24
3 × 3 =	9	3 × 9 =	27	7 × 3 =	21
3 × 4 =	12	3 × 4 =	12	3 × 2 =	6
3 × 5 =	15	3 × 6 =	18	3 × 10 =	30
3 × 6 =	18	3 × 8 =	24	8 × 3 =	24
3 × 7 =	21	3 × 10 =	30	3 × 0 =	0
3 × 8 =	24	3 × 1 =	3	1 × 3 =	3
3 × 9 =	27	3 × 0 =	0	3 × 3 =	9
3 × 10 =	30	3 × 2 =	6	3 × 9 =	27

All the 4s

You should know these:

1 × 4 = 4   2 × 4 = 8   3 × 4 = 12   4 × 4 = 16   5 × 4 = 20   10 × 4 = 40

How many altogether?

6 sets of four are 24   six fours are 24   6 × 4 = 24

How many altogether?

7 sets of four are 28   seven fours are 28   7 × 4 = 28

How many altogether?

8 sets of four are 32   eight fours are 32   8 × 4 = 32

How many altogether?

9 sets of four are 36   nine fours are 36   9 × 4 = 36

36

All the 4s again

You should know all of the four times table by now.
1 × 4 = 4   2 × 4 = 8   3 × 4 = 12   4 × 4 = 16   5 × 4 = 20
6 × 4 = 24   7 × 4 = 28   8 × 4 = 32   9 × 4 = 36   10 × 4 = 40
Say these to yourself a few times.

Cover the four times table with a sheet of paper so you can't see the numbers.
Write the answers. Be as fast as you can, but get them right!

1 × 4 =	4	5 × 4 =	20	6 × 4 =	24
2 × 4 =	8	7 × 4 =	28	9 × 4 =	36
3 × 4 =	12	9 × 4 =	36	4 × 1 =	4
4 × 4 =	16	3 × 4 =	12	5 × 4 =	20
5 × 4 =	20	6 × 4 =	24	4 × 7 =	28
6 × 4 =	24	8 × 4 =	32	3 × 4 =	12
7 × 4 =	28	10 × 4 =	40	2 × 4 =	8
8 × 4 =	32	1 × 4 =	4	10 × 4 =	40
9 × 4 =	36	4 × 4 =	16	4 × 3 =	12
10 × 4 =	40	2 × 4 =	8	4 × 6 =	24
4 × 1 =	4	4 × 5 =	20	4 × 5 =	20
4 × 2 =	8	4 × 7 =	28	4 × 8 =	32
4 × 3 =	12	4 × 9 =	36	7 × 4 =	28
4 × 4 =	16	4 × 4 =	16	4 × 2 =	8
4 × 5 =	20	4 × 6 =	24	4 × 10 =	40
4 × 6 =	24	4 × 8 =	32	8 × 4 =	32
4 × 7 =	28	4 × 10 =	40	4 × 0 =	0
4 × 8 =	32	4 × 1 =	4	1 × 4 =	4
4 × 9 =	36	4 × 0 =	0	4 × 4 =	16
4 × 10 =	40	4 × 2 =	8	4 × 9 =	36

37 — Speed trials

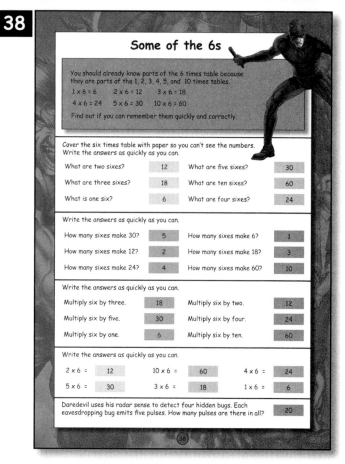

You should know all of the 1, 2, 3, 4, 5, and 10 times tables by now, but how quickly can you do them? Ask someone to time you as you do this page. Remember, you must be fast but also correct.

4 x 2 = 8	6 x 3 = 18	
8 x 3 = 24	3 x 4 = 12	
7 x 4 = 28	7 x 5 = 35	7 x 2 = 14
6 x 5 = 30	3 x 10 = 30	6 x 3 = 18
8 x 10 = 80	1 x 2 = 2	5 x 4 = 20
8 x 2 = 16	7 x 3 = 21	4 x 5 = 20
5 x 3 = 15	4 x 4 = 16	3 x 10 = 30
9 x 4 = 36	6 x 5 = 30	2 x 2 = 4
5 x 5 = 25	4 x 10 = 40	1 x 3 = 3
7 x 10 = 70	6 x 2 = 12	0 x 4 = 0
0 x 2 = 0	5 x 3 = 15	10 x 5 = 50
4 x 3 = 12	8 x 4 = 32	9 x 2 = 18
6 x 4 = 24	0 x 5 = 0	8 x 3 = 24
3 x 5 = 15	2 x 10 = 20	7 x 4 = 28
4 x 10 = 40	7 x 2 = 14	6 x 5 = 30
7 x 2 = 14	8 x 3 = 24	5 x 10 = 50
3 x 3 = 9	9 x 4 = 36	4 x 0 = 0
2 x 4 = 8	5 x 5 = 25	3 x 2 = 6
7 x 5 = 35	7 x 10 = 70	2 x 8 = 16
9 x 10 = 90	5 x 2 = 10	1 x 9 = 9

38 — Some of the 6s

You should already know parts of the 6 times table because they are parts of the 1, 2, 3, 4, 5, and 10 times tables.

1 x 6 = 6   2 x 6 = 12   3 x 6 = 18
4 x 6 = 24   5 x 6 = 30   10 x 6 = 60

Find out if you can remember them quickly and correctly.

Cover the six times table with paper so you can't see the numbers. Write the answers as quickly as you can.

What are two sixes?	12	What are five sixes?	30
What are three sixes?	18	What are ten sixes?	60
What is one six?	6	What are four sixes?	24

Write the answers as quickly as you can.

How many sixes make 30?	5	How many sixes make 6?	1
How many sixes make 12?	2	How many sixes make 18?	3
How many sixes make 24?	4	How many sixes make 60?	10

Write the answers as quickly as you can.

Multiply six by three.	18	Multiply six by two.	12
Multiply six by five.	30	Multiply six by four.	24
Multiply six by one.	6	Multiply six by ten.	60

Write the answers as quickly as you can.

2 x 6 = 12	10 x 6 = 60	4 x 6 = 24
5 x 6 = 30	3 x 6 = 18	1 x 6 = 6

Daredevil uses his radar sense to detect four hidden bugs. Each eavesdropping bug emits five pulses. How many pulses are there in all? **20**

39 — The rest of the 6s

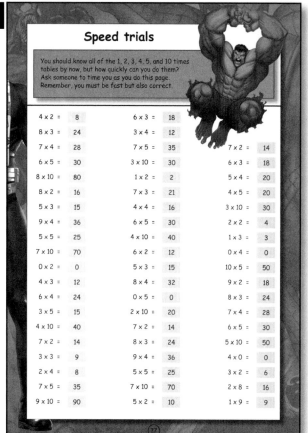

You need to learn these:

6 x 6 = 36   7 x 6 = 42
8 x 6 = 48   9 x 6 = 54

Have no fear! It's only a question of adding 6!

This work will help you remember the 6 times table.

Complete these sequences.

6   12   18   24   30   **36**   **42**   **48**   **54**

5 x 6 = 30 so 6 x 6 = 30 plus another 6 = **36**

18   24   30   **36**   **42**   **48**   **54**   **60**

6 x 6 = 36 so 7 x 6 = 36 plus another 6 = **42**

6   12   18   **24**   **30**   **36**   **42**   48   **54**   60

7 x 6 = 42 so 8 x 6 = 42 plus another 6 = **48**

6   12   18   24   30   **36**   **42**   **48**   **54**   60

8 x 6 = 48 so 9 x 6 = 48 plus another 6 = **54**

6   **12**   **18**   24   **30**   **36**   42   **48**   **54**   60

Test yourself on the rest of the 6 times table.
Cover the above part of the page with a sheet of paper.

What are six sixes?	36	What are eight sixes?	48
What are seven sixes?	42	What are nine sixes?	54

8 x 6 = **48**   7 x 6 = **42**   6 x 6 = **36**   9 x 6 = **54**

40 — Practice the 6s

You should know all of the 6 times table now, but how quickly can you remember it? Ask someone to time you as you do this page. Remember, you must be fast but also correct.

1 x 6 = 6	2 x 6 = 12	7 x 6 = 42
2 x 6 = 12	4 x 6 = 24	3 x 6 = 18
3 x 6 = 18	6 x 6 = 36	9 x 6 = 54
4 x 6 = 24	8 x 6 = 48	6 x 4 = 24
5 x 6 = 30	10 x 6 = 60	1 x 6 = 6
6 x 6 = 36	1 x 6 = 6	6 x 2 = 12
7 x 6 = 42	3 x 6 = 18	6 x 8 = 48
8 x 6 = 48	5 x 6 = 30	0 x 6 = 0
9 x 6 = 54	7 x 6 = 42	6 x 3 = 18
10 x 6 = 60	9 x 6 = 54	5 x 6 = 30
6 x 1 = 6	6 x 3 = 18	6 x 7 = 42
6 x 2 = 12	6 x 5 = 30	2 x 6 = 12
6 x 3 = 18	6 x 7 = 42	6 x 9 = 54
6 x 4 = 24	6 x 9 = 54	4 x 6 = 24
6 x 5 = 30	6 x 2 = 12	8 x 6 = 48
6 x 6 = 36	6 x 4 = 24	10 x 6 = 60
6 x 7 = 42	6 x 6 = 36	6 x 5 = 30
6 x 8 = 48	6 x 8 = 48	6 x 0 = 0
6 x 9 = 54	6 x 10 = 60	6 x 1 = 6
6 x 10 = 60	6 x 0 = 0	6 x 6 = 36

Speed trials

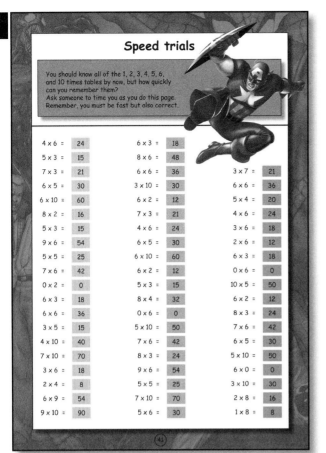

You should know all of the 1, 2, 3, 4, 5, 6, and 10 times tables by now, but how quickly can you remember them?
Ask someone to time you as you do this page.
Remember, you must be fast but also correct.

4 x 6 =	24	6 x 3 =	18		
5 x 3 =	15	8 x 6 =	48		
7 x 3 =	21	6 x 6 =	36	3 x 7 =	21
6 x 5 =	30	3 x 10 =	30	6 x 6 =	36
6 x 10 =	60	6 x 2 =	12	5 x 4 =	20
8 x 2 =	16	7 x 3 =	21	4 x 6 =	24
5 x 3 =	15	4 x 6 =	24	3 x 6 =	18
9 x 6 =	54	6 x 5 =	30	2 x 6 =	12
5 x 5 =	25	6 x 10 =	60	6 x 3 =	18
7 x 6 =	42	6 x 2 =	12	0 x 6 =	0
0 x 2 =	0	5 x 3 =	15	10 x 5 =	50
6 x 3 =	18	8 x 4 =	32	6 x 2 =	12
6 x 6 =	36	0 x 6 =	0	8 x 3 =	24
3 x 5 =	15	5 x 10 =	50	7 x 6 =	42
4 x 10 =	40	7 x 6 =	42	6 x 5 =	30
7 x 10 =	70	8 x 3 =	24	5 x 10 =	50
3 x 6 =	18	9 x 6 =	54	6 x 0 =	0
2 x 4 =	8	5 x 5 =	25	3 x 10 =	30
6 x 9 =	54	7 x 10 =	70	2 x 8 =	16
9 x 10 =	90	5 x 6 =	30	1 x 8 =	8

Some of the 7s

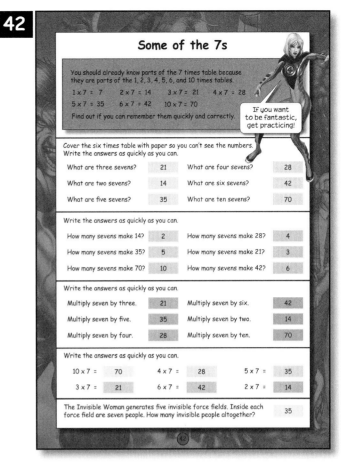

You should already know parts of the 7 times table because they are parts of the 1, 2, 3, 4, 5, and 10 times tables.

1 x 7 = 7	2 x 7 = 14	3 x 7 = 21	4 x 7 = 28
5 x 7 = 35	6 x 7 = 42	10 x 7 = 70	

Find out if you can remember them quickly and correctly.

> If you want to be fantastic, get practicing!

Cover the six times table with paper so you can't see the numbers. Write the answers as quickly as you can.

What are three sevens?	21	What are four sevens?	28
What are two sevens?	14	What are six sevens?	42
What are five sevens?	35	What are ten sevens?	70

Write the answers as quickly as you can.

How many sevens make 14?	2	How many sevens make 28?	4
How many sevens make 35?	5	How many sevens make 21?	3
How many sevens make 70?	10	How many sevens make 42?	6

Write the answers as quickly as you can.

Multiply seven by three.	21	Multiply seven by six.	42
Multiply seven by five.	35	Multiply seven by two.	14
Multiply seven by four.	28	Multiply seven by ten.	70

Write the answers as quickly as you can.

10 x 7 =	70	4 x 7 =	28	5 x 7 =	35
3 x 7 =	21	6 x 7 =	42	2 x 7 =	14

The Invisible Woman generates five invisible force fields. Inside each force field are seven people. How many invisible people altogether? 35

The rest of the 7s

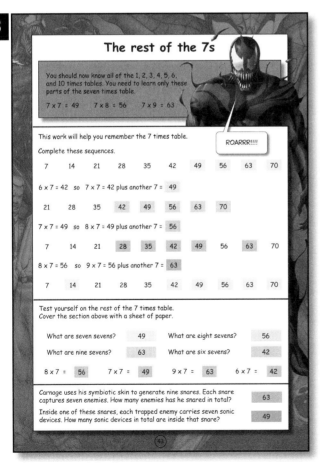

You should now know all of the 1, 2, 3, 4, 5, 6, and 10 times tables. You need to learn only these parts of the seven times table.

7 x 7 = 49   7 x 8 = 56   7 x 9 = 63

> ROARRR!!!!

This work will help you remember the 7 times table.

Complete these sequences.

7   14   21   28   35   42   49   56   63   70

6 x 7 = 42 so 7 x 7 = 42 plus another 7 = 49

21   28   35   42   49   56   63   70

7 x 7 = 49 so 8 x 7 = 49 plus another 7 = 56

7   14   21   28   35   42   49   56   63   70

8 x 7 = 56 so 9 x 7 = 56 plus another 7 = 63

7   14   21   28   35   42   49   56   63   70

Test yourself on the rest of the 7 times table. Cover the section above with a sheet of paper.

What are seven sevens?	49	What are eight sevens?	56
What are nine sevens?	63	What are six sevens?	42

8 x 7 =	56	7 x 7 =	49	9 x 7 =	63	6 x 7 =	42

Carnage uses his symbiotic skin to generate nine snares. Each snare captures seven enemies. How many enemies has he snared in total? 63

Inside one of these snares, each trapped enemy carries seven sonic devices. How many sonic devices in total are inside that snare? 49

Practice the 7s

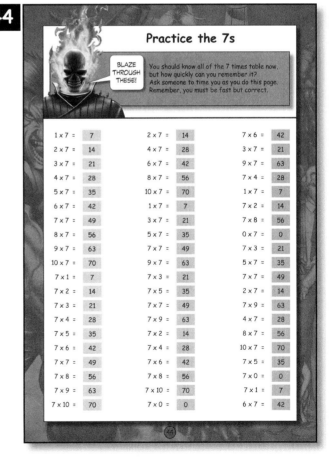

> BLAZE THROUGH THESE!

You should know all of the 7 times table now, but how quickly can you remember it?
Ask someone to time you as you do this page.
Remember, you must be fast but correct.

1 x 7 =	7	2 x 7 =	14	7 x 6 =	42
2 x 7 =	14	4 x 7 =	28	3 x 7 =	21
3 x 7 =	21	6 x 7 =	42	9 x 7 =	63
4 x 7 =	28	8 x 7 =	56	7 x 4 =	28
5 x 7 =	35	10 x 7 =	70	1 x 7 =	7
6 x 7 =	42	1 x 7 =	7	7 x 2 =	14
7 x 7 =	49	3 x 7 =	21	7 x 8 =	56
8 x 7 =	56	5 x 7 =	35	0 x 7 =	0
9 x 7 =	63	7 x 7 =	49	7 x 3 =	21
10 x 7 =	70	9 x 7 =	63	5 x 7 =	35
7 x 1 =	7	7 x 3 =	21	7 x 7 =	49
7 x 2 =	14	7 x 5 =	35	2 x 7 =	14
7 x 3 =	21	7 x 7 =	49	7 x 9 =	63
7 x 4 =	28	7 x 9 =	63	4 x 7 =	28
7 x 5 =	35	7 x 2 =	14	8 x 7 =	56
7 x 6 =	42	7 x 4 =	28	10 x 7 =	70
7 x 7 =	49	7 x 6 =	42	7 x 5 =	35
7 x 8 =	56	7 x 8 =	56	7 x 0 =	0
7 x 9 =	63	7 x 10 =	70	7 x 1 =	7
7 x 10 =	70	7 x 0 =	0	6 x 7 =	42

Speed trials

You should know all of the 1, 2, 3, 4, 5, 6, 7, and 10 times tables now, but how quickly can you remember them? Ask someone to time you as you do this page. Remember, you must be fast but also correct.

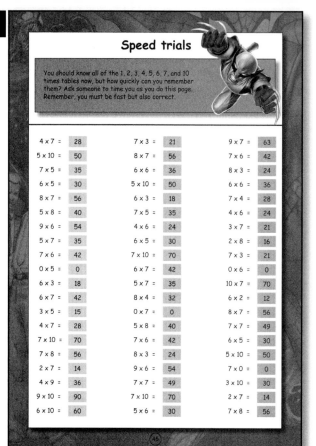

4 x 7 = 28	7 x 3 = 21	9 x 7 = 63
5 x 10 = 50	8 x 7 = 56	7 x 6 = 42
7 x 5 = 35	6 x 6 = 36	8 x 3 = 24
6 x 5 = 30	5 x 10 = 50	6 x 6 = 36
8 x 7 = 56	6 x 3 = 18	7 x 4 = 28
5 x 8 = 40	7 x 5 = 35	4 x 6 = 24
9 x 6 = 54	4 x 6 = 24	3 x 7 = 21
5 x 7 = 35	6 x 5 = 30	2 x 8 = 16
7 x 6 = 42	7 x 10 = 70	7 x 3 = 21
0 x 5 = 0	6 x 7 = 42	0 x 6 = 0
6 x 3 = 18	5 x 7 = 35	10 x 7 = 70
6 x 7 = 42	8 x 4 = 32	6 x 2 = 12
3 x 5 = 15	0 x 7 = 0	8 x 7 = 56
4 x 7 = 28	5 x 8 = 40	7 x 7 = 49
7 x 10 = 70	7 x 6 = 42	6 x 5 = 30
7 x 8 = 56	8 x 3 = 24	5 x 10 = 50
2 x 7 = 14	9 x 6 = 54	7 x 0 = 0
4 x 9 = 36	7 x 7 = 49	3 x 10 = 30
9 x 10 = 90	7 x 10 = 70	2 x 7 = 14
6 x 10 = 60	5 x 6 = 30	7 x 8 = 56

Some of the 8s

You should already know some of the 8 times table because it is part of the 1, 2, 3, 4, 5, 6, 7, and 10 times tables.

1 x 8 = 8	2 x 8 = 16	3 x 8 = 24	4 x 8 = 32
5 x 8 = 40	6 x 8 = 48	7 x 8 = 56	10 x 8 = 80

Find out if you can remember them.

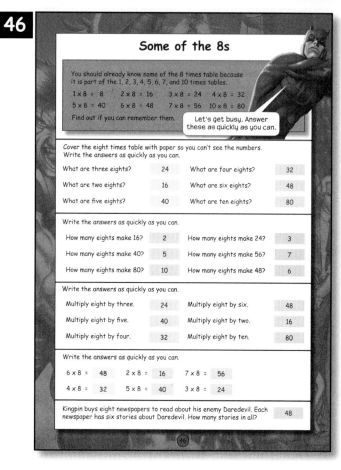

Let's get busy. Answer these as quickly as you can.

Cover the eight times table with paper so you can't see the numbers. Write the answers as quickly as you can.

What are three eights?	24	What are four eights?	32
What are two eights?	16	What are six eights?	48
What are five eights?	40	What are ten eights?	80

Write the answers as quickly as you can.

How many eights make 16?	2	How many eights make 24?	3
How many eights make 40?	5	How many eights make 56?	7
How many eights make 80?	10	How many eights make 48?	6

Write the answers as quickly as you can.

Multiply eight by three.	24	Multiply eight by six.	48
Multiply eight by five.	40	Multiply eight by two.	16
Multiply eight by four.	32	Multiply eight by ten.	80

Write the answers as quickly as you can.

6 x 8 = 48	2 x 8 = 16	7 x 8 = 56
4 x 8 = 32	5 x 8 = 40	3 x 8 = 24

Kingpin buys eight newspapers to read about his enemy Daredevil. Each newspaper has six stories about Daredevil. How many stories in all? 48

The rest of the 8s

You need to learn only these parts of the eight times table.

8 x 8 = 64   9 x 8 = 72

This work will help you remember the 8 times table.

Complete these sequences.

8   16   24   32   40   48   56   64   72   80

7 x 8 = 56 so 8 x 8 = 56 plus another 8 = 64

24   32   40   48   56   64   72   80

8 x 8 = 64 so 9 x 8 = 64 plus another 8 = 72

8   16   24   32   40   48   56   64   72   80

8   16   24   32   40   48   56   64   72   80

Test yourself on the rest of the 8 times table.
Cover the section above with a sheet of paper.

What are seven eights?	56	What are eight eights?	64
What are nine eights?	72	What are eight sixes?	48

8 x 8 = 64	9 x 8 = 72	8 x 9 = 72	10 x 8 = 80

What number multiplied by 8 gives the answer 72? 9

A number multiplied by 8 gives the answer 64. What is the number? 8

A shopkeeper arranges Doctor Strange masks in piles of 8. How many masks will there be in 10 piles? 80

How many 8s make 56? 7

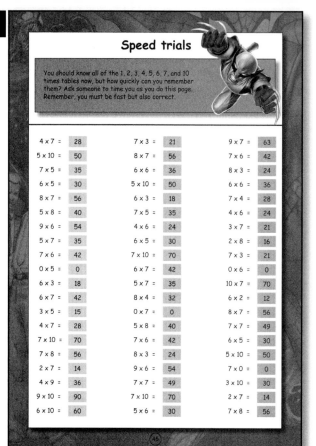

Practice the 8s

You should know all of the 8 times table now, but how quickly can you remember it? Ask someone to time you as you do this page. Be fast but also correct.

1 x 8 = 8	2 x 8 = 16	8 x 6 = 48
2 x 8 = 16	4 x 8 = 32	3 x 8 = 24
3 x 8 = 24	6 x 8 = 48	9 x 8 = 72
4 x 8 = 32	8 x 8 = 64	8 x 4 = 32
5 x 8 = 40	10 x 8 = 80	1 x 8 = 8
6 x 8 = 48	1 x 8 = 8	8 x 2 = 16
7 x 8 = 56	3 x 8 = 24	7 x 8 = 56
8 x 8 = 64	5 x 8 = 40	0 x 8 = 0
9 x 8 = 72	7 x 8 = 56	8 x 3 = 24
10 x 8 = 80	9 x 8 = 72	5 x 8 = 40
8 x 1 = 8	8 x 3 = 24	8 x 8 = 64
8 x 2 = 16	8 x 5 = 40	2 x 8 = 16
8 x 3 = 24	8 x 7 = 56	8 x 9 = 72
8 x 4 = 32	8 x 9 = 72	4 x 8 = 32
8 x 5 = 40	8 x 2 = 16	8 x 6 = 48
8 x 6 = 48	8 x 4 = 32	10 x 8 = 80
8 x 7 = 56	8 x 6 = 48	8 x 5 = 40
8 x 8 = 64	8 x 8 = 64	8 x 0 = 0
8 x 9 = 72	8 x 10 = 80	8 x 1 = 8
8 x 10 = 80	8 x 0 = 0	6 x 8 = 48

49

Speed trials

You should know all of the 1, 2, 3, 4, 5, 6, 7, 8, and 10 times tables now, but how quickly can you remember them? Ask someone to time you as you do this page. Be fast but also correct.

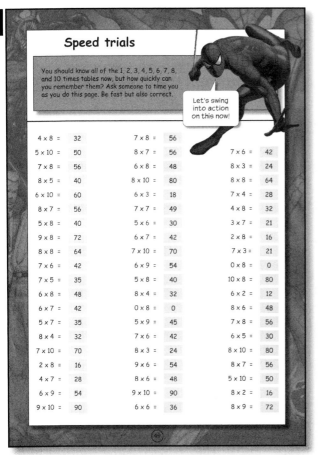

Let's swing into action on this now!

4 x 8 =	32	7 x 8 =	56		
5 x 10 =	50	8 x 7 =	56	7 x 6 =	42
7 x 8 =	56	6 x 8 =	48	8 x 3 =	24
8 x 5 =	40	8 x 10 =	80	8 x 8 =	64
6 x 10 =	60	6 x 3 =	18	7 x 4 =	28
8 x 7 =	56	7 x 7 =	49	4 x 8 =	32
5 x 8 =	40	5 x 6 =	30	3 x 7 =	21
9 x 8 =	72	6 x 7 =	42	2 x 8 =	16
8 x 8 =	64	7 x 10 =	70	7 x 3 =	21
7 x 6 =	42	6 x 9 =	54	0 x 8 =	0
7 x 5 =	35	5 x 8 =	40	10 x 8 =	80
6 x 8 =	48	8 x 4 =	32	6 x 2 =	12
6 x 7 =	42	0 x 8 =	0	8 x 6 =	48
5 x 7 =	35	5 x 9 =	45	7 x 8 =	56
8 x 4 =	32	7 x 6 =	42	6 x 5 =	30
7 x 10 =	70	8 x 3 =	24	8 x 10 =	80
2 x 8 =	16	9 x 6 =	54	8 x 7 =	56
4 x 7 =	28	8 x 6 =	48	5 x 10 =	50
6 x 9 =	54	9 x 10 =	90	8 x 2 =	16
9 x 10 =	90	6 x 6 =	36	8 x 9 =	72

50

Some of the 9s

You should already know nearly all of the 9 times table because it is part of the 1, 2, 3, 4, 5, 6, 7, 8, and 10 times tables.

1 x 9 = 9   2 x 9 = 18   3 x 9 = 27   4 x 9 = 36   5 x 9 = 45
6 x 9 = 54   7 x 9 = 63   8 x 9 = 72   10 x 9 = 90

Find out if you can remember them quickly and correctly.

What are three nines?	27	What are eight nines?	72
What are seven nines?	63	What are four nines?	36
What are six nines?	54	What are five nines?	45

Write the answers as quickly as you can.

How many nines equal 18?	2	How many nines equal 54?	6
How many nines equal 90?	10	How many nines equal 63?	7
How many nines equal 72?	8	How many nines equal 36?	4

Write the answers as quickly as you can.

Multiply nine by seven.	63	Multiply nine by ten.	90
Multiply nine by two.	18	Multiply nine by five.	45
Multiply nine by six.	54	Multiply nine by four.	36
Multiply nine by three.	27	Multiply nine by eight.	72

Write the answers as quickly as you can.

6 x 9 =	54	2 x 9 =	18
5 x 9 =	45	3 x 9 =	27
0 x 9 =	0	7 x 9 =	63

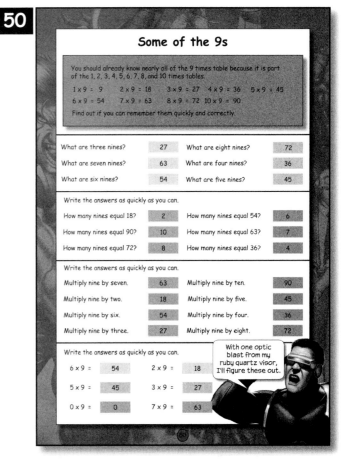

With one optic blast from my ruby quartz visor, I'll figure these out.

The rest of the 9s

You need to learn only this part of the nine times table.

9 x 9 = 81

This work will help you remember the nine times table.

Complete these sequences.

9   18   27   36   45   54   63   72   81   90

8 x 9 = 72 so 9 x 9 = 72 plus another 9 = 81

27   36   45   54   63   72   81   90

9   18   27   36   45   54   63   72   81   90

9   18   27   36   45   54   63   72   81   90

Look for a pattern in the nine times table.

1 x 9 = 09
2 x 9 = 18
3 x 9 = 27
4 x 9 = 36
5 x 9 = 45
6 x 9 = 54
7 x 9 = 63
8 x 9 = 72
9 x 9 = 81
10 x 9 = 90

I can't see any patterns. Can you?

Write down any patterns you can see. (There are more than one.)

The digits in every answer have a sum of 9.
If we take the first number of every answer, from top to bottom, we get 0, 1, 2, 3, 4, 5, 6, 7, 8, 9.
If we take the second number of every answer, from bottom to top, we get 0, 1, 2, 3, 4, 5, 6, 7, 8, 9.
The first and last answers are opposites (09 and 90), the second and second last answers are opposites (18 and 81), and so on.

Practice the 9s

HA!

You should know all of the 9 times table now, but how quickly can you remember it? Ask someone to time you as you do this page. Be fast and correct.

1 x 9 =	9	2 x 9 =	18	9 x 6 =	54
2 x 9 =	18	4 x 9 =	36	3 x 9 =	27
3 x 9 =	27	6 x 9 =	54	9 x 9 =	81
4 x 9 =	36	8 x 9 =	72	9 x 4 =	36
5 x 9 =	45	10 x 9 =	90	1 x 9 =	9
6 x 9 =	54	1 x 9 =	9	9 x 2 =	18
7 x 9 =	63	3 x 9 =	27	7 x 9 =	63
8 x 9 =	72	5 x 9 =	45	0 x 9 =	0
9 x 9 =	81	7 x 9 =	63	9 x 3 =	27
10 x 9 =	90	9 x 9 =	81	5 x 9 =	45
9 x 1 =	9	9 x 3 =	27	9 x 9 =	81
9 x 2 =	18	9 x 5 =	45	2 x 9 =	18
9 x 3 =	27	9 x 7 =	63	8 x 9 =	72
9 x 4 =	36	9 x 2 =	18	4 x 9 =	36
9 x 5 =	45	9 x 4 =	36	9 x 7 =	63
9 x 6 =	54	9 x 6 =	54	10 x 9 =	90
9 x 7 =	63	9 x 8 =	72	9 x 5 =	45
9 x 8 =	72	9 x 10 =	90	9 x 0 =	0
9 x 9 =	81	9 x 0 =	0	9 x 1 =	9
9 x 10 =	90	9 x 9 =	81	6 x 9 =	54

Encourage children to notice patterns. It does not matter how they express these. One pattern is to deduct 1 from the number being multiplied. This gives the first digit of the answer. Then deduct this first digit from 9 to get the second digit of the answer.

53

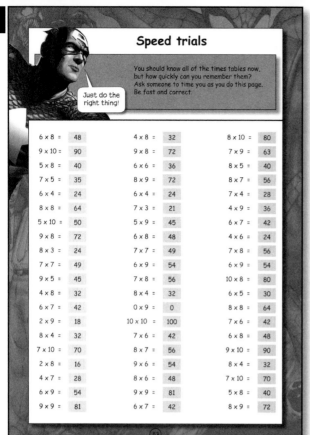

Speed trials

You should know all of the times tables now, but how quickly can you remember them? Ask someone to time you as you do this page. Be fast and correct.

Just do the right thing!

6 x 8 = 48	4 x 8 = 32	8 x 10 = 80
9 x 10 = 90	9 x 8 = 72	7 x 9 = 63
5 x 8 = 40	6 x 6 = 36	8 x 5 = 40
7 x 5 = 35	8 x 9 = 72	8 x 7 = 56
6 x 4 = 24	6 x 4 = 24	7 x 4 = 28
8 x 8 = 64	7 x 3 = 21	4 x 9 = 36
5 x 10 = 50	5 x 9 = 45	6 x 7 = 42
9 x 8 = 72	6 x 8 = 48	4 x 6 = 24
8 x 3 = 24	7 x 7 = 49	7 x 8 = 56
7 x 7 = 49	6 x 9 = 54	6 x 9 = 54
9 x 5 = 45	7 x 8 = 56	10 x 8 = 80
4 x 8 = 32	8 x 4 = 32	6 x 5 = 30
6 x 7 = 42	0 x 9 = 0	8 x 8 = 64
2 x 9 = 18	10 x 10 = 100	7 x 6 = 42
8 x 4 = 32	7 x 6 = 42	6 x 8 = 48
7 x 10 = 70	8 x 7 = 56	9 x 10 = 90
2 x 8 = 16	9 x 6 = 54	8 x 4 = 32
4 x 7 = 28	8 x 6 = 48	7 x 10 = 70
6 x 9 = 54	9 x 9 = 81	5 x 8 = 40
9 x 9 = 81	6 x 7 = 42	8 x 9 = 72

54

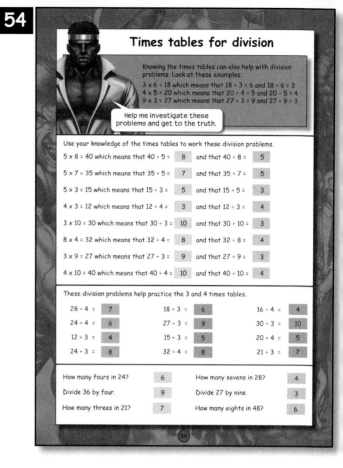

Times tables for division

Knowing the times tables can also help with division problems. Look at these examples.
3 x 6 = 18 which means that 18 ÷ 3 = 6 and 18 ÷ 6 = 3
4 x 5 = 20 which means that 20 ÷ 4 = 5 and 20 ÷ 5 = 4
9 x 3 = 27 which means that 27 ÷ 3 = 9 and 27 ÷ 9 = 3

Help me investigate these problems and get to the truth.

Use your knowledge of the times tables to work these division problems.

5 x 8 = 40 which means that 40 ÷ 5 = 8 and that 40 ÷ 8 = 5
5 x 7 = 35 which means that 35 ÷ 5 = 7 and that 35 ÷ 7 = 5
5 x 3 = 15 which means that 15 ÷ 3 = 5 and that 15 ÷ 5 = 3
4 x 3 = 12 which means that 12 ÷ 4 = 3 and that 12 ÷ 3 = 4
3 x 10 = 30 which means that 30 ÷ 3 = 10 and that 30 ÷ 10 = 3
8 x 4 = 32 which means that 32 ÷ 4 = 8 and that 32 ÷ 8 = 4
3 x 9 = 27 which means that 27 ÷ 3 = 9 and that 27 ÷ 9 = 3
4 x 10 = 40 which means that 40 ÷ 4 = 10 and that 40 ÷ 10 = 4

These division problems help practice the 3 and 4 times tables.

28 ÷ 4 = 7	18 ÷ 3 = 6	16 ÷ 4 = 4
24 ÷ 4 = 6	27 ÷ 3 = 9	30 ÷ 3 = 10
12 ÷ 3 = 4	15 ÷ 3 = 5	20 ÷ 4 = 5
24 ÷ 3 = 8	32 ÷ 4 = 8	21 ÷ 3 = 7

How many fours in 24? 6	How many sevens in 28? 4
Divide 36 by four. 9	Divide 27 by nine. 3
How many threes in 21? 7	How many eights in 48? 6

55

Times tables for division

This page will help you remember times tables by dividing by 2, 3, 4, 5, and 10.

20 ÷ 5 = 4   18 ÷ 3 = 6   60 ÷ 10 = 6

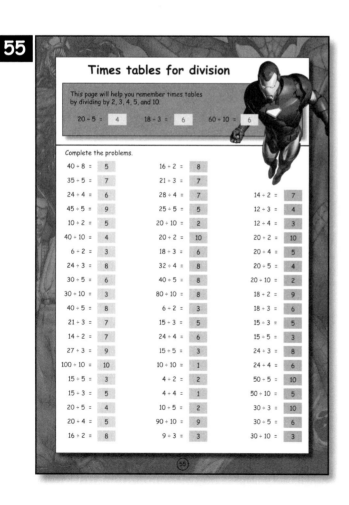

Complete the problems.

40 ÷ 8 = 5	16 ÷ 2 = 8	
35 ÷ 5 = 7	21 ÷ 3 = 7	
24 ÷ 4 = 6	28 ÷ 4 = 7	14 ÷ 2 = 7
45 ÷ 5 = 9	25 ÷ 5 = 5	12 ÷ 3 = 4
10 ÷ 2 = 5	20 ÷ 10 = 2	12 ÷ 4 = 3
40 ÷ 10 = 4	20 ÷ 2 = 10	20 ÷ 2 = 10
6 ÷ 2 = 3	18 ÷ 3 = 6	20 ÷ 4 = 5
24 ÷ 3 = 8	32 ÷ 4 = 8	20 ÷ 5 = 4
30 ÷ 5 = 6	40 ÷ 5 = 8	20 ÷ 10 = 2
30 ÷ 10 = 3	80 ÷ 10 = 8	18 ÷ 2 = 9
40 ÷ 5 = 8	6 ÷ 2 = 3	18 ÷ 3 = 6
21 ÷ 3 = 7	15 ÷ 3 = 5	15 ÷ 3 = 5
14 ÷ 2 = 7	24 ÷ 4 = 6	15 ÷ 5 = 3
27 ÷ 3 = 9	15 ÷ 5 = 3	24 ÷ 3 = 8
100 ÷ 10 = 10	10 ÷ 10 = 1	24 ÷ 4 = 6
15 ÷ 5 = 3	4 ÷ 2 = 2	50 ÷ 5 = 10
15 ÷ 3 = 5	4 ÷ 4 = 1	50 ÷ 10 = 5
20 ÷ 5 = 4	10 ÷ 5 = 2	30 ÷ 3 = 10
20 ÷ 4 = 5	90 ÷ 10 = 9	30 ÷ 5 = 6
16 ÷ 2 = 8	9 ÷ 3 = 3	30 ÷ 10 = 3

56

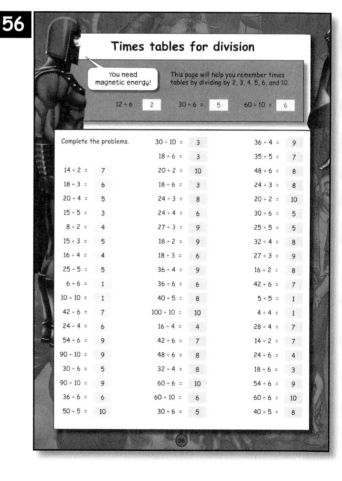

Times tables for division

You need magnetic energy!

This page will help you remember times tables by dividing by 2, 3, 4, 5, 6, and 10.

12 ÷ 6 = 2   30 ÷ 6 = 5   60 ÷ 10 = 6

Complete the problems.		
	30 ÷ 10 = 3	36 ÷ 4 = 9
	18 ÷ 6 = 3	35 ÷ 5 = 7
14 ÷ 2 = 7	20 ÷ 2 = 10	48 ÷ 6 = 8
18 ÷ 3 = 6	18 ÷ 6 = 3	24 ÷ 3 = 8
20 ÷ 4 = 5	24 ÷ 3 = 8	20 ÷ 2 = 10
15 ÷ 5 = 3	24 ÷ 4 = 6	30 ÷ 6 = 5
8 ÷ 2 = 4	27 ÷ 3 = 9	25 ÷ 5 = 5
15 ÷ 3 = 5	18 ÷ 2 = 9	32 ÷ 4 = 8
16 ÷ 4 = 4	18 ÷ 3 = 6	27 ÷ 3 = 9
25 ÷ 5 = 5	36 ÷ 4 = 9	16 ÷ 2 = 8
6 ÷ 6 = 1	36 ÷ 6 = 6	42 ÷ 6 = 7
10 ÷ 10 = 1	40 ÷ 5 = 8	5 ÷ 5 = 1
42 ÷ 6 = 7	100 ÷ 10 = 10	4 ÷ 4 = 1
24 ÷ 4 = 6	16 ÷ 4 = 4	28 ÷ 4 = 7
54 ÷ 6 = 9	42 ÷ 6 = 7	14 ÷ 2 = 7
90 ÷ 10 = 9	48 ÷ 6 = 8	24 ÷ 6 = 4
30 ÷ 6 = 5	32 ÷ 4 = 8	18 ÷ 6 = 3
90 ÷ 10 = 9	60 ÷ 6 = 10	54 ÷ 6 = 9
36 ÷ 6 = 6	60 ÷ 10 = 6	60 ÷ 6 = 10
50 ÷ 5 = 10	30 ÷ 6 = 5	40 ÷ 5 = 8

Times tables for division

This page will help you remember times tables by dividing by 2, 3, 4, 5, 6, 7, and 10.

42 ÷ 7 = 6   21 ÷ 7 = 3   70 ÷ 7 = 10

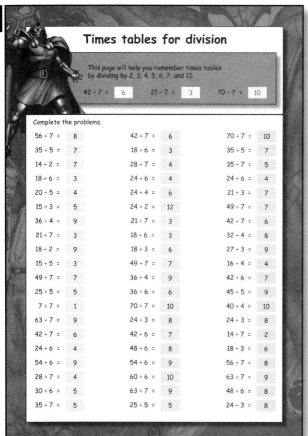

Complete the problems.

56 ÷ 7 = 8	42 ÷ 7 = 6	70 ÷ 7 = 10
35 ÷ 5 = 7	18 ÷ 6 = 3	35 ÷ 5 = 7
14 ÷ 2 = 7	28 ÷ 7 = 4	35 ÷ 7 = 5
18 ÷ 6 = 3	24 ÷ 6 = 4	24 ÷ 6 = 4
20 ÷ 5 = 4	24 ÷ 4 = 6	21 ÷ 3 = 7
15 ÷ 3 = 5	24 ÷ 2 = 12	49 ÷ 7 = 7
36 ÷ 4 = 9	21 ÷ 7 = 3	42 ÷ 7 = 6
21 ÷ 7 = 3	18 ÷ 6 = 3	32 ÷ 4 = 8
18 ÷ 2 = 9	18 ÷ 3 = 6	27 ÷ 3 = 9
15 ÷ 5 = 3	49 ÷ 7 = 7	16 ÷ 4 = 4
49 ÷ 7 = 7	36 ÷ 4 = 9	42 ÷ 6 = 7
25 ÷ 5 = 5	36 ÷ 6 = 6	45 ÷ 5 = 9
7 ÷ 7 = 1	70 ÷ 7 = 10	40 ÷ 4 = 10
63 ÷ 7 = 9	24 ÷ 3 = 8	24 ÷ 3 = 8
42 ÷ 7 = 6	42 ÷ 6 = 7	14 ÷ 7 = 2
24 ÷ 6 = 4	48 ÷ 6 = 8	18 ÷ 3 = 6
54 ÷ 6 = 9	54 ÷ 6 = 9	56 ÷ 7 = 8
28 ÷ 7 = 4	60 ÷ 6 = 10	63 ÷ 7 = 9
30 ÷ 6 = 5	63 ÷ 7 = 9	48 ÷ 6 = 8
35 ÷ 7 = 5	25 ÷ 5 = 5	24 ÷ 3 = 8

Times tables for division

This page will help you remember times tables by dividing by 2, 3, 4, 5, 6, 7, 8, and 9.

28 ÷ 7 = 4   32 ÷ 8 = 4   27 ÷ 9 = 3

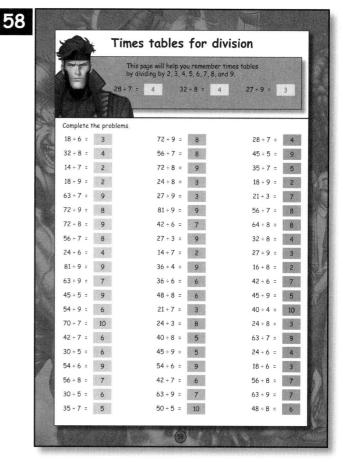

Complete the problems.

18 ÷ 6 = 3	72 ÷ 9 = 8	28 ÷ 7 = 4
32 ÷ 8 = 4	56 ÷ 7 = 8	45 ÷ 5 = 9
14 ÷ 7 = 2	72 ÷ 8 = 9	35 ÷ 7 = 5
18 ÷ 9 = 2	24 ÷ 8 = 3	18 ÷ 9 = 2
63 ÷ 7 = 9	27 ÷ 9 = 3	21 ÷ 3 = 7
72 ÷ 9 = 8	81 ÷ 9 = 9	56 ÷ 7 = 8
72 ÷ 8 = 9	42 ÷ 6 = 7	64 ÷ 8 = 8
56 ÷ 7 = 8	27 ÷ 3 = 9	32 ÷ 8 = 4
24 ÷ 6 = 4	14 ÷ 7 = 2	27 ÷ 9 = 3
81 ÷ 9 = 9	36 ÷ 4 = 9	16 ÷ 8 = 2
63 ÷ 9 = 7	36 ÷ 6 = 6	42 ÷ 6 = 7
45 ÷ 5 = 9	48 ÷ 8 = 6	45 ÷ 9 = 5
54 ÷ 9 = 6	21 ÷ 7 = 3	40 ÷ 4 = 10
70 ÷ 7 = 10	24 ÷ 3 = 8	24 ÷ 8 = 3
42 ÷ 7 = 6	40 ÷ 8 = 5	63 ÷ 7 = 9
30 ÷ 5 = 6	45 ÷ 9 = 5	24 ÷ 6 = 4
54 ÷ 6 = 9	54 ÷ 6 = 9	18 ÷ 6 = 3
56 ÷ 8 = 7	42 ÷ 7 = 6	56 ÷ 8 = 7
30 ÷ 5 = 6	63 ÷ 9 = 7	63 ÷ 9 = 7
35 ÷ 7 = 5	50 ÷ 5 = 10	48 ÷ 8 = 6

Times tables for practice grids

This is a times tables grid.

X	3	4	5	6
7	21	28	35	42
8	24	32	40	48

Square up to the task!

Complete each times tables grid.

X	1	3	5	7	9
2	2	6	10	14	18
3	3	9	15	21	27

X	4	6
6	24	36
7	28	42
8	32	48

X	6	7	8	9	10
3	18	21	24	27	30
4	24	28	32	36	40
5	30	35	40	45	50

X	5	7	10	4	2
3	15	21	30	12	6
5	25	35	50	20	10
7	35	49	70	28	14

Don't get grid lock!

X	2	6	4	7
5	10	30	20	35
10	20	60	40	70

X	8	5	9	6
9	72	45	81	54
7	56	35	63	42

Times tables practice grids

Here are more times tables grids.

X	2	4	6
3	6	12	18
7	14	28	42

STREEEETCH your mind....

X	8	3	7	2
5	40	15	35	10
6	48	18	42	12
8	64	24	56	16

X	2	3	4	5	7
4	8	12	16	20	28
6	12	18	24	30	42
8	16	24	32	40	56

X	2	3	4	5
8	16	24	32	40
9	18	27	36	45

Target the right answer!

X	10	9	8	7
5	50	45	40	35
7	70	63	56	49
9	90	81	72	63

X	3	6
2	6	12
3	9	18
4	12	24
5	15	30
6	18	36
7	21	42

X	2	4	6	8
1	2	4	6	8
3	6	12	18	24
5	10	20	30	40
7	14	28	42	56
9	18	36	54	72
0	0	0	0	0

Times tables practice grids

Here are some other times tables grids.

X	7	8	9	10
7	49	56	63	70
8	56	64	72	80

X	9	8	7	6	5	4
9	81	72	63	54	45	36
8	72	64	56	48	40	32
7	63	56	49	42	35	28

X	2	5	7	9
4	8	20	28	36
6	12	30	42	54
8	16	40	56	72

X	3	5	7
2	6	10	14
8	24	40	56
6	18	30	42
0	0	0	0
4	12	20	28
7	21	35	49

X	8	7	9	6
7	56	49	63	42
9	72	63	81	54
0	0	0	0	0
10	80	70	90	60
8	64	56	72	48
6	48	42	54	36

Line 'em up, fill in the grids, and make it snappy!

62

Speed trials

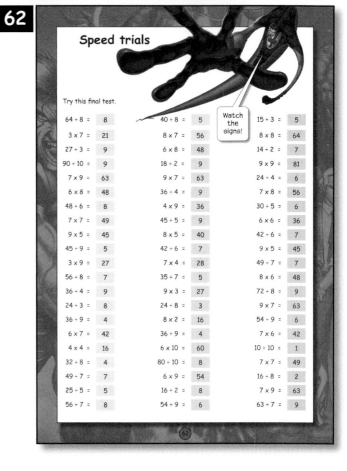

Try this final test.

Watch the signs!

64 ÷ 8 = 8	40 ÷ 8 = 5	15 ÷ 3 = 5
3 x 7 = 21	8 x 7 = 56	8 x 8 = 64
27 ÷ 3 = 9	6 x 8 = 48	14 ÷ 2 = 7
90 ÷ 10 = 9	18 ÷ 2 = 9	9 x 9 = 81
7 x 9 = 63	9 x 7 = 63	24 ÷ 4 = 6
6 x 8 = 48	36 ÷ 4 = 9	7 x 8 = 56
48 ÷ 6 = 8	4 x 9 = 36	30 ÷ 5 = 6
7 x 7 = 49	45 ÷ 5 = 9	6 x 6 = 36
9 x 5 = 45	8 x 5 = 40	42 ÷ 6 = 7
45 ÷ 9 = 5	42 ÷ 6 = 7	9 x 5 = 45
3 x 9 = 27	7 x 4 = 28	49 ÷ 7 = 7
56 ÷ 8 = 7	35 ÷ 7 = 5	8 x 6 = 48
36 ÷ 4 = 9	9 x 3 = 27	72 ÷ 8 = 9
24 ÷ 3 = 8	24 ÷ 8 = 3	9 x 7 = 63
36 ÷ 9 = 4	8 x 2 = 16	54 ÷ 9 = 6
6 x 7 = 42	36 ÷ 9 = 4	7 x 6 = 42
4 x 4 = 16	6 x 10 = 60	10 ÷ 10 = 1
32 ÷ 8 = 4	80 ÷ 10 = 8	7 x 7 = 49
49 ÷ 7 = 7	6 x 9 = 54	16 ÷ 8 = 2
25 ÷ 5 = 5	16 ÷ 2 = 8	7 x 9 = 63
56 ÷ 7 = 8	54 ÷ 9 = 6	63 ÷ 7 = 9

63

Addition, multiplication, and division

I KNOW you can do it!

Write the missing number in the box.

8 + ? = 8   5 x ? = 5
8 + [0] = 8   5 x [1] = 5

Write the missing number in the box.

3 + 12 = 15	17 + 7 = 24	12 + 7 = 19	16 + 0 = 16
4 + 8 = 12	12 x 1 = 12	1 x 9 = 9	0 + 6 = 6
25 + 15 = 40	35 ÷ 7 = 5	12 + 5 = 17	4 + 5 = 9
15 + 60 = 75	14 + 7 = 21	22 + 30 = 52	48 + 9 = 57
5 x 6 = 30	12 ÷ 4 = 3	50 ÷ 5 = 10	8 x 6 = 48
9 x 6 = 54	90 ÷ 18 = 5	43 x 10 = 430	36 ÷ 9 = 4

Write the missing number in the box.

3 x (6 x 4) = (3 x ?) x 4
3 x (6 x 4) = (3 x 6) x 4

(2 x 5) x 9 = ? x (5 x 9)
(2 x 5) x 9 = 2 x (5 x 9)

(7 x 9) x 3 = 7 x (? x 3)
(7 x 9) x 3 = 7 x (9 x 3)

8 x (8 x 7) = (8 x 8) x ?
8 x (8 x 7) = (8 x 8) x 7

5 x (10 + 3) = (5 x 10) + (? x 3)
5 x (10 + 3) = (5 x 10) + (5 x 3)

(8 + 6) x 7 = (8 x 7) + (6 x ?)
(8 + 6) x 7 = (8 x 7) + (6 x 7)

9 x (5 + 12) = (? x 5) + (? x 12)
9 x (5 + 12) = (9 x 5) + (9 x 12)

(3 + 7) x 2 = (? x 2) + (7 x 2)
(3 + 7) x 2 = (3 x 2) + (7 x 2)

Children may have difficulty understanding the distributive property. Perform the operations to show tham that 5 x (10 + 3) = (5 x 10) + (5 x 3).

Place value to 10,000,000

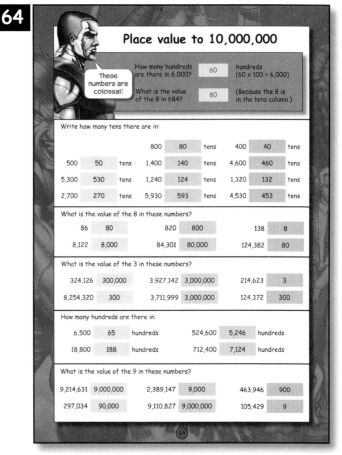

These numbers are colossal!

How many hundreds are there in 6,000? [60] hundreds (60 x 100 = 6,000)

What is the value of the 8 in 684? [80] (Because the 8 is in the tens column.)

Write how many tens there are in:

800	80 tens		400	40 tens	
500	50 tens	1,400	140 tens	4,600	460 tens
5,300	530 tens	1,240	124 tens	1,320	132 tens
2,700	270 tens	5,930	593 tens	4,530	453 tens

What is the value of the 8 in these numbers?

86	80	
820	800	
138	8	
8,122	8,000	84,301	80,000	124,382	80

What is the value of the 3 in these numbers?

324,126	300,000	3,927,142	3,000,000	214,623	3
8,254,320	300	3,711,999	3,000,000	124,372	300

How many hundreds are there in:

6,500	65 hundreds	524,600	5,246 hundreds	
18,800	188 hundreds	712,400	7,124 hundreds	

What is the value of the 9 in these numbers?

9,214,631	9,000,000	2,389,147	9,000	463,946	900
297,034	90,000	9,110,827	9,000,000	105,429	9

Explain to children that finding how many tens there are in a number is the same as dividing by 10. In the number 400, for example, there are 40 tens, because 400 divided by 10 is 40.

Multiplying and dividing by 10

Write the answer in the box. To multiply by 10, add a zero.

$42 \times 10 =$ 420 $68 \div 10 =$ 6.8

Jump to it!

Write the product in the box.

$84 \times 10 =$ 840	$13 \times 10 =$ 130	
$36 \times 10 =$ 360	$58 \times 10 =$ 580	$54 \times 10 =$ 540
$256 \times 10 =$ 2,560	$412 \times 10 =$ 4,120	$836 \times 10 =$ 8,360
$4,700 \times 10 =$ 47,000	$687 \times 10 =$ 6,870	$2,145 \times 10 =$ 21,450

Write the quotient in the box. To divide by 10, move the decimal point one place left.

$82 \div 10 =$ 8.2	$58 \div 10 =$ 5.8	$38 \div 10 =$ 3.8
$19 \div 10 =$ 1.9	$79 \div 10 =$ 7.9	$82 \div 10 =$ 8.2
$245 \div 10 =$ 24.5	$367 \div 10 =$ 36.7	$279 \div 10 =$ 27.9
$379 \div 10 =$ 37.9	$924 \div 10 =$ 92.4	$674 \div 10 =$ 67.4

Find the missing factor.

24 $\times 10 = 240$	75 $\times 10 = 750$	99 $\times 10 = 990$
37 $\times 10 = 370$	14 $\times 10 = 140$	35 $\times 10 = 350$
55 $\times 10 = 550$	87 $\times 10 = 870$	76 $\times 10 = 760$

Find the dividend.

47 $\div 10 = 4.7$	78 $\div 10 = 7.8$	47 $\div 10 = 4.7$
257 $\div 10 = 25.7$	99 $\div 10 = 9.9$	807 $\div 10 = 80.7$
409 $\div 10 = 40.9$	679 $\div 10 = 67.9$	269 $\div 10 = 26.9$

Multiplying a number by 10 is the same as adding a 0 to it. Dividing by 10 moves the decimal point one place to the left. Whole numbers (e.g. 58) can be written with a decimal point (58.0). In the last two sections, the inverse operation also gives the answer.

66

Ordering sets of measures

Write these measures in order, from least to greatest.

Sort it out!

4,100 km	34 km	1,621 km	347 km	6 km	879 km
6 km	34 km	347 km	879 km	1,621 km	4,100 km

Write these amounts in order, from least to greatest.

$416	$15,940	$1,504	$826	$37,532
$416	$826	$1,504	$15,940	$37,532
7,200 mi	720 mi	27,410 mi	15 mi	247 mi
15 mi	247 mi	720 mi	7,200 mi	27,410 mi
1,327 lb	9,565 lb	32,942 lb	752,247 lb	556 lb
556 lb	1,327 lb	9,565 lb	32,942 lb	752,247 lb
8,940 yrs	20,316 yrs	8,520 yrs	320 yrs	4,681 yrs
320 yrs	4,681 yrs	8,520 yrs	8,940 yrs	20,316 yrs
14,632 kg	8,940 kg	175 kg	217,846 kg	75,126 kg
175 kg	8,940 kg	14,632 kg	75,126 kg	217,846 kg
9,420 km	764 km	25,811 km	114,243 km	7,240 km
764 km	7,240 km	9,420 km	25,811 km	114,243 km
$4,212	$37,227	$1,365,240	$950	$143,822
$950	$4,212	$37,227	$143,822	$1,365,240
24,091 ft	59,473 ft	1,237 ft	426 ft	837,201 ft
426 ft	1,237 ft	24,091 ft	59,473 ft	837,201 ft
2,330 oz	103,427 oz	9,625 oz	847 oz	47,632 oz
847 oz	2,330 oz	9,625 oz	47,632 oz	103,427 oz
7,340 m	249 m	12,746 m	32 m	17,407,321 m
32 m	249 m	7,340 m	12,746 m	17,407,321 m
$12,111	$12,493	$43	$430	$5,672
$43	$430	$5,672	$12,111	$12,493

You may need to help children identify the significant digit when sorting a group of numbers. In some cases, when the significant digits are the same, it will be necessary to compare the digits to the right of the significant digit.

67

Appropriate units of measure

Choose the best units to measure the length of each item.

inches	feet	yards
notebook	car	swimming pool
inches	feet	yards

Choose the best units to measure the length of each item.

	inches	feet	yards
TV set	bicycle	toothbrush	football field
inches	feet	inches	yards
shoe	backyard	canoe	fence
inches	feet or yards	feet	yards

The height of a door is about 7 feet

The height of a pencil is about 7 inches

The height of a flagpole is about 7 yards

My seventh sense tells me that you can do this.

Choose the best units to measure the weight of each item.

	ounces	pounds	tons
kitten	train	tomato	sweatshirt
ounces	tons	ounces	ounces
hamburger	elephant	refrigerator	
ounces	tons	pounds	

The weight of a tennis ball is about 2 ounces

The weight of a bag of potatoes is about 5 pounds

The weight of a truck is about 4 tons

Children might come up with their own examples of items that measure about 1 inch, 1 foot, and 1 yard, as well as items that weigh about 1 ounce, 1 pound, and 1 ton. They can use these as benchmarks to find the appropriate unit.

Identifying patterns

Continue each pattern.

Intervals of 6:	2	8	14	20	26	32
Intervals of 3:	26	23	20	17	14	11

Continue each pattern.

0	10	20	30	40	50	60
5	10	15	20	25	30	35
5	7	9	11	13	15	17
3	10	17	24	31	38	45
4	7	10	13	16	19	22
1	9	17	25	33	41	49

It's time for action!

Continue each pattern.

46	42	38	34	30	26	22
33	29	25	21	17	13	9
65	60	55	50	45	40	35
50	43	36	29	22	15	8
28	25	22	19	16	13	10
49	42	35	28	21	14	7

Continue each pattern.

5	7	9	11	13	15	17
56	53	50	47	44	41	38
3	8	13	18	23	28	33
47	40	33	26	19	12	5
1	4	7	10	13	16	19
81	72	63	54	45	36	27

Point out that some of the patterns show an increase and some a decrease. Children should see what operation turns the first number into the second, and the second number into the third. They can then continue the pattern.

Recognizing multiples

My heightened senses make uncovering things real easy.

Circle the multiples of ten. For example, 2 x 10 = 20, so circle 20.

14   (20)   25   (30)   47   (60)

Circle the multiples of 6.

| 20 | (24) | 56 | (72) | 26 | 35 |
| 1 | 3 | (6) | 16 | 32 | (36) |

Circle the multiples of 7.

| (14) | 17 | (35) | 27 | 47 | (49) |
| (63) | (42) | 52 | 37 | 64 | 71 |

Circle the multiples of 8.

| 18 | 54 | (64) | 35 | (72) | (8) |
| 25 | 31 | (48) | 84 | (32) | 28 |

Circle the multiples of 9.

| 64 | (81) | (36) | 35 | 33 | 98 |
| (45) | 53 | (27) | (18) | 92 | 106 |

Circle the multiples of 10.

| 44 | 37 | (30) | 29 | (50) | (100) |
| 15 | 35 | (60) | 46 | (90) | 45 |

Circle the multiples of 11.

| 45 | (33) | 87 | 98 | (99) | 60 |
| 24 | (44) | 65 | 54 | (66) | (121) |

Circle the multiples of 12.

| 23 | 34 | (48) | 74 | (24) | (60) |
| (72) | 66 | 29 | 109 | (108) | (132) |

Success on this page bascially depends on a knowledge of multiplication tables. Where children experience difficulty, it may be necesssary to reinforce multiplication tables.

70

Using information in tables

Use the table to answer the questions.

MARVEL HEROES FAVORITE SPORTS

Sport	Number of votes
Basketball	5
Soccer	10
Softball	4
Swimming	7

How many Marvel heroes voted for swimming?   7

What is the most popular sport?   soccer

Use the table to answer the questions.

APPEARANCES IN MARVEL COMICS

Character	April	May	June
Cyclops	5	9	11
Magneto	7	2	9
Rogue	3	1	12
Wolverine	8	8	10

How many times did Wolverine appear in May?   8

Who appeared 9 times in June?   Magneto

How many times did Cyclops appear in April, May, and June?   25

Complete the table and answer the questions.

SUPERHERO OLYMPIC MEDALS

Superhero	Gold	Silver	Bronze	Total
Human Torch	3	4	9	16
Invisible Woman	6	6	4	16
Mister Fanstastic	12	8	7	27
Black Panther	10	8	10	28
Spider-Man	9	5	4	18
Wolverine	8	4	4	16

How many more gold medals did Wolverine win than bronze medals?   4

Which Marvel hero won the most bronze medals?   Black Panther

Which Marvel hero won three times as many bronze medals as gold medals?   Human Torch

Am I the winner?

On this page, children have to read, compare data, or manipulate information in a table. To answer the questions about the third table, children must first complete the final column.

71

Coordinate graphs

Remember to write the coordinates for the x-axis first.

A   (2, 5)
B   (3, 3)
C   (5, 2)

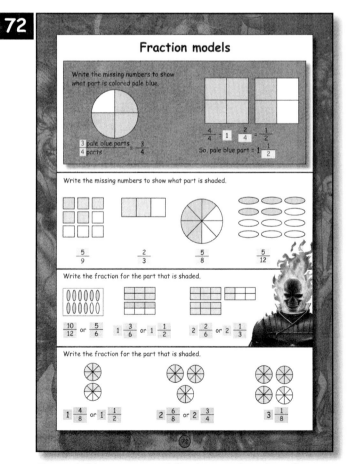

Write the coordinates for each icon.

▲   (2, 5)
■   (5, 4)
●   (1, 3)
★   (3, 2)
⬟   (1, 1)

Write the coordinates for each letter.

A   (3, 2)
B   (2, 4)
C   (4, 6)
D   (5, 4)
E   (5, 1)

Surf into shape!

Most errors on this page result from children using the incorrect order for coordinate pairs. Make sure children know that the x-coordinate is always written before the y-coordinate.

Fraction models

Write the missing numbers to show what part is colored pale blue.

$\frac{3 \text{ pale blue parts}}{4 \text{ parts}} = \frac{3}{4}$

$\frac{4}{4} = 1$ $\frac{2}{4} = \frac{1}{2}$

So, pale blue part = $1\frac{1}{2}$

Write the missing numbers to show what part is shaded.

$\frac{5}{9}$ $\frac{2}{3}$ $\frac{5}{8}$ $\frac{5}{12}$

Write the fraction for the part that is shaded.

$\frac{10}{12}$ or $\frac{5}{6}$ $1\frac{3}{6}$ or $1\frac{1}{2}$ $2\frac{2}{6}$ or $2\frac{1}{3}$

Write the fraction for the part that is shaded.

$1\frac{4}{8}$ or $1\frac{1}{2}$ $2\frac{6}{8}$ or $2\frac{3}{4}$ $3\frac{1}{8}$

Some children may need further explanation of the models of mixed numbers. Point out that when all the parts of a model are shaded, the model shows the number 1.

Converting fractions and decimals

Write these fractions as decimals.

$\frac{6}{10}$ = 0.6

$\frac{4}{100}$ = 0.04

Write these decimals as fractions.

0.2 = $\frac{2}{10}$ = $\frac{1}{5}$

0.53 = $\frac{53}{100}$

Even small numbers don't escape me.

Write these fractions as decimals.

$\frac{7}{10}$ = 0.7 $\frac{1}{10}$ = 0.1 $\frac{3}{10}$ = 0.3

$\frac{2}{10}$ = 0.2 $\frac{8}{10}$ = 0.8 $\frac{5}{10}$ = 0.5

$\frac{1}{2}$ = $\frac{5}{10}$ = 0.5 $\frac{9}{10}$ = 0.9 $\frac{4}{10}$ = 0.4

Write these decimals as fractions.

0.4 = $\frac{4}{10}$ = $\frac{2}{5}$ 0.5 = $\frac{5}{10}$ = $\frac{1}{2}$ 0.6 = $\frac{6}{10}$ = $\frac{3}{5}$

0.7 = $\frac{7}{10}$ 0.2 = $\frac{2}{10}$ = $\frac{1}{5}$ 0.3 = $\frac{3}{10}$

0.1 = $\frac{1}{10}$ 0.8 = $\frac{8}{10}$ = $\frac{4}{5}$ 0.9 = $\frac{9}{10}$

Change these fractions to decimals.

$\frac{3}{100}$ = 0.03 $\frac{1}{100}$ = 0.01 $\frac{7}{100}$ = 0.07

$\frac{25}{100}$ = 0.25 $\frac{15}{100}$ = 0.15 $\frac{49}{100}$ = 0.49

$\frac{56}{100}$ = 0.56 $\frac{24}{100}$ = 0.24 $\frac{72}{100}$ = 0.72

Change these decimals to fractions.

0.83 = $\frac{83}{100}$ 0.91 = $\frac{91}{100}$ 0.73 = $\frac{73}{100}$

0.39 = $\frac{39}{100}$ 0.43 = $\frac{43}{100}$ 0.17 = $\frac{17}{100}$

A number line showing tenths with their decimal equivalents can help children. If they neglect to include the zeros when converting fractions such as 7/100 to 0.07, ask them to convert the decimal back to the fraction to realize their error.

74

Factors of numbers from 31 to 65

The factors of 40 are: 1   2   4   5   8   20   40

Circle the factors of 56:   1   2   3   4   5   6   7   8   14   28   32   56

Find all the factors of each number if you DARE!

Find all the factors of each number.

The factors of 31 are   1, 31

The factors of 47 are   1, 47

The factors of 35 are   1, 5, 7, 35

The factors of 50 are   1, 2, 5, 10, 25, 50

The factors of 42 are   1, 2, 3, 6, 7, 14, 21, 42

The factors of 52 are   1, 2, 4, 13, 26, 52

The factors of 48 are   1, 2, 3, 4, 6, 8, 12, 16, 24, 48

The factors of 60 are   1, 2, 3, 4, 5, 6, 10, 12, 15, 20, 30, 60

Circle all the factors of each number.

Which numbers are factors of 14?

1   2   3   4   5   6   7   8   9   10   11   12   13   14

Which numbers are factors of 45?

1   3   4   5   8   9   12   15   16   21   24   36   40   44   45

Which numbers are factors of 61?

1   3   4   5   6   10   15   16   18   20   24   29   30   61

Which numbers are factors of 65?

1   2   4   5   6   8   9   10   12   13   14   15   30   60   65

Some numbers have only factors of 1 and themselves. They are called prime numbers. Write all the prime numbers between 31 and 65 in the box.

31, 37, 41, 43, 47, 53, 59, 61

Children often miss some of the factors of large numbers. Encourage a systematic method to find factors. Remind children that 1 and the number itself are factors of a number. If necessary, discuss prime numbers with them.

75

Writing equivalent fractions

Make these fractions equal by writing in the missing number.

$\frac{40}{100}$ = $\frac{4}{10}$ = $\frac{2}{5}$ $\frac{5}{15}$ = $\frac{1}{3}$

You've gotta understand fractions to divide the spoils.

Make these fractions equal by writing in the missing number.

$\frac{20}{100}$ = $\frac{2}{10}$ $\frac{4}{5}$ = $\frac{8}{10}$ $\frac{5}{9}$ = $\frac{10}{18}$

$\frac{2}{20}$ = $\frac{1}{10}$ $\frac{2}{3}$ = $\frac{8}{12}$ $\frac{5}{100}$ = $\frac{1}{20}$

$\frac{11}{14}$ = $\frac{22}{28}$ $\frac{5}{6}$ = $\frac{15}{18}$ $\frac{2}{8}$ = $\frac{1}{4}$

$\frac{2}{12}$ = $\frac{1}{6}$ $\frac{9}{21}$ = $\frac{3}{7}$ $\frac{6}{20}$ = $\frac{3}{10}$

$\frac{7}{8}$ = $\frac{28}{32}$ $\frac{5}{20}$ = $\frac{1}{4}$ $\frac{5}{8}$ = $\frac{10}{16}$

$\frac{5}{25}$ = $\frac{1}{5}$ $\frac{25}{100}$ = $\frac{5}{20}$ $\frac{6}{30}$ = $\frac{1}{5}$

$\frac{5}{30}$ = $\frac{1}{6}$ $\frac{12}{14}$ = $\frac{6}{7}$ $\frac{1}{5}$ = $\frac{2}{10}$

$\frac{9}{18}$ = $\frac{1}{2}$ $\frac{40}{100}$ = $\frac{2}{5}$ $\frac{25}{30}$ = $\frac{5}{6}$

$\frac{3}{8}$ = $\frac{9}{24}$ $\frac{4}{100}$ = $\frac{1}{25}$ $\frac{1}{3}$ = $\frac{5}{15}$

$\frac{1}{12}$ = $\frac{2}{24}$ = $\frac{3}{36}$ = $\frac{4}{48}$ = $\frac{5}{60}$ = $\frac{6}{72}$

$\frac{20}{100}$ = $\frac{5}{25}$ = $\frac{2}{10}$ = $\frac{1}{5}$ = $\frac{10}{50}$ = $\frac{40}{200}$

$\frac{2}{5}$ = $\frac{6}{15}$ = $\frac{8}{20}$ = $\frac{4}{10}$ = $\frac{20}{50}$ = $\frac{40}{100}$

$\frac{1}{6}$ = $\frac{2}{12}$ = $\frac{3}{18}$ = $\frac{4}{24}$ = $\frac{5}{30}$ = $\frac{6}{36}$

$\frac{2}{3}$ = $\frac{16}{24}$ = $\frac{24}{36}$ = $\frac{14}{21}$ = $\frac{6}{9}$ = $\frac{200}{300}$

If children have any problems, point out that fractions retain the same value if you multiply the numerator and denominator by the same number or divide the numerator and denominator by the same number.

Properties of polygons

Circle the polygon that has two pairs of parallel sides.

Read the description and circle the polygon.

All the angles are right angles, but not all the sides are the same length.

Exactly three pairs of parallel sides.

Exactly one pair of sides is parallel.

All the sides are the same length, and all the angles are right angles.

All the sides are the same length, and all the angles are the same.

If children answer questions incorrectly, make sure they understand the concepts of parallel lines, lengths of sides of a polygon, equal angles, and right angles.

Naming polygons

Polygons are named for the number of sides they have.

triangle quadrilateral pentagon hexagon octagon

Quadrilaterals, which have four sides, can be different shapes.

rectangle rhombus square parallelogram trapezoid

Circle the quadrilaterals.

Write the name of each polygon in the box.

parallelogram octagon triangle pentagon square

hexagon rhombus rectangle trapezoid triangle

The questions on this page require children to identify
and name various polygons. Children may have difficulty
differentiating among a square, a parallelogram, a
rectangle, and a rhombus. Explain that they are all
particular kinds of parallelogams.

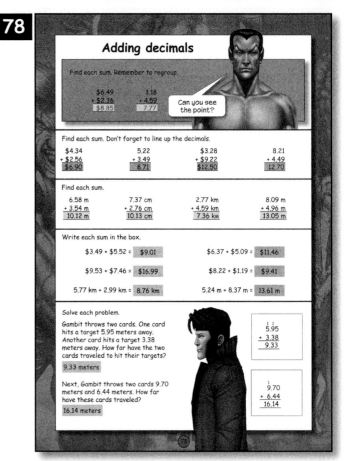

78

Adding decimals

Find each sum. Remember to regroup.

$6.49	3.18
+ $2.36	+ 4.59
$8.85	7.77

Can you see the point?

Find each sum. Don't forget to line up the decimals.

$4.34	5.22	$3.28	8.21
+ $2.56	+ 3.49	+ $9.22	+ 4.49
$6.90	8.71	$12.50	12.70

Find each sum.

6.58 m	7.37 cm	2.77 km	8.09 m
+ 3.54 m	+ 2.76 cm	+ 4.59 km	+ 4.96 m
10.12 m	10.13 cm	7.36 km	13.05 m

Write each sum in the box.

$3.49 + $5.52 = $9.01 $6.37 + $5.09 = $11.46

$9.53 + $7.46 = $16.99 $8.22 + $1.19 = $9.41

5.77 km + 2.99 km = 8.76 km   5.24 m + 8.37 m = 13.61 m

Solve each problem.

Gambit throws two cards. One card
hits a target 5.95 meters away.
Another card hits a target 3.38
meters away. How far have the two
cards traveled to hit their targets?

9.33 meters

| 1 1 |
| 5.95 |
| + 3.38 |
| 9.33 |

Next, Gambit throws two cards 9.70
meters and 6.44 meters. How far
have these cards traveled?

16.14 meters

| 1 |
| 9.70 |
| + 6.44 |
| 16.14 |

Children may place the decimal point incorrectly in
sums that are presented horizontally (such as those
in the third section). Have them rewrite the problems
vertically, lining up the decimal points. Remind children
to regroup when necessary.

79

Adding decimals

Find each sum. Remember to regroup.

$5.96	6.92 cm
+ $2.83	+ 1.68 cm
$8.79	8.60 cm

It's not the end of the world...I should know!

Find each sum.

$9.57	$7.96	$5.73	$6.49
+ $9.99	+ $4.78	+ $9.97	+ $3.88
$19.56	$12.74	$15.70	$10.37

Find each sum.

9.98	7.34 cm	3.04 km	7.40 m
+ 8.09	+ 9.91 cm	+ 5.76 km	+ 4.19 m
18.07	17.25 cm	8.80 km	11.59 m

Write each sum in the box.

6.49 + 5.03 = 11.52 $2.04 + $9.97 = $12.01

$9.58 + $8.32 = $17.90   2.04 m + 4.83 m = 6.87 m

$9.19 + $5.26 = $14.45   1.29 + 4.83 = 6.12

Solve each problem.

Daniel buys a Doom mask for $3.99
and a Galactus mask for $2.75. How
much has he spent?

$6.74

| 1 1 |
| 3.99 |
| + 2.75 |
| 6.74 |

Daniel goes to another store.
There he sees that Doom masks
cost $2.49 each. If he bought two
masks, how much would Daniel pay?

$4.98

| 2.49 |
| + 2.49 |
| 4.98 |

When the final decimal place of a sum is zero, it can be
written, as in the second example, but it can also be
omitted—unless the sum is an amount of dollars.

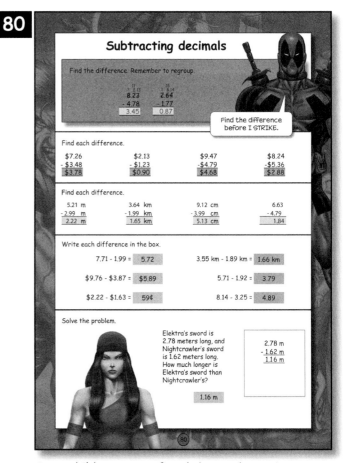

80

Subtracting decimals

Find the difference. Remember to regroup.

7 11	1 14
8.23	2.64
- 4.78	- 1.77
3.45	0.87

Find the difference before I STRIKE.

Find each difference.

$7.26	$2.13	$9.47	$8.24
- $3.48	- $1.23	- $4.79	- $5.36
$3.78	$0.90	$4.68	$2.88

Find each difference.

5.21 m	3.64 km	9.12 cm	6.63
- 2.99 m	- 1.99 km	- 3.99 cm	- 4.79
2.22 m	1.65 km	5.13 cm	1.84

Write each difference in the box.

7.71 - 1.99 = 5.72   3.55 km - 1.89 km = 1.66 km

$9.76 - $3.87 = $5.89   5.71 - 1.92 = 3.79

$2.22 - $1.63 = 59¢   8.14 - 3.25 = 4.89

Solve the problem.

Elektra's sword is
2.78 meters long, and
Nightcrawler's sword
is 1.62 meters long.
How much longer is
Elektra's sword than
Nightcrawler's?

1.16 m

| 2.78 m |
| - 1.62 m |
| 1.16 m |

Some children are confused about subtracting
decimals. Show them that once they line up the decimal
points, they can simply subtract the digits, lining up the
decimal point of the answer.

81

Subtracting decimals

Find each difference. Remember to regroup.

$$\begin{array}{r} \overset{6}{\cancel{7}}.\overset{1}{\cancel{2}}3 \\ -1.94 \\ \hline 5.29 \end{array}$$

$$\begin{array}{r} \overset{11}{\cancel{6}}.\overset{1}{\cancel{2}}3 \\ -2.84 \\ \hline 3.39 \end{array}$$

The heat is turning up... get adding.

Find each difference.

$8.24	6.31	$4.23	8.91
- $2.87	- 2.89	-$2.24	- 5.92
$5.37	$3.42	$1.99	$2.99

Find each difference.

6.23	7.48 m	6.33 km	9.11 cm
-2.24	-3.49 m	-2.94 km	-1.32 cm
3.99	3.99 m	3.39 km	7.79 cm

Write each difference in the box.

6.14 - 3.17 = 2.97   7.42 - 4.57 = 2.85

7.51 - 6.59 = 0.92 $3.39 - $1.47 = $1.92

$7.14 - $3.46 = $3.68 $6.23 - $5.34 = $0.89

Solve each problem.

Spider-Man shoots a web 7.95 meters onto a wall. He climbs up 3.62 meters. How far has he left to climb?

4.33 meters

$$\begin{array}{r} 7.95 \\ -3.62 \\ \hline 4.33 \end{array}$$

Spider-Man shoots a web 11.51 meters onto a wall. He climbs up 8.69 meters. How far has he left to climb?

2.82 meters

$$\begin{array}{r} \overset{10}{\cancel{1}}\overset{14}{\cancel{1}}.\overset{4}{\cancel{5}}\overset{11}{\cancel{1}} \\ -8.69 \\ \hline 2.82 \end{array}$$

This page follows from the previous page. You may need to remind children that they can regroup across a decimal point in the same way as they would if the decimal point were not there.

82

Multiplying by one-digit numbers

Find each product. Remember to regroup.

465	391	178
x 3	x 4	x 4
1,395	1,564	712

Under my hypnotic control, I guarantee you'll find each product.

Find each product.

573	920	438	813
x 3	x 2	x 3	x 2
1,719	1,840	1,314	1,626
582	832	405	396
x 4	x 3	x 5	x 6
2,328	2,496	2,025	2,376

Find each product.

317	224	543	218
x 3	x 3	x 4	x 3
951	672	2,172	654
128	276	798	365
x 4	x 5	x 6	x 6
512	1,380	4,788	2,190
100	373	882	954
x 5	x 4	x 4	x 3
500	1,492	3,528	2,862

Solve each problem.

Hightown middle school has 255 students. The high school has 6 times as many students. How many students are there at the high school?   **1,530 students**

$$\begin{array}{r} \overset{3}{}\overset{3}{}255 \\ x\ 6 \\ \hline 1,530 \end{array}$$

A train can carry 375 passengers. How many can it carry on four trips?   **1,500**

six trips?   **2,250**

$$\begin{array}{r} \overset{3}{}\overset{2}{}375 \\ x\ 4 \\ \hline 1,500 \end{array} \qquad \begin{array}{r} \overset{4}{}\overset{3}{}375 \\ x\ 6 \\ \hline 2,250 \end{array}$$

Make sure children understand the convention of multiplication, i.e. mulitply the ones first and work left. Problems on this page may result from gaps in knowledge of the 2, 3, 4, 5, and 6 times tables. Errors will also occur if children neglect to regroup.

83

Multiplying by one-digit numbers

Find each product. Remember to regroup.

465	823	755
x 6	x 8	x 9
2,790	6,584	6,795

Bigger and better!

Find each product.

395	734	826	943
x 7	x 8	x 8	x 9
2,765	5,872	6,608	8,487
643	199	823	546
x 7	x 6	x 7	x 8
4,501	1,194	5,761	4,368

Find each product.

502	377	845	222
x 7	x 8	x 8	x 9
3,514	3,016	6,760	1,998
473	224	606	514
x 9	x 8	x 6	x 7
4,257	1,792	3,636	3,598
500	800	900	200
x 9	x 9	x 9	x 9
4,500	7,200	8,100	1,800

Solve each problem.

A crate holds 230 oxygen cylinders. How many cylinders are there in 8 crates?   **1,840 cylinders**

$$\begin{array}{r} \overset{2}{}230 \\ x\ 8 \\ \hline 1,840 \end{array}$$

The Blackbird flies 4,570 miles a month on missions. How many miles does it fly in 6 months?   **27,420 miles**

$$\begin{array}{r} \overset{3}{}\overset{4}{}4,570 \\ x\ 6 \\ \hline 27,420 \end{array}$$

Problems encountered will be similar to the previous page. Gaps in knowledge of the 6, 7, 8, and 9 times table will result in errors.

84

Division with remainders

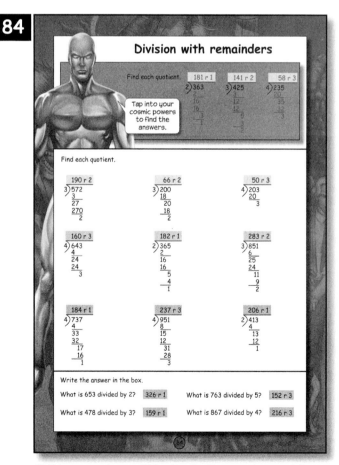

Find each quotient.

$$2\overline{)363} = 181\ r\ 1 \qquad 3\overline{)425} = 141\ r\ 2 \qquad 4\overline{)235} = 58\ r\ 3$$

Tap into your cosmic powers to find the answers.

Find each quotient.

$$\begin{array}{r} 190\ r\ 2 \\ 3\overline{)572} \\ 3 \\ \hline 27 \\ 270 \\ \hline 2 \end{array} \qquad \begin{array}{r} 66\ r\ 2 \\ 3\overline{)200} \\ 18 \\ \hline 20 \\ 18 \\ \hline 2 \end{array} \qquad \begin{array}{r} 50\ r\ 3 \\ 4\overline{)203} \\ 20 \\ \hline 3 \end{array}$$

$$\begin{array}{r} 160\ r\ 3 \\ 4\overline{)643} \\ 4 \\ \hline 24 \\ 24 \\ \hline 3 \end{array} \qquad \begin{array}{r} 182\ r\ 1 \\ 2\overline{)365} \\ 2 \\ \hline 16 \\ 16 \\ \hline 5 \\ 4 \\ \hline 1 \end{array} \qquad \begin{array}{r} 283\ r\ 2 \\ 3\overline{)851} \\ 6 \\ \hline 25 \\ 24 \\ \hline 11 \\ 9 \\ \hline 2 \end{array}$$

$$\begin{array}{r} 184\ r\ 1 \\ 4\overline{)737} \\ 4 \\ \hline 33 \\ 32 \\ \hline 17 \\ 16 \\ \hline 1 \end{array} \qquad \begin{array}{r} 237\ r\ 3 \\ 4\overline{)951} \\ 8 \\ \hline 15 \\ 12 \\ \hline 31 \\ 28 \\ \hline 3 \end{array} \qquad \begin{array}{r} 206\ r\ 1 \\ 2\overline{)413} \\ 4 \\ \hline 13 \\ 12 \\ \hline 1 \end{array}$$

Write the answer in the box.

What is 653 divided by 2? **326 r 1**   What is 763 divided by 5? **152 r 3**

What is 478 divided by 3? **159 r 1**   What is 867 divided by 4? **216 r 3**

Children may have difficulty finding quotients with remainders. Have them perform long division until the remaining value to be divided is less than the divisor. That value is the remainder. Make sure that the digits in the answer line up correctly, as shown.

85

Division with remainders

Find each quotient.

62 r 5	84 r 4	66 r 3
9)563	8)676	7)465

Get cracking!

Find each quotient.

71 r 6	81 r 6
7)503	8)654

129 r 3	17 r 2	71 r 5
6)777	7)121	6)431

44 r 8	73 r 5	33 r 1
9)404	8)589	6)199

Write the answer in the box.

What is 759 divided by 7? **108 r 3**   Divide 941 by 9. **104 r 5**

What is 463 divided by 8? **57 r 7**   Divide 232 by 6. **38 r 4**

This page is similar to the previous page, but the divisors are numbers greater that 5. Children will need to know their 6, 7, 8, and 9 times tables.

86

Real-life problems

Elektra spent $4.68 at the store and had $4.77 left. How much did she start with?   **$9.45**

$$\begin{array}{r} \overset{1\ 1}{4.77} \\ + 4.68 \\ \hline 9.45 \end{array}$$

Jean Grey saves $30.00 a week. How much will she have if she saves all of it for 8 weeks?   **$240**

$$\begin{array}{r} 30.00 \\ \times\ \ \ 8 \\ \hline 240.00 \end{array}$$

Madripoor theater charges $4 for each matinee ticket. If it sells 560 tickets for a matinee performance, how much money does it take in?   **$2,240**

$$\begin{array}{r} \overset{2}{560} \\ \times\ \ \ 4 \\ \hline 2,240 \end{array}$$

Peter Parker has saved $9.69. His friend has saved $3.24 less. How much does his friend have?   **$6.45**

$$\begin{array}{r} 9.69 \\ -\ 3.24 \\ \hline 6.45 \end{array}$$

The cost for 9 children to see a Blade film is $54. How much does each child pay? If only 6 children go, what will the cost be?   **$6 per child $36 for 6 children**

6)54

$6 \times 6 = 36$

Rogue has $12.95. Colossus gives her another $3.64, and she goes out and buys a coffee for $3.25. How much does she have left?   **$13.34**

$$\begin{array}{r} \overset{1}{12.95} \\ + 3.64 \\ \hline 16.59 \end{array}$$

$$\begin{array}{r} 16.59 \\ -\ 3.25 \\ \hline 13.34 \end{array}$$

Wolverine has $60 in savings. He decides to spend $\frac{1}{4}$ of it. How much will he have left?   **$45**

$60 \div 4 = 15$

$60 - 15 = 45$

This page requires children to apply skills they have learned. If they are unsure about what operation to use, discuss whether they expect the answer to be larger or smaller. This can help them decide whether to add, subtract, multiply, or divide.

87

Real-life problems

The Fantastic Four have an hour to find their spaceship. They spend $\frac{1}{3}$ of the time checking satellite data. How many minutes is that?   **20 minutes**

1 hr = 60 min

3)60 20

While chasing a crook, Spider-Man uses two 2 long swings of 18.7 m and 21.9 m. How far does he swing altogether?   **4.06 m**

$$\begin{array}{r} \overset{1\ 1}{1.87} \\ + 2.19 \\ \hline 4.06 \end{array}$$

Captain America finds a vial of poison containing 400 ml. He takes out $\frac{1}{4}$ to test. How much is left?   **300 ml**

$400 \div 4 = 100$

$400 - 100 = 300$

Quicksilver runs 140 m in 7 seconds. At that speed, how far did he run in 1 second?   **20 m**

$140 \div 7 = 20$

The S.H.I.E.L.D Helicarrier carries 2.25 tons of cargo. If 1.68 tons is left in the hold, how much has been dropped off?   **0.57 kg**

$$\begin{array}{r} 2.25 \\ -\ 1.68 \\ \hline 0.57 \end{array}$$

She-Hulk's gamma-charger emits 25 pulses of gamma rays every 15 minutes. How many pulses are produced in 1 hour?   **100**

1 hr = 60 min

$60 \div 15 = 4$

$$\begin{array}{r} \overset{2}{25} \\ \times\ \ \ 4 \\ \hline 100 \end{array}$$

A computer in The Blackbird is 41.63 cm wide, and next to it is a printer that is 48.37 cm wide. How much space is left on the shelf for a scanner if the shelf is 1.5 m wide?   **60 cm**

1.5 m = 150 cm

$$\begin{array}{r} \overset{1\ 1\ 1}{41.63} \\ - 48.37 \\ \hline 90.00 \end{array} \quad \begin{array}{r} 150 \\ -\ 90 \\ \hline 60 \end{array}$$

This page deals with units other than money. As on the previous page, children have to decide what operation to use. Note that solving the final problem requires two operations.

Perimeters of squares and rectangles

Find the perimeter of this rectangle.   5 in.

To find the perimeter of a rectangle or a square, add the lengths of the four sides.   3 in.

5 in. + 5 in. + 3 in. + 3 in. = 16 in.   **5 in.**

Find the perimeters of these rectangles and squares.

3 ft / 3 ft   **8 in.**

3 ft / 3 ft   **12 in.**

2 in. / 3 in.   **10 in.**

1 ft

5 ft / 4 ft   **18 ft.**

2 mi / 2 mi   **8 mi**

6 cm / 4 cm   **20 cm**

5 in. / 5 in.   **20 in.**

5 m / 3 m   **16 m**

2 km / 2 km   **8 km**

Make sure that children do not simply add the lengths of two sides of a figure rather than all four sides. You may want to help children realize that the perimeter of a square can be found by multiplying the length of one side by 4.

Problems involving time

The Beast spends 35 minutes studying genetics each day. How many minutes does he spend studying genetics from Monday through Friday? **175 minutes**

$$\begin{array}{r} 2 \\ 35 \\ \times\ 5 \\ \hline 175 \end{array}$$

Colossus spends 175 minutes eating breakfast from Monday through Friday. How long does he spend eating breakfast each day? **35 minutes**

$$5\overline{)175}$$

Professor Xavier works in the Combat Operation Center from 9 A.M. to 5 P.M. He leaves for lunch from noon until 1 P.M. How many hours does he work in the center from Monday to Friday? **35 hours**

$9 \rightarrow 5 = 8\,h$
$8 - 1 = 7$
$7 \times 5 = 35$

Patch walks by Madripoor Harbor for 15 minutes every morning and 10 minutes every evening. How many minutes does he walk in a 7-day week? **175 minutes**

$$\begin{array}{r} 15 \\ +10 \\ \hline 25 \end{array} \qquad \begin{array}{r} 25 \\ \times\ 7 \\ \hline 175 \end{array}$$

It takes 2 hours for one Avenger to file a report. If the report is divided equally between four Avengers, how long will it take to complete? **30 minutes**

$2 \times 60 = 120$

$$\begin{array}{r} 30 \\ 4\overline{)120} \\ 12 \\ \hline 00 \end{array}$$

Mister Fantastic spent 7 days fixing the computers at Baxter Building. If he worked a total of 56 hours and he divided the work equally among the seven days, how long did he work each day? **8 hours**

$56 \div 7 = 8$

It took Doctor Strange 45 hours to build a new computer circuit. If he spent 5 hours a day working on it, how many days did it take? **9 days**

$45 \div 5 = 9$

How many hours a day would he have worked to finish it in 5 days? **9 hours**

$45 \div 5 = 9$

For the third problem, check that children divide by 4 rather than 3.

90

Using bar graphs

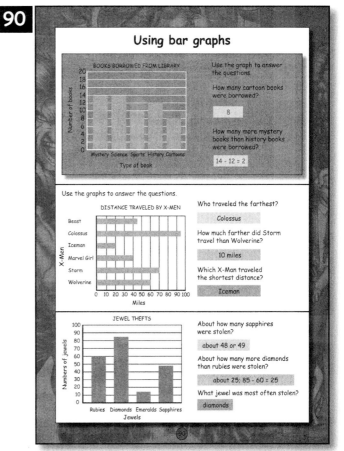

BOOKS BORROWED FROM LIBRARY

Use the graph to answer the questions.

How many cartoon books were borrowed? **8**

How many more mystery books than history books were borrowed? **14 - 12 = 2**

Use the graphs to answer the questions.

DISTANCE TRAVELED BY X-MEN

Who traveled the farthest? **Colossus**

How much farther did Storm travel than Wolverine? **10 miles**

Which X-Man traveled the shortest distance? **Iceman**

JEWEL THEFTS

About how many sapphires were stolen? **about 48 or 49**

About how many more diamonds than rubies were stolen? **about 25; 85 - 60 = 25**

What jewel was most often stolen? **diamonds**

On this page, children have to find specific entries, compare data, or manipulate information read from a bar graph. Some children may need to be reassured that a horizontal bar graph can be read in much the same way as a vertical bar graph.

91

Congruency

Congruent triangles are triangles that are exactly the same shape and size. Triangles are congruent if the corresponding sides are the same and the three corresponding angles are the same. **a and c**

Look at these triangles from a different angle!

Which triangles are congruent? **b and f**

Which triangles are congruent? **a, c, and e; d and g**

You may want to discuss with children the fact that a triangle with congruent corresponding sides also has congruent corresponding angles.

92

Lines of symmetry

How many lines of symmetry does this figure have? **6**

Six lines can be drawn, each of which divides the figure in half.

How many lines of symmetry do these figures have?

4 **6** **5**

2 **5** **2**

6 **8** **1**

Make sure that children understand that the lines of symmetry of the figures on this page could be between opposite vertices, between the mid-points of opposite sides, or between vertices and mid-points of their opposite sides.

93

Writing equivalent number sentences

Write a multiplication sentence that goes with 30 ÷ 6 = 5.
  6 x 5 = 30 or 5 x 6 = 30

Write a related subtraction sentence for 7 + 12 = 19.
  19 - 7 = 12 or 19 - 12 = 7

However you add it up, I'm always formidable.

Write a related subtraction sentence for each sentence.

27 + 14 = 41	41 - 14 = 27 or 41 - 27 = 14
33 + 12 = 45	45 - 33 = 12 or 45 - 12 = 33
16 + 12 = 28	28 - 12 = 16 or 28 - 16 = 12

Write a related addition sentence for each sentence.

55 - 34 = 21	21 + 34 = 55 or 34 + 21 = 55
82 - 23 = 59	23 + 59 = 82 or 59 + 23 = 82
45 - 20 = 25	20 + 25 = 45 or 25 + 20 = 45

Write a related multiplication sentence for each sentence.

28 ÷ 7 = 4	7 x 4 = 28 or 4 x 7 = 28
45 ÷ 9 = 5	5 x 9 = 45 or 9 x 5 = 45
64 ÷ 2 = 32	2 x 32 = 64 or 32 x 2 = 64

Write a related division sentence for each sentence.

8 x 6 = 48	48 ÷ 6 = 8 or 48 ÷ 8 = 6
7 x 12 = 84	84 ÷ 12 = 7 or 84 ÷ 7 = 12
9 x 5 = 45	45 ÷ 9 = 5 or 48 ÷ 5 = 9

If children answer any questions incorrectly, have them check their answers to find out if they have written sentences that do not express facts.

94

Multiplying and dividing

Write the answer in the box.
  26 x 100 = 2,600   400 ÷ 100 = 4

Write the answer in the box.

34 x 10 =	340	41 x 10 =	410	56 x 10 =	560
95 x 100 =	9,500	36 x 100 =	3,600	75 x 100 =	7,500
413 x 10 =	4,130	204 x 10 =	2,040	524 x 10 =	5,240
787 x 100 =	78,700	834 x 100 =	83,400	254 x 100 =	25,400

Write the quotient in the box.

120 ÷ 10 =	12	260 ÷ 10 =	26	480 ÷ 10 =	48
500 ÷ 100 =	5	800 ÷ 10 =	80	700 ÷ 100 =	7
20 ÷ 10 =	2	30 ÷ 10 =	3	60 ÷ 10 =	6
800 ÷ 100 =	8	100 ÷ 100 =	1	900 ÷ 100 =	9

Write the number that has been multiplied by 100.

46	x 100 = 4,600	723	x 100 = 72,300
325	x 100 = 32,500	250	x 100 = 25,000
12	x 100 = 1,200	456	x 100 = 45,600
84	x 100 = 8,400	623	x 100 = 62,300

Write the number that has been divided by 100.

300	÷ 100 = 3	700	÷ 100 = 7
1,200	÷ 100 = 12	1,800	÷ 100 = 18
8,700	÷ 100 = 87	2,300	÷ 100 = 23
1,000	÷ 100 = 10	6,400	÷ 100 = 64

Go! Go! Go!

Children should realize that multiplying a whole number by 10 or 100 means writing one or two zeros at the end of it. To divide a multiple of 10 by 10, take the final zero off the number. The two final sections require use of the inverse operation.

95

Ordering sets of measures

Write these amounts in order, from least to greatest.

75 cm	320 mm	3 km	6 m	340mm
320 mm	340 mm	75 cm	6 m	3 km

Write these amounts in order, from least to greatest.

600¢	$4.00	$5.50	350¢	640¢
350¢	$4.00	$5.50	600¢	640¢
10 qt	1 gal	12 pt	2 gal	3 qt
3 qt	1 gal	12 pt	2 gal	10 qt
115 min	2 hr	210 min	¾ hr	1 hr
¾ hr	1 hr	115 min	2 hr	210 min
2,500 m	2 km	1,000 cm	20 m	1,000 m
1,000 cm	20 m	1,000 m	2 km	2,500 m
$240	3,500¢	$125.00	4,600¢	$50.00
3,500¢	4,600¢	$50.00	$125.00	$240
8 ft	1 yd	24 in.	72 in.	7 ft
24 in.	1 yd	72 in.	7 ft	8 ft
6 qt	8 pt	3 gal	1 qt	4 pt
1 qt	4 pt	6 qt	8 pt	3 gal
2 hr	65 min	1½ hr	100 min	150 min
65 min	1½ hr	100 min	2 hr	150 min
44 mm	4 cm	4 m	4 km	40 cm
4 cm	44 mm	40 cm	4 m	4 km
4 yd	36 in.	2 ft	29 in.	2 yd
2 ft	29 in.	36 in.	2 yd	4 yd
6 pt	1 gal	9 qt	7 qt	10 pt
6 pt	1 gal	10 pt	7 qt	9 qt

Most errors will result from a lack of understanding of the relationships between measures written using different units. Look out for confusion between large numbers of small units and small numbers of large units, such as 350¢ and $4.00.

96

Decimal models

Fill in the grid to show the decimal.

1	3 tenths	1.6

1	0.33	1 and 9 hundredths

Fill in the grid to show the decimal.

0.7	3 tenths	1	1 and 7 tenths

0.23	1 and 37 hundredths	72 hundredths	0.62

Write the decimal represented by the grid.

1.2	0.5	1.01

Children may have difficulty understanding that the zero in a number such as 1.01 is needed. If they write such a number incorrectly, show them that their answer actually represents a different number.

97

Identifying patterns

Continue each pattern.

Steps of 2:	$\frac{1}{2}$	$2\frac{1}{2}$	$4\frac{1}{2}$	$6\frac{1}{2}$	$8\frac{1}{2}$	$10\frac{1}{2}$
Steps of 5:	3.5	8.5	13.5	18.5	23.5	28.5

Continue each pattern.

$5\frac{1}{2}$	$10\frac{1}{2}$	$15\frac{1}{2}$	$20\frac{1}{2}$	$25\frac{1}{2}$	$30\frac{1}{2}$
$2\frac{1}{4}$	$4\frac{1}{4}$	$6\frac{1}{4}$	$8\frac{1}{4}$	$10\frac{1}{4}$	$12\frac{1}{4}$
$8\frac{1}{3}$	$9\frac{1}{3}$	$10\frac{1}{3}$	$11\frac{1}{3}$	$12\frac{1}{3}$	$13\frac{1}{3}$
$65\frac{3}{4}$	$55\frac{3}{4}$	$45\frac{3}{4}$	$35\frac{3}{4}$	$25\frac{3}{4}$	$15\frac{3}{4}$
$44\frac{1}{2}$	$40\frac{1}{2}$	$36\frac{1}{2}$	$32\frac{1}{2}$	$28\frac{1}{2}$	$24\frac{1}{2}$
$4\frac{2}{3}$	$7\frac{2}{3}$	$10\frac{2}{3}$	$13\frac{2}{3}$	$16\frac{2}{3}$	$19\frac{2}{3}$
7.5	6.5	5.5	4.5	3.5	2.5
29.3	26.3	23.3	20.3	17.3	14.3
82.6	73.6	64.6	55.6	46.6	37.6
6.4	10.4	14.4	18.4	22.4	26.4
14.2	16.2	18.2	20.2	22.2	24.2
21.8	28.8	35.8	42.8	49.8	56.8
$13\frac{3}{4}$	$19\frac{3}{4}$	$25\frac{3}{4}$	$31\frac{3}{4}$	$37\frac{3}{4}$	$43\frac{3}{4}$
57.5	48.5	39.5	30.5	21.5	12.5
$11\frac{1}{2}$	$10\frac{1}{2}$	$9\frac{1}{2}$	$8\frac{1}{2}$	$7\frac{1}{2}$	$6\frac{1}{2}$
8.4	11.4	14.4	17.4	20.4	23.4

I can't spot the pattern. Get me some help with these.

97

Although the patterns here are formed by adding or subtracting whole numbers, the items in each are mixed numbers or decimals.The operation that turns the first number into the second, and the second into the third can be used to continue the pattern.

98

Products with odd and even numbers

Find the products of these numbers.

4 and 5 The product of 4 and 5 is 20. 6 and 7 The product of 6 and 7 is 42.

Find the products of these odd and even numbers.

3 and 4	The product of 3 and 4 is 12.	2 and 3	The product of 2 and 3 is 6.
7 and 4	The product of 7 and 4 is 28.	8 and 3	The product of 8 and 3 is 24.
6 and 3	The product of 6 and 3 is 18.	9 and 2	The product of 9 and 2 is 18.
10 and 3	The product of 10 and 3 is 30.	12 and 5	The product of 12 and 5 is 60.

What do you notice about your answers? The product of odd and even numbers is always an even number.

Find the products of these odd numbers.

3 and 5	The product of 3 and 5 is 15.	3 and 9	The product of 3 and 9 is 27.
5 and 7	The product of 5 and 7 is 35.	7 and 3	The product of 7 and 3 is 21.
5 and 11	The product of 5 and 11 is 55.	9 and 7	The product of 9 and 7 is 63.
9 and 5	The product of 9 and 5 is 45.	1 and 5	The product of 1 and 5 is 5.

What do you notice about your answers? The product of two odd numbers is always an odd number.

Find the products of these even numbers.

4 and 2	The product of 4 and 2 is 8.	4 and 6	The product of 4 and 6 is 24.
2 and 6	The product of 2 and 6 is 12.	4 and 8	The product of 4 and 8 is 32.
10 and 2	The product of 10 and 2 is 20.	4 and 10	The product of 4 and 10 is 40.
6 and 10	The product of 6 and 10 is 60.	2 and 8	The product of 2 and 8 is 16.

What do you notice about your answers? The product of two numbers will always be even unless both numbers are odd.

98

Children may need help answering the questions on what they notice about the products. Accept any rule about products that children write as long as it indicates that they have grasped the concept.

99

Squares of numbers

Find the square of 3. $3 \times 3 = 9$

What is the area of this square? (3 in. by 3 in.) $3 \times 3 = 9$ Area = 9 in.^{2}

Find the square of these numbers.

2	$2 \times 2 = 4$	1	$1 \times 1 = 1$	10	$10 \times 10 = 100$
7	$7 \times 7 = 49$	8	$8 \times 8 = 64$	5	$5 \times 5 = 25$
9	$9 \times 9 = 81$	4	$4 \times 4 = 16$	6	$6 \times 6 = 36$

Now try these.

11	$11 \times 11 = 121$	13	$13 \times 13 = 169$	12	$12 \times 12 = 144$
20	$20 \times 20 = 400$	40	$40 \times 40 = 1,600$	30	$30 \times 30 = 900$

Find the areas of these squares.

4 in. × 4 in.: 16 in.^{2}

5 ft × 5 ft: 25 ft^2

6 cm × 6 cm: 36 cm^2

8 in. × 8 in.: 64 in.^{2}

9 ft × 9 ft: 81 ft^2

Square? Who says I'm square?

99

Make sure that children understand that area is given in square units. You may want to add lines to divide the square in the example into quarters, to show 4 square inches. Check that they are in fact squaring the numbers, and not multiplying by two.

100

Factors of numbers from 66 to 100

The factors of 66 are: 1 2 3 6 11 22 33 66

Circle the factors of 94: ① ② 28 32 43 (47) 71 86 (94)

Write the factors of each number in the box.

The factors of 70 are	1, 2, 5, 7, 10, 14, 35, 70
The factors of 83 are	1, 83
The factors of 63 are	1, 3, 7, 9, 21, 63
The factors of 85 are	1, 5, 17, 85
The factors of 75 are	1, 3, 5, 15, 25, 75
The factors of 99 are	1, 3, 9, 11, 33, 99
The factors of 69 are	1, 3, 23, 69
The factors of 72 are	1, 2, 3, 4, 6, 8, 9, 12, 18, 24, 36, 72
The factors of 96 are	1, 2, 3, 4, 6, 8, 12, 16, 24, 32, 48, 96

Consider all the factors when you're planning a crime caper.

Circle the factors.

Which numbers are factors of 68?

① ② 3 ④ 5 6 7 8 9 11 12 ⑰ ㉞ 35 62 (68)

Which numbers are factors of 95?

① 2 3 4 ⑤ 15 16 17 ⑲ 24 59 85 90 (95) 96

Which numbers are factors of 88?

① ② 3 ④ 5 6 ⑧ 10 ⑪ 15 ㉒ 33 38 ㊹ 87 (88)

Which numbers are factors of 73?

① 2 3 4 6 8 9 10 12 13 14 15 37 42 (73)

A prime number has only two factors, 1 and itself. Write all the prime numbers between 66 and 100 in the box.

67, 71, 73, 79, 83, 89, 97

100

Children often miss some of the factors of large numbers. Encourage a systematic method of finding factors. Children may forget that 1 and the number itself are factors of a number. If necessary, discuss prime numbers with children.

101

Renaming fractions

Rename these improper fractions as mixed numbers in simplest form.

$$\frac{19}{10} = 1\frac{9}{10} \qquad \frac{26}{6} = 4\frac{1}{3}$$

Rename this improper fraction as a mixed number in simplest form.

$$\frac{18}{10} = 1\frac{8}{10} = 1\frac{4}{5}$$

Rename these improper fractions as mixed numbers in simplest form.

$\frac{17}{4} = 4\frac{1}{4}$ $\frac{14}{10} = 1\frac{2}{5}$ $\frac{27}{5} = 5\frac{2}{5}$

$\frac{19}{12} = 1\frac{7}{12}$ $\frac{22}{10} = 2\frac{1}{5}$ $\frac{17}{6} = 2\frac{5}{6}$

$\frac{19}{6} = 3\frac{1}{6}$ $\frac{24}{5} = 4\frac{4}{5}$ $\frac{13}{3} = 4\frac{1}{3}$

$\frac{11}{4} = 2\frac{3}{4}$ $\frac{19}{2} = 9\frac{1}{2}$ $\frac{14}{9} = 1\frac{5}{9}$

$\frac{9}{8} = 1\frac{1}{8}$ $\frac{11}{6} = 1\frac{5}{6}$ $\frac{15}{7} = 2\frac{1}{7}$

$\frac{15}{8} = 1\frac{7}{8}$ $\frac{43}{4} = 10\frac{3}{4}$ $\frac{11}{5} = 2\frac{1}{5}$

$\frac{16}{10} = 1\frac{3}{5}$ $\frac{36}{8} = 4\frac{1}{2}$ $\frac{18}{8} = 2\frac{1}{4}$

$\frac{35}{10} = 3\frac{1}{2}$ $\frac{22}{6} = 3\frac{2}{3}$ $\frac{24}{20} = 1\frac{1}{5}$

$\frac{26}{8} = 3\frac{1}{4}$ $\frac{20}{8} = 2\frac{1}{2}$ $\frac{16}{12} = 1\frac{1}{3}$

$\frac{35}{15} = 2\frac{1}{3}$ $\frac{22}{4} = 5\frac{1}{2}$

$\frac{28}{24} = 1\frac{1}{6}$ $\frac{32}{6} = 5\frac{1}{3}$

$\frac{18}{12} = 1\frac{1}{2}$ $\frac{50}{4} = 12\frac{1}{2}$

There's nothing improper here!

To change improper fractions to mixed numbers children should divide the numerator by the denominator and place the remainder over the denominator. Help them simplify answers by finding common factors for the numerator and denominator.

102

Ordering sets of decimals

Write these decimals in order, from least to greatest.

0.54	0.27	2.11	1.45	3.72	2.17
0.27	0.54	1.45	2.11	2.17	3.72

Write these decimals in order, from least to greatest.

6.63	2.14	5.6	3.91	1.25
1.25	2.14	3.91	5.6	6.63
0.95	0.79	8.25	7.63	7.49
0.79	0.95	7.49	7.63	8.25
1.05	2.36	1.09	2.41	7.94
1.05	1.09	2.36	2.41	7.94
3.92	5.63	2.29	4.62	5.36
2.29	3.92	4.62	5.36	5.63
27.71	21.87	27.28	21.78	27.09
21.78	21.87	27.09	27.28	27.71

Write these decimals in order, from least to greatest.

110.75 km	65.99 km	94.36 km	76.91 km	87.05 km
65.99 km	76.91 km	87.05 km	94.36 km	110.75 km
$65.25	$32.40	$11.36	$32.04	$65.99
$11.36	$32.04	$32.40	$65.25	$65.99
19.51 m	16.15 m	15.53 m	12.65 m	24.24 m
12.65 m	15.53 m	16.15 m	19.51 m	24.24 m
4.291	8.921	8.291	10.651	7.351
4.291	7.351	8.291	8.921	10.651
1.34 cm	0.98 cm	0.89 cm	1.43 cm	1.09 cm
0.89 cm	0.98 cm	1.09 cm	1.34 cm	1.43 cm

Children should take special care when they order sets that include numbers with similar digits that have different place values. Make sure that they understand how place value defines a number.

103

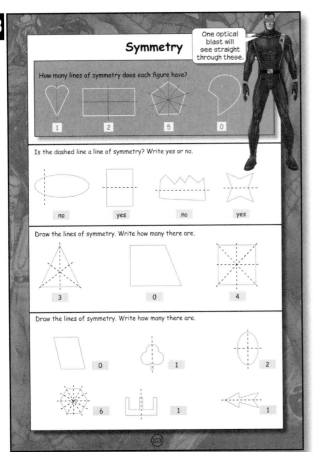

Symmetry

One optical blast will see straight through these.

How many lines of symmetry does each figure have?

1   2   5   0

Is the dashed line a line of symmetry? Write yes or no.

no   yes   no   yes

Draw the lines of symmetry. Write how many there are.

3   0   4

Draw the lines of symmetry. Write how many there are.

0   1   2

6   1   1

Children may have difficulty understanding that a line of symmetry in a pentagon passes through the mid-point of a side and the opposite vertex. Place a pocket mirror upright along a line of symmetry to show how the reflection completes the figure.

104

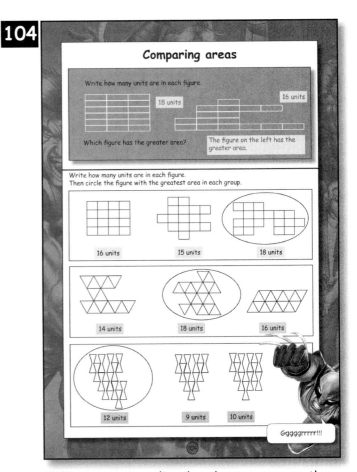

Comparing areas

Write how many units are in each figure.

18 units   16 units

Which figure has the greater area?   The figure on the left has the greater area.

Write how many units are in each figure. Then circle the figure with the greatest area in each group.

16 units   15 units   18 units

14 units   18 units   16 units

12 units   9 units   10 units

Gggggrrrrr!!!

Children may not realize that they can compare the areas of irregular figures. Make sure that they take care to count the units in each figure, rather than incorrectly assuming that the longest or tallest figure has the greatest area.

105

Probability

Use the table to answer the questions.

PROFESSOR X's TIES

Color	Number of ties
Red	4
Blue	4
Green	5
Yellow	6
Black	3

If Professor X picks a tie without looking, which color is he most likely to pick?
yellow

Which color is Professor X as likely to pick as red?
blue

Use the table to answer the questions.

ROGUE'S SKIRTS

Yellow	Blue	Red	Green
卌 卌	卌 II	卌 卌	卌 卌 卌

If Rogue picks a skirt without looking, is she more likely to choose a yellow skirt or a green skirt?
green

Which color is she least likely to pick?
blue

Use the graph to answer the questions.

JELLYBEAN COLORS
(bar graph: Number of jellybeans vs Colors — Green, Yellow, Pink, Red, Orange)

If you pick a jellybean without looking, which color will you most probably pick?
red

Are you more likely to pick a pink jellybean or a yellow jellybean?
yellow

Which color jellybean are you as likely to pick as on orange one?
green

Children must read the tally table and the bar graph to compare the numbers of items. Make sure they understand that there is an equal probability of picking either of two items if there is the same number of each.

106

Column addition

Find these sums. Regroup if needed.

4,612 km	$455
1,096 km	$644
2,363 km	$327
+ 1,374 km	+ $923
9,445 km	$2,349

Find these sums.

8,010 mi	3,852 mi	2,112 mi	4,352 mi
7,793 mi	4,534 mi	6,231 mi	3,920 mi
1,641 mi	1,512 mi	1,573 mi	8,439 mi
+ 7,684 mi	+ 3,756 mi	+ 3,141 mi	+ 1,348 mi
25,128 mi	13,654 mi	13,057 mi	18,059 mi

$4,721	$3,654	$8,171	$4,563
$8,342	$5,932	$1,475	$2,395
$1,711	$6,841	$7,760	$1,486
+ $2,365	+ $4,736	+ $8,102	+ $6,374
$17,139	$21,163	$25,508	$14,818

8,690 m	6,329 m	5,245 m	6,431 m
5,243 m	3,251 m	2,845 m	7,453 m
6,137 m	2,642 m	1,937 m	4,650 m
+ 5,843 m	+ 4,823 m	+ 5,610 m	+ 3,782 m
25,913 m	17,045 m	15,637 m	22,316 m

539 yd	206 yd	481 yd	735 yd
965 yd	812 yd	604 yd	234 yd
774 yd	619 yd	274 yd	391 yd
+ 347 yd	+ 832 yd	+ 976 yd	+ 863 yd
2,625 yd	2,469 yd	2,335 yd	2,223 yd

763 lb	944 lb	817 lb	746 lb
861 lb	835 lb	591 lb	201 lb
608 lb	391 lb	685 lb	432 lb
+ 671 lb	+ 105 lb	+ 245 lb	+ 309 lb
2,903 lb	2,275 lb	2,338 lb	1,688 lb

This page requires children to perform basic addition. However, with a larger number of addends, there is a greater possibility of neglecting to regroup correctly.

107

Column addition

Find these sums. Regroup if needed.

$3,614	2,534
$4,159	3,120
$3,522	7,459
$2,100	6,102
+ $3,461	+ 8,352
$16,856	27,567

Everything adds up!

Find these sums.

3,846 km	2,510 km	3,144 km	1,475 km
1,769 km	1,734 km	2,345 km	2,653 km
6,837 km	5,421 km	8,479 km	2,765 km
1,593 km	3,205 km	1,004 km	3,742 km
+ 3,276 km	+ 2,365 km	+ 6,310 km	+ 5,905 km
17,321 km	15,235 km	21,282 km	16,540 km

$4,468	$3,823	$7,525	$8,618
$3,533	$9,275	$7,875	$3,453
$6,400	$3,669	$4,256	$4,404
$8,675	$2,998	$5,752	$4,361
+ $2,901	+ $7,564	+ $2,594	+ $5,641
$25,977	$27,329	$28,002	$26,477

1,480 m	4,527 m	3,063 m	8,741 m
6,366 m	8,309 m	8,460 m	6,334 m
1,313 m	6,235 m	2,712 m	3,231 m
3,389 m	4,487 m	3,756 m	6,063 m
+ 4,592 m	+ 4,065 m	+ 5,650 m	+ 4,096 m
17,140 m	27,623 m	23,641 m	28,465 m

3,742 mi	2,739 mi	8,463 mi	8,596 mi
2,785 mi	6,517 mi	5,641 mi	5,430 mi
7,326 mi	6,014 mi	9,430 mi	8,379 mi
1,652 mi	7,115 mi	8,204 mi	2,943 mi
+ 5,753 mi	+ 2,704 mi	+ 6,326 mi	+ 1,081 mi
21,258 mi	25,089 mi	38,064 mi	26,429 mi

This page is similar to the previous one, but children must find the sum of a larger number of addends.

108

Adding fractions

Write the sum in simplest form.

$$\frac{1}{8} + \frac{5}{8} = \frac{6}{8} = \frac{3}{4} \qquad \frac{3}{5} + \frac{3}{5} = \frac{6}{5} = 1\frac{1}{5}$$

Write the sum in simplest form.

$$\frac{2}{3} + \frac{2}{3} = \frac{4}{3} = 1\frac{1}{3} \qquad \frac{1}{8} + \frac{5}{8} = \frac{6}{8} = \frac{3}{4}$$

$$\frac{1}{4} + \frac{1}{4} = \frac{2}{4} = \frac{1}{2} \qquad \frac{5}{7} + \frac{1}{7} = \frac{6}{7}$$

$$\frac{3}{7} + \frac{5}{7} = \frac{8}{7} = 1\frac{1}{7} \qquad \frac{1}{12} + \frac{3}{12} = \frac{4}{12} = \frac{1}{3}$$

$$\frac{7}{13} + \frac{7}{13} = \frac{14}{13} = 1\frac{1}{13} \qquad \frac{5}{11} + \frac{9}{11} = \frac{14}{11} = 1\frac{3}{11}$$

$$\frac{9}{10} + \frac{7}{10} = \frac{16}{10} = \frac{8}{5} = 1\frac{3}{5} \qquad \frac{5}{18} + \frac{4}{18} = \frac{9}{18} = \frac{1}{2}$$

$$\frac{3}{8} + \frac{5}{8} = \frac{8}{8} = 1 \qquad \frac{5}{9} + \frac{5}{9} = \frac{10}{9} = 1\frac{1}{9}$$

$$\frac{5}{16} + \frac{7}{16} = \frac{12}{16} = \frac{3}{4} \qquad \frac{4}{15} + \frac{7}{15} = \frac{11}{15}$$

$$\frac{8}{9} + \frac{7}{9} = \frac{15}{9} = \frac{5}{3} = 1\frac{2}{3} \qquad \frac{2}{5} + \frac{1}{5} = \frac{3}{5}$$

Normally, I'm a fraction of this size!

$$\frac{4}{11} + \frac{5}{11} = \frac{9}{11} \qquad \frac{1}{8} + \frac{5}{8} = \frac{6}{8} = \frac{3}{4}$$

$$\frac{5}{6} + \frac{5}{6} = \frac{10}{6} = \frac{5}{3} = 1\frac{2}{3} \qquad \frac{3}{4} + \frac{3}{4} = \frac{6}{4} = \frac{3}{2} = 1\frac{1}{2}$$

$$\frac{2}{5} + \frac{4}{5} = \frac{6}{5} = 1\frac{1}{5} \qquad \frac{4}{15} + \frac{7}{15} = \frac{11}{15}$$

$$\frac{5}{12} + \frac{5}{12} = \frac{10}{12} = \frac{5}{6} \qquad \frac{7}{12} + \frac{11}{12} = \frac{18}{12} = \frac{9}{6} = 1\frac{3}{6} = 1\frac{1}{2}$$

$$\frac{8}{14} + \frac{5}{14} = \frac{13}{14} \qquad \frac{9}{14} + \frac{9}{14} = \frac{18}{14} = \frac{9}{7} = 1\frac{2}{7}$$

$$\frac{1}{7} + \frac{4}{7} = \frac{5}{7} \qquad \frac{1}{7} + \frac{5}{7} = \frac{6}{7}$$

Some children may incorrectly add both the numerators and the denominators. Demonstrate that only the numerators should be added when the fractions have the same denominators: $1/2 + 1/2$ equals $2/2$ or 1, not $2/4$.

109

Adding fractions

Write the sum in simplest form.

$\frac{1}{12} + \frac{3}{4} = \frac{1}{12} + \frac{9}{12} = \frac{10}{12} = \frac{5}{6}$ $\frac{3}{5} + \frac{7}{10} = \frac{6}{10} + \frac{7}{10} = \frac{13}{10} = 1\frac{3}{10}$

Write the sum in simplest form.

$\frac{1}{6} + \frac{2}{3} = \frac{1}{6} + \frac{4}{6} = \frac{5}{6}$

$\frac{1}{10} + \frac{1}{2} = \frac{1}{10} + \frac{5}{10} = \frac{6}{10} = \frac{3}{5}$

$\frac{8}{12} + \frac{5}{24} = \frac{16}{24} + \frac{5}{24} = \frac{21}{24} = \frac{7}{8}$ $\frac{6}{10} + \frac{7}{30} = \frac{18}{30} + \frac{7}{30} = \frac{25}{30} = \frac{5}{6}$

$\frac{5}{6} + \frac{9}{12} = \frac{10}{12} + \frac{9}{12} = \frac{19}{12} = 1\frac{7}{12}$ $\frac{7}{12} + \frac{7}{36} = \frac{21}{36} + \frac{7}{36} = \frac{28}{36} = \frac{7}{9}$

$\frac{5}{7} + \frac{7}{14} = \frac{10}{14} + \frac{7}{14} = \frac{17}{14} = 1\frac{3}{14}$ $\frac{7}{12} + \frac{5}{6} = \frac{7}{12} + \frac{10}{12} = \frac{17}{12} = 1\frac{5}{12}$

$\frac{4}{9} + \frac{2}{3} = \frac{4}{9} + \frac{6}{9} = \frac{10}{9} = 1\frac{1}{9}$ $\frac{19}{25} + \frac{2}{5} = \frac{19}{25} + \frac{10}{25} = \frac{29}{25} = 1\frac{4}{25}$

$\frac{5}{8} + \frac{5}{24} = \frac{15}{24} + \frac{5}{24} = \frac{20}{24} = \frac{5}{6}$ $\frac{2}{3} + \frac{7}{15} = \frac{10}{15} + \frac{7}{15} = \frac{17}{15} = 1\frac{2}{15}$

$\frac{4}{5} + \frac{3}{10} = \frac{8}{10} + \frac{3}{10} = \frac{11}{10} = 1\frac{1}{10}$ $\frac{7}{8} + \frac{1}{2} = \frac{7}{8} + \frac{4}{8} = \frac{11}{8} = 1\frac{3}{8}$

$\frac{11}{14} + \frac{9}{28} = \frac{22}{28} + \frac{9}{28} = \frac{31}{28} = 1\frac{3}{28}$ $\frac{7}{8} + \frac{3}{16} = \frac{14}{16} + \frac{3}{16} = \frac{17}{16} = 1\frac{1}{16}$

$\frac{3}{10} + \frac{7}{20} = \frac{6}{20} + \frac{7}{20} = \frac{13}{20}$ $\frac{25}{33} + \frac{5}{11} = \frac{25}{33} + \frac{15}{33} = \frac{40}{33} = 1\frac{7}{33}$

Give me a hand with these sums.

On this page, children must rename fractions so that both addends have the same denominator. They should also be aware that they must simplify the sum when necessary.

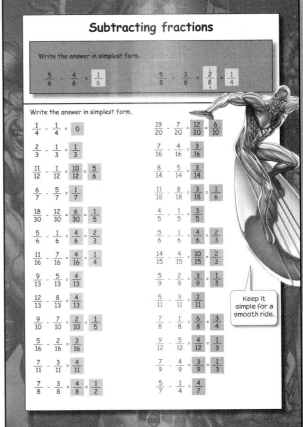

110

Subtracting fractions

Write the answer in simplest form.

$\frac{5}{6} - \frac{4}{6} = \frac{1}{6}$ $\frac{5}{8} - \frac{3}{8} = \frac{2}{8} = \frac{1}{4}$

Write the answer in simplest form.

$\frac{1}{4} - \frac{1}{4} = 0$ $\frac{19}{20} - \frac{7}{20} = \frac{12}{20} = \frac{6}{10}$

$\frac{2}{3} - \frac{2}{3} = \frac{1}{3}$ $\frac{7}{16} - \frac{4}{16} = \frac{3}{16}$

$\frac{11}{12} - \frac{1}{12} = \frac{10}{12} = \frac{5}{6}$ $\frac{8}{14} - \frac{5}{14} = \frac{3}{14}$

$\frac{6}{7} - \frac{5}{7} = \frac{1}{7}$ $\frac{11}{18} - \frac{8}{18} = \frac{3}{18} = \frac{1}{6}$

$\frac{18}{30} - \frac{12}{30} = \frac{6}{30} = \frac{1}{5}$ $\frac{4}{5} - \frac{1}{5} = \frac{3}{5}$

$\frac{5}{6} - \frac{1}{6} = \frac{4}{6} = \frac{2}{3}$ $\frac{5}{6} - \frac{1}{6} = \frac{4}{6} = \frac{2}{3}$

$\frac{11}{16} - \frac{7}{16} = \frac{4}{16} = \frac{1}{4}$ $\frac{14}{15} - \frac{4}{15} = \frac{10}{15} = \frac{2}{3}$

$\frac{9}{13} - \frac{5}{13} = \frac{4}{13}$ $\frac{5}{9} - \frac{2}{9} = \frac{3}{9} = \frac{1}{3}$

$\frac{12}{13} - \frac{8}{13} = \frac{4}{13}$ $\frac{5}{11} - \frac{3}{11} = \frac{2}{11}$

$\frac{9}{10} - \frac{7}{10} = \frac{2}{10} = \frac{1}{5}$ $\frac{7}{8} - \frac{1}{8} = \frac{6}{8} = \frac{3}{4}$

$\frac{5}{16} - \frac{2}{16} = \frac{3}{16}$ $\frac{9}{12} - \frac{5}{12} = \frac{4}{12} = \frac{1}{3}$

$\frac{7}{11} - \frac{3}{11} = \frac{4}{11}$ $\frac{7}{9} - \frac{4}{9} = \frac{3}{9} = \frac{1}{3}$

$\frac{7}{8} - \frac{3}{8} = \frac{4}{8} = \frac{1}{2}$ $\frac{5}{7} - \frac{1}{7} = \frac{4}{7}$

Keep it simple for a smooth ride.

On this page, children subtract fractions that have the same denominators. If they neglect to simplify their answers, help them find common factors in the numerator and denominator.

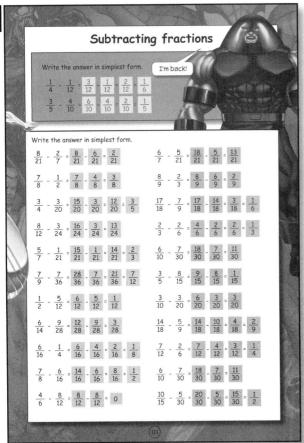

111

Subtracting fractions

I'm back!

Write the answer in simplest form.

$\frac{1}{4} - \frac{1}{12} = \frac{3}{12} - \frac{1}{12} = \frac{2}{12} = \frac{1}{6}$

$\frac{3}{5} - \frac{4}{10} = \frac{6}{10} - \frac{4}{10} = \frac{2}{10} = \frac{1}{5}$

Write the answer in simplest form.

$\frac{8}{21} - \frac{2}{7} = \frac{8}{21} - \frac{6}{21} = \frac{2}{21}$ $\frac{6}{7} - \frac{5}{21} = \frac{18}{21} - \frac{5}{21} = \frac{13}{21}$

$\frac{7}{8} - \frac{1}{2} = \frac{7}{8} - \frac{4}{8} = \frac{3}{8}$ $\frac{8}{9} - \frac{2}{3} = \frac{8}{9} - \frac{6}{9} = \frac{2}{9}$

$\frac{3}{4} - \frac{3}{20} = \frac{15}{20} - \frac{3}{20} = \frac{12}{20} = \frac{3}{5}$ $\frac{17}{18} - \frac{7}{9} = \frac{17}{18} - \frac{14}{18} = \frac{3}{18} = \frac{1}{6}$

$\frac{8}{12} - \frac{3}{24} = \frac{16}{24} - \frac{3}{24} = \frac{13}{24}$ $\frac{2}{3} - \frac{2}{6} = \frac{4}{6} - \frac{2}{6} = \frac{2}{6} = \frac{1}{3}$

$\frac{5}{7} - \frac{1}{21} = \frac{15}{21} - \frac{1}{21} = \frac{14}{21} = \frac{2}{3}$ $\frac{6}{10} - \frac{7}{30} = \frac{18}{30} - \frac{7}{30} = \frac{11}{30}$

$\frac{7}{9} - \frac{7}{36} = \frac{28}{36} - \frac{7}{36} = \frac{21}{36} = \frac{7}{12}$ $\frac{3}{5} - \frac{8}{15} = \frac{9}{15} - \frac{8}{15} = \frac{1}{15}$

$\frac{1}{2} - \frac{5}{12} = \frac{6}{12} - \frac{5}{12} = \frac{1}{12}$ $\frac{3}{10} - \frac{3}{20} = \frac{6}{20} - \frac{3}{20} = \frac{3}{20}$

$\frac{6}{14} - \frac{9}{28} = \frac{12}{28} - \frac{9}{28} = \frac{3}{28}$ $\frac{14}{18} - \frac{5}{9} = \frac{14}{18} - \frac{10}{18} = \frac{4}{18} = \frac{2}{9}$

$\frac{6}{16} - \frac{1}{4} = \frac{6}{16} - \frac{4}{16} = \frac{2}{16} = \frac{1}{8}$ $\frac{7}{12} - \frac{2}{6} = \frac{7}{12} - \frac{4}{12} = \frac{3}{12} = \frac{1}{4}$

$\frac{7}{8} - \frac{6}{16} = \frac{14}{16} - \frac{6}{16} = \frac{8}{16} = \frac{1}{2}$ $\frac{6}{10} - \frac{7}{30} = \frac{18}{30} - \frac{7}{30} = \frac{11}{30}$

$\frac{4}{6} - \frac{8}{12} = \frac{8}{12} - \frac{8}{12} = 0$ $\frac{10}{15} - \frac{5}{30} = \frac{20}{30} - \frac{5}{30} = \frac{15}{30} = \frac{1}{2}$

On this page, children must write both fractions with the same denominator before subtracting. If necessary, point out that fractions have the same value as long as you multiply the numerator and denominator by the same number.

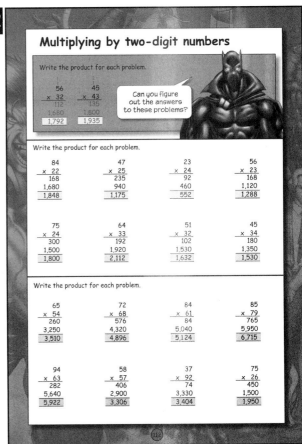

112

Multiplying by two-digit numbers

Write the product for each problem.

Can you figure out the answers to these problems?

```
   56        45
 x 32      x 43
  112       135
1,680     1,800
1,792     1,935
```

Write the product for each problem.

```
   84        47        23        56
 x 22      x 25      x 24      x 23
  168       235        92       168
1,680       940       460     1,120
1,848     1,175       552     1,288


   75        64        51        45
 x 24      x 33      x 32      x 34
  300       192       102       180
1,500     1,920     1,530     1,350
1,800     2,112     1,632     1,530
```

Write the product for each problem.

```
   65        72        84        85
 x 54      x 68      x 61      x 79
  260       576        84       765
3,250     4,320     5,040     5,950
3,510     4,896     5,124     6,715


   94        58        37        75
 x 63      x 57      x 92      x 26
  282       406        74       450
5,640     2,900     3,330     1,500
5,922     3,306     3,404     1,950
```

Children should understand that multiplying a number by 32 is the same as multiplying the number by 2, and by 30, and then adding the two products.

Multiplying by two-digit numbers

Write the product for each problem.

```
   38          68
 x 88        x 98
  304         544
3 040        6 120
─────       ─────
3,344       6,664
```

Write the product for each problem.

```
   86          76          94          99
 x 98        x 78        x 69        x 65
  688         608         846         495
7,740       5,320       5,640       5,940
─────       ─────       ─────       ─────
8,428       5,928       6,486       6,435
```

```
   74          67          94          87
 x 33        x 76        x 79        x 49
  222         402         846         783
2,220       4,690       6,580       3,480
─────       ─────       ─────       ─────
2,442       5,092       7,426       4,263
```

Write the product for each problem.

```
   46          84          87          58
 x 67        x 71        x 79        x 63
  322          84         783         174
2,760       5,880       6,090       3,480
─────       ─────       ─────       ─────
3,082       5,964       6,873       3,654
```

```
   73          79          96          48
 x 98        x 87        x 78        x 27
  584         553         768         336
6,570       6,320       6,720         960
─────       ─────       ─────       ─────
7,154       6,873       7,488       1,296
```

This page gives further practice of multiplication as on the previous page. Make sure that children do not neglect to regroup when necessary.

Dividing by one-digit numbers

```
Find the quotient. Estimate your answer first.      89 r 1
                                                  3)268
3 x 100 = 300, so the quotient will be               24
less than 100.                                        28
3 x 80 = 240 and 3 x 90 = 270, so the                 27
quotient will be between 80 and 90.                    1
```

Find the quotients. Remember to estimate your answers first.

```
   233 r 1          205 r 3          201 r 2
2)467            4)823            3)605
  4                8                6
  67               023             005
   6                20               3
   7                 3               2
   6
   1
```

Make a good guess then check it out...QUICKLY!

```
   73 r 1           86 r 1          162 r 2
2)147            3)259            5)812
  14               24               5
   07              19               32
    6              18               30
    1               1               12
                                    10
                                     2
```

```
   246 r 1          101 r 2          296 r 1
3)739            4)406            2)593
  6                4                4
  13               006             19
  12                 4             18
   19                2             13
   18                              12
    1                               1
```

Children may have difficulty finding quotients with remainders. Have them perform long division until the remaining value to be divided is less than the divisor. That value is the remainder. Make sure that the digits in the answer line up correctly, as shown.

Dividing by one-digit numbers

```
Find the quotient. Estimate your answer first.     105 r 7
                                                 8)847
8 x 100 = 800, so the quotient will be              8
more than 100.                                       04
8 x 110 = 880, so the quotient will be               0
between 100 and 110.                                 47
                                                     40
                                                      7
```

Find the quotients. Remember to estimate your answers first.

```
   122 r 1          66 r 3           117 r 5
6)733            7)465            8)941
  6                42               8
  13               45               14
  12               42                8
  13                3               61
  12                                56
   1                                 5
```

```
   66 r 4           80 r 6           71 r 2
8)532            7)566            7)499
  48               56               49
  52               06               09
  48                                 7
   4                                 2
```

I just love dividing up the spoils of battle!

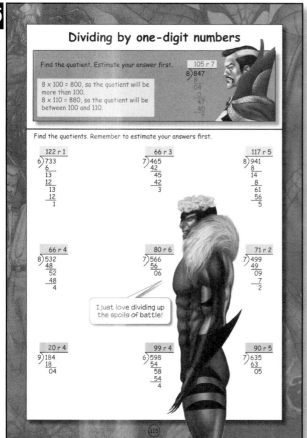

```
   20 r 4           99 r 4           90 r 5
9)184            6)598            7)635
  18               54               63
   04              58               05
                   54
                    4
```

This page is similar to the previous page, but the divisors are numbers greater than 5. Children will need to know their 6, 7, 8, and 9 times tables. Make sure that the digits in the answer line up correctly, as shown.

Real-life problems

Find the answer to each problem.

Jean spends $42.99 on new shoes. Scott spends $76.54 on gifts. How much more does he spend than Jean?

```
   14
  5 4 14
  76.54
- 42.99
──────
  33.55       $33.55
```

Professor X buys some new equipment. He spends $99 a day for 16 days. How much does he spend?

```
    99
  x 16
  ────
   594
   990
 ─────
 1,584       $1,584
```

Black Cat has $5,762 in stocks and $3,247 in her bank. How much does she have altogether?

$9,009

```
   5,762
 + 3,247
 ───────
   9,009
```

A shop in Chicago takes in $9,651 on a Saturday. It is burgled by Black Cat, who steals $3,247. How much does the Chicago shop have left?

$6,404

```
    4 11
  9,6̸5̸1
 - 3,247
 ───────
   6,404
```

117 S.H.I.E.L.D. agents claim $2 each for their expenses, and 251 agents claim $3 each, how much did the agents claim altogether?

$987

```
   117    251    234
  x  2   x  3    753
  ────   ────   ────
   234    753    987
```

Jean Grey has $50. She spends $2.50 on candies, $5.75 on flowers, and $24.25 on new shoes. How much money does she have left?

$17.50

```
  11 1
  24.25      4 9 10
   5.75     5̸0.0̸0̸
 + 2.50    - 32.50
 ──────    ───────
  32.50      17.50
```

Agent Zero earns $1,200 a day as a mercenary. How much will he earn in 5 days?

$6,000

```
   1,200
   x   5
 ───────
   6,000
```

The third and fourth problems on this page require multiple steps to reach the correct answers. If children have difficulty, help them plan out methods to solve the problems.

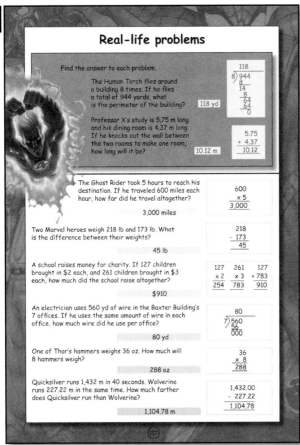

Real-life problems

Find the answer to each problem.

The Human Torch flies around a building 8 times. If he flies a total of 944 yards, what is the perimeter of the building? **118 yd**

$$8)\overline{944}$$
$$\begin{array}{r}118\\ \underline{8}\\ 14\\ \underline{8}\\ 64\\ \underline{64}\\ 0\end{array}$$

Professor X's study is 5.75 m long and his dining room is 4.37 m long. If he knocks out the wall between the two rooms to make one room, how long will it be? **10.12 m**

$$\begin{array}{r}5.75\\ +\ 4.37\\ \hline 10.12\end{array}$$

The Ghost Rider took 5 hours to reach his destination. If he traveled 600 miles each hour, how far did he travel altogether? **3,000 miles**

$$\begin{array}{r}600\\ \times\ 5\\ \hline 3,000\end{array}$$

Two Marvel heroes weigh 218 lb and 173 lb. What is the difference between their weights? **45 lb**

$$\begin{array}{r}218\\ -\ 173\\ \hline 45\end{array}$$

A school raises money for charity. If 127 children brought in $2 each, and 261 children brought in $3 each, how much did the school raise altogether? **$910**

$$\begin{array}{r}127\\ \times\ 2\\ \hline 254\end{array}\quad \begin{array}{r}261\\ \times\ 3\\ \hline 783\end{array}\quad \begin{array}{r}127\\ +\ 783\\ \hline 910\end{array}$$

An electrician uses 560 yd of wire in the Baxter Building's 7 offices. If he uses the same amount of wire in each office, how much wire did he use per office? **80 yd**

$$7)\overline{560}\quad \begin{array}{r}80\\ 56\\ \hline 000\end{array}$$

One of Thor's hammers weighs 36 oz. How much will 8 hammers weigh? **288 oz**

$$\begin{array}{r}36\\ \times\ 8\\ \hline 288\end{array}$$

Quicksilver runs 1,432 m in 40 seconds. Wolverine runs 227.22 m in the same time. How much farther does Quicksilver run than Wolverine? **1,104.78 m**

$$\begin{array}{r}1,432.00\\ -\ 227.22\\ \hline 1,104.78\end{array}$$

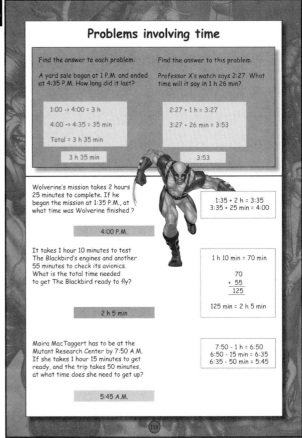

Problems involving time

Find the answer to each problem.

A yard sale began at 1 P.M. and ended at 4:35 P.M. How long did it last?

1:00 -> 4:00 = 3 h
4:00 -> 4:35 = 35 min
Total = 3 h 35 min

3 h 35 min

Find the answer to this problem.

Professor X's watch says 2:27. What time will it say in 1 h 26 min?

2:27 + 1 h = 3:27
3:27 + 26 min = 3:53

3:53

Wolverine's mission takes 2 hours 25 minutes to complete. If he began the mission at 1:35 P.M., at what time was Wolverine finished?

1:35 + 2 h = 3:35
3:35 + 25 min = 4:00

4:00 P.M.

It takes 1 hour 10 minutes to test The Blackbird's engines and another 55 minutes to check its avionics. What is the total time needed to get The Blackbird ready to fly?

1 h 10 min = 70 min

$$\begin{array}{r}70\\ +\ 55\\ \hline 125\end{array}$$

125 min = 2 h 5 min

2 h 5 min

Moira MacTaggert has to be at the Mutant Research Center by 7:50 A.M. If she takes 1 hour 15 minutes to get ready, and the trip takes 50 minutes, at what time does she need to get up?

7:50 - 1 h = 6:50
6:50 - 15 min = 6:35
6:35 - 50 min = 5:45

5:45 A.M.

You may need to help children understand time periods so that they can manage the questions more easily. For example, borrowing an hour in a subtraction problem is the same as borrowing 60 minutes.

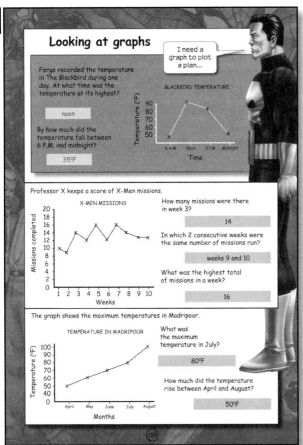

Looking at graphs

I need a graph to plot a plan...

Forge recorded the temperature in The Blackbird during one day. At what time was the temperature at its highest? **noon**

BLACKBIRD TEMPERATURE

By how much did the temperature fall between 6 P.M. and midnight? **35°F**

Professor X keeps a score of X-Men missions.

X-MEN MISSIONS

How many missions were there in week 3? **14**

In which 2 consecutive weeks were the same number of missions run? **weeks 9 and 10**

What was the highest total of missions in a week? **16**

The graph shows the maximum temperatures in Madripoor.

TEMPERATURE IN MADRIPOOR

What was the maximum temperature in July? **80°F**

How much did the temperature rise between April and August? **50°F**

On this page, children are required to find two or more pieces of information on a graph. They then have to compare or find the difference in value. In the first question, make sure that children understand the meaning of consecutive.

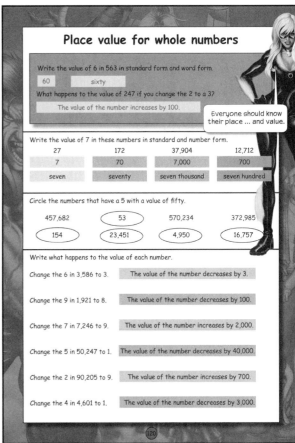

Place value for whole numbers

Write the value of 6 in 563 in standard form and word form. **60** **sixty**

What happens to the value of 247 if you change the 2 to a 3? **The value of the number increases by 100.**

Everyone should know their place ... and value.

Write the value of 7 in these numbers in standard and number form.

27	172	37,904	12,712
7	70	7,000	700
seven	seventy	seven thousand	seven hundred

Circle the numbers that have a 5 with a value of fifty.

457,682	53	570,234	372,985
154	23,451	4,950	16,757

Write what happens to the value of each number.

Change the 6 in 3,586 to 3. **The value of the number decreases by 3.**

Change the 9 in 1,921 to 8. **The value of the number decreases by 100.**

Change the 7 in 7,246 to 9. **The value of the number increases by 2,000.**

Change the 5 in 50,247 to 1. **The value of the number decreases by 40,000.**

Change the 2 in 90,205 to 9. **The value of the number increases by 700.**

Change the 4 in 4,601 to 1. **The value of the number decreases by 3,000.**

Children may need help completing the final section of the page. If so, help them work through the first question of the section. Have children write the new number for each question before trying to find the answer.

Place value for decimals

Write the value of 5 in 7.53 in standard form and word form.
| 0.5 | 5 tenths |

What happens to the value of 3.48 if you change the 8 to 1?
The value of the number decreases by 0.07.

Write the value of the 8 in these numbers in standard and written form.

2.8	0.18	875.04	8.12
0.8	0.08	800	8
eight tenths	eight hundredths	eight hundred	eight

0.98	581.65	18.95	3.86
0.08	80	8	0.8
eight hundredths	eighty	eight	eight tenths

Write what happens to the value of each number.

Change the 6 in 12,586 to 3.	The value of the number decreases by 3.
Change the 2 in 1.02 to 6.	The value increases by 4 hundredths.
Change the 3 in 3,460 to 9.	The value of the number increases by 6,000.
Change the 3 in 328.45 to 1.	The value of the number decreases by 200.

Circle the numbers that have a 5 with the value of 5 hundredths.

555.52   (99.95)   16.53   (5.35)   52.59

Circle the numbers that have an 8 with a value of 8 tenths.

557.68   (2.8)   (75.82)   8.09   (557.86)

Circle the numbers that have a 3 with the value of 3 tenths.

(3,603.3)   0.93   32.45   (5.33)   23.53

This page is similar to the previous one, but involves decimals rather than whole numbers. For the second section of questions, it may help children to write the new numbers and then find the difference between them and the original numbers.

Reading tally charts

Use the chart to answer the questions.

PET PREFERENCES
Pet	Number
Dog	卌 卌 ||||
Cat	卌 卌 卌	
Fish	卌 |||

What is the most popular pet for X-Men?
cats

How many more prefer dogs than fish?
14 - 8 = 6

Use the chart to answer the question.

APPEARANCES IN MARVEL
Wolverine	Lizard	Rogue	Spider-Man
卌 卌 卌 ||||	卌 |||	卌 卌		卌 卌 卌 卌

Which characters appeared more than 12 times?
Wolverine and Spider-Man

How many times did Rogue appear?
11

How many more times did Wolverine appear than Rogue?
8

Use the chart to answer the questions.

SNACKS CHOSEN BY S.H.I.E.L.D AGENTS
Carrots	Fries	Cookies	Pretzels
||||	卌 卌 |||	卌 卌 卌 ||	卌 卌 卌 卌 ||

What snack did fewer than 12 agents choose?
carrots

How many chose the most popular snack?
22

What is the total number of agents who chose fries and cookies?
30

If children have difficulty reading tally charts, show them that they can count by 5s for groups of tallies that are crossed out.

Volumes of cubes

This cube is 1 cm long, 1 cm high, and 1 cm wide. We say it has a volume of 1 cubic centimeter (1 cm³). If we put 4 of these cubes together, the new shape has a volume of 4 cm³.

These shapes are made of 1 cm³ cubes. What are their volumes?

3 cm³	3 cm³	8 cm³
4 cm³	4 cm³	5 cm³
6 cm³	5 cm³	4 cm³

To find the volume of some of the shapes on this page, children must visualize in order to determine how many blocks cannot be seen in the illustrations. In the third and sixth shapes there is one block that is not shown.

Acute and obtuse angles

A right angle forms a square corner.

An obtuse angle is greater than a right angle.

An acute angle is less than a right angle.

I don't like tight corners.

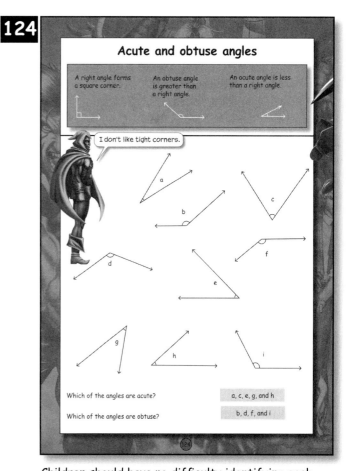

Which of the angles are acute?
a, c, e, g, and h

Which of the angles are obtuse?
b, d, f, and i

Children should have no difficulty identifying each angle if they compare it to a right angle. Since an angle is made up of two rays, remind children to put arrows on the ends of their angles (as shown).

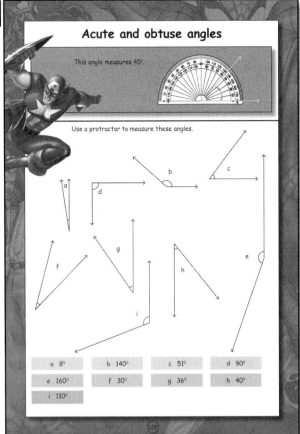

125

Acute and obtuse angles

This angle measures 45°.

Use a protractor to measure these angles.

a 8°	b 140°	c 51°	d 90°
e 160°	f 30°	g 36°	h 40°
i 110°			

If children make errors on this page, the most likely reasons are that they have placed the protractor inaccurately above the vertex of the angle or that they have read the protractor from the wrong direction.

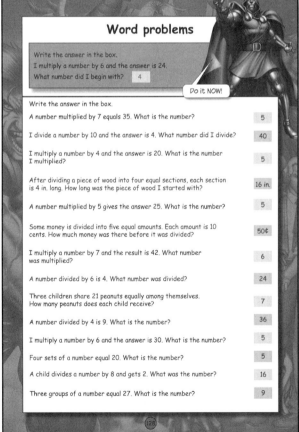

126

Addition fact families

Circle the number sentence that is in the same fact family as the first pair.

24 - 10 = 12	12 - 6 = 6	(10 + 12 = 24)	12 + 12 = 24
12 + 10 = 24			
10 - 8 = 2	8 + 10 = 18	(10 - 2 = 8)	18 - 10 = 8
8 + 2 = 10			

Circle the number sentence that is in the same fact family as the first pair.

Me and my alien costume make a great pair.

7 + 8 = 15	8 - 7 = 1	(15 - 8 = 7)	7 + 5 = 12
8 + 7 = 15			
15 - 6 = 9	(15 - 9 = 6)	15 + 6 = 21	21 - 15 = 6
9 + 6 = 15			
14 - 5 = 9	9 - 3 = 6	14 + 9 = 23	(5 + 9 = 14)
14 - 9 = 5			
7 + 9 = 16	(16 - 9 = 7)	16 + 9 = 25	7 + 16 = 23
9 + 7 = 16			
19 - 9 = 10	9 + 3 = 12	(9 + 10 = 19)	18 - 8 = 10
19 - 10 = 9			
6 + 7 = 13	13 + 6 = 19	(13 - 6 = 7)	7 + 13 = 20
13 - 7 = 6			

Write the fact family for every group of numbers.

7, 12, 5	6, 10, 4	5, 13, 8
5 + 7 = 12	4 + 6 = 10	5 + 8 = 13
7 + 5 = 12	6 + 4 = 10	8 + 5 = 13
12 - 7 = 5	10 - 6 = 4	13 - 8 = 5
12 - 5 = 7	10 - 4 = 6	13 - 5 = 8

Children should understand that subtraction "undoes" addition. You may want to use counters to show the addition fact families.

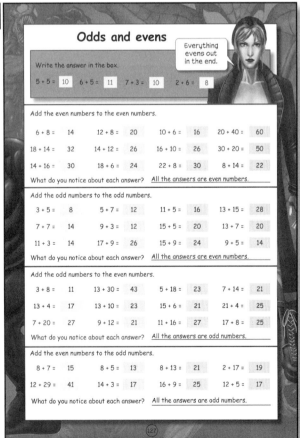

127

Odds and evens

Everything evens out in the end.

Write the answer in the box.

5 + 5 = 10   6 + 5 = 11   7 + 3 = 10   2 + 6 = 8

Add the even numbers to the even numbers.

6 + 8 =	14	12 + 8 =	20	10 + 6 =	16	20 + 40 =	60
18 + 14 =	32	14 + 12 =	26	16 + 10 =	26	30 + 20 =	50
14 + 16 =	30	18 + 6 =	24	22 + 8 =	30	8 + 14 =	22

What do you notice about each answer? <u>All the answers are even numbers.</u>

Add the odd numbers to the odd numbers.

3 + 5 =	8	5 + 7 =	12	11 + 5 =	16	13 + 15 =	28
7 + 7 =	14	9 + 3 =	12	15 + 5 =	20	13 + 7 =	20
11 + 3 =	14	17 + 9 =	26	15 + 9 =	24	9 + 5 =	14

What do you notice about each answer? <u>All the answers are even numbers.</u>

Add the odd numbers to the even numbers.

3 + 8 =	11	13 + 30 =	43	5 + 18 =	23	7 + 14 =	21
13 + 4 =	17	13 + 10 =	23	15 + 6 =	21	21 + 4 =	25
7 + 20 =	27	9 + 12 =	21	11 + 16 =	27	17 + 8 =	25

What do you notice about each answer? <u>All the answers are odd numbers.</u>

Add the even numbers to the odd numbers.

8 + 7 =	15	8 + 5 =	13	8 + 13 =	21	2 + 17 =	19
12 + 29 =	41	14 + 3 =	17	16 + 9 =	25	12 + 5 =	17

What do you notice about each answer? <u>All the answers are odd numbers.</u>

Children should notice that adding two even numbers results in an even number and adding two odd numbers results in an odd number. Adding an odd and an even number gives an odd number. The order in which numbers are added is not important.

128

Word problems

Write the answer in the box.
I multiply a number by 6 and the answer is 24.
What number did I begin with?   4

Do it NOW!

Write the answer in the box.

A number multiplied by 7 equals 35. What is the number?	5
I divide a number by 10 and the answer is 4. What number did I divide?	40
I multiply a number by 4 and the answer is 20. What is the number I multiplied?	5
After dividing a piece of wood into four equal sections, each section is 4 in. long. How long was the piece of wood I started with?	16 in.
A number multiplied by 5 gives the answer 25. What is the number?	5
Some money is divided into five equal amounts. Each amount is 10 cents. How much money was there before it was divided?	50¢
I multiply a number by 7 and the result is 42. What number was multiplied?	6
A number divided by 6 is 4. What number was divided?	24
Three children share 21 peanuts equally among themselves. How many peanuts does each child receive?	7
A number divided by 4 is 9. What is the number?	36
I multiply a number by 6 and the answer is 30. What is the number?	5
Four sets of a number equal 20. What is the number?	5
A child divides a number by 8 and gets 2. What was the number?	16
Three groups of a number equal 27. What is the number?	9

Some children find these sorts of problems difficult even if they are good with times tables and division. Many of the problems require the children to perform the inverse operation. Have children check their answers to make sure they are correct.

Word problems

Write the answer in the box.

Phoenix is given ten dimes. How much money does she have altogether? `$1`

Write the answer in the box.

Four helicopters carry a total of 100 spies. How many spies are in each helicopter? `25`

The Beast has a box containing 6 computer disks. How many boxes would he need to buy to have 18 disks? `3`

Peter Parker is given three bags of candy. There are 20 pieces of candy in each bag. How many pieces of candy does Peter have in total? `60`

There are 210 planets in a solar system and the Silver Surfer visits 60. How many has he not visited in the system? `150`

Rogue, Daredevil, and Dazzler win the lottery and share $900 equally among themselves. How much does each receive? `$300`

A truck contains 50 barrels of oil. It delivers 27 barrels to Kingpin. How many barrels are left on the truck? `23`

Gambit has a collection of 150 cards. He gives 35 of them to a friend. How many cards does he have left? `115`

When Storm multiplies her apartment number by 4, the result is 76. What is her apartment number? `19`

One Marvel comic costs $1.80. How much will three comics cost? `$5.40`

The Hulk transforms 20 times on Monday, 30 times on Tuesday, and 40 times on Wednesday. How many times has he transformed altogether in these three days? `90`

Rogue's car trip is supposed to be 70 miles long but her car breaks down half-way. How far has she traveled? `35 mi`

Blade battles with 32 vampires. Only 13 vampires escape. How many vampires has Blade defeated? `19`

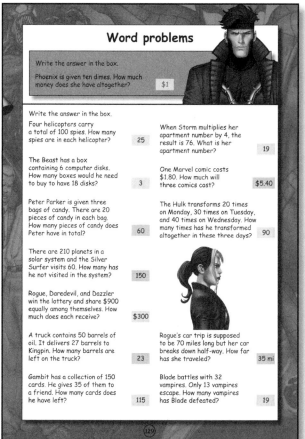

Children will need to think carefully about how they will solve each problem. If they have difficulty, talk each problem through with them.

Multiples

Circle the multiples of 3.

4   7   (9)   14   20   (24)

Circle the multiples of 3.

8	11	16	(18)	(24)	(27)	31	35
10	20	(30)	40	50	(60)	70	80
1	(3)	5	7	(9)	11	13	(15)
2	5	8	11	14	17	20	23
4	11	(15)	19	26	(30)	34	41
0	(3)	(9)	(12)	(15)	(21)	(24)	(30)
11	19	(30)	41	49	(60)	71	79
5	10	16	20	26	31	40	47
2	7	13	17	(21)	25	(33)	(60)

Circle the multiples of 4.

2	7	11	15	19	23	(28)	31
2	(4)	6	(8)	10	(12)	14	(16)
1	3	5	7	9	11	13	15
5	10	15	(20)	25	30	35	(40)
(8)	(16)	22	30	34	(40)	(48)	54
3	6	9	(12)	15	18	21	(24)
9	11	(12)	15	(16)	18		
11	13	15	17	19	(20)		
18	(24)	30	(36)	42	(48)		

Children may not know the rule for finding a multiple of 3: if the digits of a number add up to a multiple of 3, then the number itself is a multiple of 3. For example, 2 + 7 = 9, which is a multiple of 3, so 27 is a multiple of 3 (and so is 72).

Factors

Write the factors of each number.

6   `1, 2, 3, 6`   8   `1, 2, 4, 8`

You've only got one chance.

Write the factors of each number.

9	1, 3, 9	10	1, 2, 5, 10	12	1, 2, 3, 4, 6, 12
4	1, 2, 4	3	1, 3	14	1, 2, 7, 14
5	1, 5	15	1, 3, 5, 15	17	1, 17
7	1, 7	20	1, 2, 4, 5, 10, 20	19	1, 19
13	1, 13	24	1, 2, 3, 4, 6, 8, 12, 24	11	1, 11
2	1, 2	30	1, 2, 3, 5, 6, 10, 15, 30	16	1, 2, 4, 8, 16

Write the factors of each number.

1	1	4	1, 2, 4	16	1, 2, 4, 8, 16
25	1, 5, 25	36	1,2,3,4,6,9,12,18,36	49	1, 7, 49
64	1, 2, 4, 8, 16, 32, 64	81	1, 3, 9, 27, 81	100	1,2,4,5,10,20,25,50,100

Do you notice anything about the number of factors each of the numbers has? Each number has an odd number of factors.
Do you know the name for these special numbers?   These are squares.

Write the factors of each number.

7	1, 7	3	1, 3	13	1, 13
2	1, 2	11	1, 11	5	1, 5
29	1, 29	19	1, 19	37	1, 37
17	1, 17	31	1, 31	23	1, 23

Do you notice anything about the number of factors each of the numbers has? The factors of each number are 1 and the number itself.
Do you know the name for these special numbers?   These are prime numbers.

Children may neglect to include 1 and the number itself as factors of a number. For larger numbers, they may not include all the factors in their answers. Point out that 1 is not a prime number.

Fractions

Write the answer in the box.

$$1\frac{1}{2} + \frac{1}{4} = 1\frac{3}{4} \qquad 2\frac{1}{4} + 3\frac{1}{2} = 5\frac{3}{4}$$

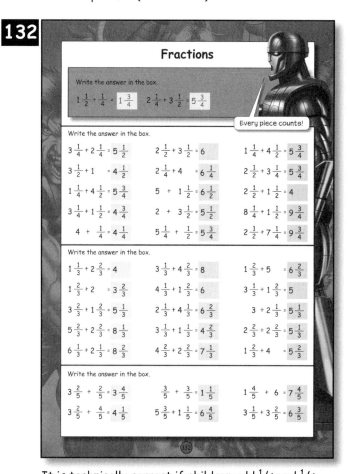

Every piece counts!

Write the answer in the box.

$3\frac{1}{4} + 2\frac{1}{4} = 5\frac{1}{2}$ $2\frac{1}{2} + 3\frac{1}{2} = 6$ $1\frac{1}{4} + 4\frac{1}{2} = 5\frac{3}{4}$

$3\frac{1}{2} + 1 = 4\frac{1}{2}$ $2\frac{1}{4} + 4 = 6\frac{1}{4}$ $2\frac{1}{2} + 3\frac{1}{4} = 5\frac{3}{4}$

$1\frac{1}{4} + 4\frac{1}{2} = 5\frac{3}{4}$ $5 + 1\frac{1}{2} = 6\frac{1}{2}$ $2\frac{1}{2} + 1\frac{1}{2} = 4$

$3\frac{1}{4} + 1\frac{1}{2} = 4\frac{3}{4}$ $2 + 3\frac{1}{2} = 5\frac{1}{2}$ $8\frac{1}{4} + 1\frac{1}{2} = 9\frac{3}{4}$

$4 + \frac{1}{4} = 4\frac{1}{4}$ $5\frac{1}{4} + \frac{1}{2} = 5\frac{3}{4}$ $2\frac{1}{2} + 7\frac{1}{4} = 9\frac{3}{4}$

Write the answer in the box.

$1\frac{1}{3} + 2\frac{2}{3} = 4$ $3\frac{1}{3} + 4\frac{2}{3} = 8$ $1\frac{2}{3} + 5 = 6\frac{2}{3}$

$1\frac{2}{3} + 2 = 3\frac{2}{3}$ $4\frac{1}{3} + 1\frac{2}{3} = 6$ $3\frac{1}{3} + 1\frac{2}{3} = 5$

$3\frac{2}{3} + 1\frac{2}{3} = 5\frac{1}{3}$ $2\frac{1}{3} + 4\frac{1}{3} = 6\frac{2}{3}$ $3 + 2\frac{1}{3} = 5\frac{1}{3}$

$5\frac{2}{3} + 2\frac{2}{3} = 8\frac{1}{3}$ $3\frac{1}{3} + 1\frac{1}{3} = 4\frac{2}{3}$ $2\frac{2}{3} + 2\frac{2}{3} = 5\frac{1}{3}$

$6\frac{1}{3} + 2\frac{1}{3} = 8\frac{2}{3}$ $4\frac{2}{3} + 2\frac{2}{3} = 7\frac{1}{3}$ $1\frac{2}{3} + 4 = 5\frac{2}{3}$

Write the answer in the box.

$3\frac{2}{5} + \frac{2}{5} = 3\frac{4}{5}$ $\frac{3}{5} + \frac{3}{5} = 1\frac{1}{5}$ $1\frac{4}{5} + 6 = 7\frac{4}{5}$

$3\frac{2}{5} + \frac{4}{5} = 4\frac{1}{5}$ $5\frac{3}{5} + 1\frac{1}{5} = 6\frac{4}{5}$ $3\frac{1}{5} + 3\frac{2}{5} = 6\frac{3}{5}$

It is technically correct if children add $\frac{1}{4}$ and $\frac{1}{4}$ to get $\frac{2}{4}$, but they should be encouraged to simplify this to $\frac{1}{2}$. Some children may not simplify improper fractions that are part of a mixed number (such as $4\frac{4}{3}$). Show them how to do this.

133

Fractions and decimals

Write each fraction as a decimal.

$2\frac{1}{10}$ = 2.1 $1\frac{2}{10}$ = 1.2 $1\frac{7}{10}$ = 1.7

Write each decimal as a fraction.

3.6 = $3\frac{6}{10}$ 1.9 = $1\frac{9}{10}$ 3.2 = $3\frac{2}{10}$

Write each fraction as a decimal.

$5\frac{1}{2}$ = 5.5	$9\frac{1}{2}$ = 9.5	$4\frac{6}{10}$ = 4.6	$11\frac{1}{2}$ = 11.5
$2\frac{1}{10}$ = 2.1	$2\frac{4}{10}$ = 2.4	$8\frac{1}{10}$ = 8.1	$5\frac{1}{2}$ = 5.5
$7\frac{8}{10}$ = 7.8	$2\frac{3}{10}$ = 2.3	$6\frac{1}{2}$ = 6.5	$8\frac{4}{10}$ = 8.4
$7\frac{4}{10}$ = 7.4	$3\frac{1}{10}$ = 3.1	$6\frac{7}{10}$ = 6.7	$1\frac{1}{2}$ = 1.5

Write each decimal as a fraction.

3.2 = $3\frac{2}{10}$	4.5 = $4\frac{1}{2}$	17.5 = $17\frac{1}{2}$	1.2 = $1\frac{2}{10}$
6.5 = $6\frac{1}{2}$	2.7 = $2\frac{7}{10}$	13.2 = $13\frac{2}{10}$	5.5 = $5\frac{1}{2}$
7.2 = $7\frac{2}{10}$	8.5 = $8\frac{1}{2}$	9.7 = $9\frac{7}{10}$	10.2 = $10\frac{2}{10}$
11.5 = $11\frac{1}{2}$	12.7 = $12\frac{7}{10}$	5.2 = $5\frac{2}{10}$	14.5 = $14\frac{1}{2}$
14.7 = $14\frac{7}{10}$	16.2 = $16\frac{2}{10}$	1.7 = $1\frac{7}{10}$	18.7 = $18\frac{7}{10}$

Write each fraction as a decimal.

$1\frac{1}{2}$ = 1.5 $2\frac{2}{10}$ = 2.2 $3\frac{3}{10}$ = 3.3

Write each decimal as a fraction.

2.5 = $2\frac{1}{2}$ 1.2 = $1\frac{2}{10}$ 3.7 = $3\frac{7}{10}$

If children have difficulty, you may want to use
a number line showing fractions and decimals.

134

Real-life problems

Write the answer in the box.

A number multiplied by 8 is 56.
What is the number?   7

I divide a number by 8 and the result is 6.
What is the number?   48

Write the answer in the box.

A number multiplied by 7 is 42.
What is the number?   6

A number divided by 8 gives
the answer 10. What was the
starting number?   80

I divide a number by 7 and
the result is 4. What number
did I begin with?   28

When 6 is multiplied by a number
the result is 42. What number
was 6 multiplied by?   7

I divide a number by 9 and
the result is 6. What number
did I begin with?   54

I multiply a number by 9 and
end up with 45. What number
did I multiply?   5

A number multiplied by itself
gives the answer 36. What is
the number?   6

I multiply a number by 9 and
the result is 81. What number
did I begin with?   9

I divide a number by 7 and
the answer is 7. What number
did I begin with?   49

When I multiply a number by 7
I end up with 56. What number
did I begin with?   8

Seven times a number is 63.
What is the number?   9

What do I have to multiply
8 by to get the result 72?   9

Six times a number is 42.
What is the number?   7

Nine times a number is 81.
What is the number?   9

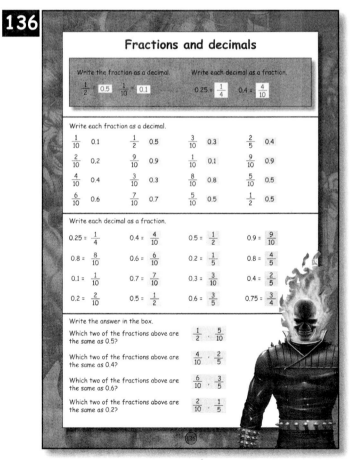

SAVE YOURSELF!
Do these as
quickly as
you can.

Some children find these sorts of problems difficult
even if they are good with times tables and division.
Many of the problems require children to perform
the inverse operation. Have them check their answers
to make sure they are correct.

135

Symmetry

The dotted line is a mirror line. Complete each shape.

Complete each shape.

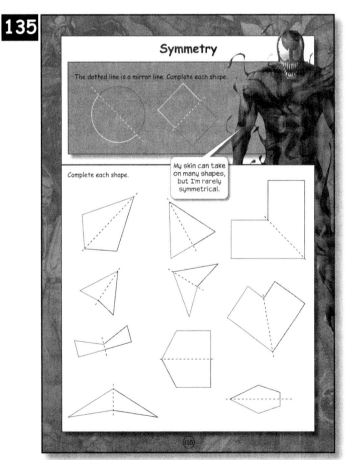

My skin can take
on many shapes,
but I'm rarely
symmetrical.

If children have difficulties with these shapes, let
them use a mirror. Even if they are confident, let them
check the shapes they have drawn with a mirror when
they finish.

136

Fractions and decimals

Write the fraction as a decimal.

$\frac{1}{2}$ = 0.5 $\frac{1}{10}$ = 0.1

Write each decimal as a fraction.

0.25 = $\frac{1}{4}$ 0.4 = $\frac{4}{10}$

Write each fraction as a decimal.

$\frac{1}{10}$ 0.1	$\frac{1}{2}$ 0.5	$\frac{3}{10}$ 0.3	$\frac{2}{5}$ 0.4
$\frac{2}{10}$ 0.2	$\frac{9}{10}$ 0.9	$\frac{1}{10}$ 0.1	$\frac{9}{10}$ 0.9
$\frac{4}{10}$ 0.4	$\frac{3}{10}$ 0.3	$\frac{8}{10}$ 0.8	$\frac{5}{10}$ 0.5
$\frac{6}{10}$ 0.6	$\frac{7}{10}$ 0.7	$\frac{5}{10}$ 0.5	$\frac{1}{2}$ 0.5

Write each decimal as a fraction.

0.25 = $\frac{1}{4}$	0.4 = $\frac{4}{10}$	0.5 = $\frac{1}{2}$	0.9 = $\frac{9}{10}$
0.8 = $\frac{8}{10}$	0.6 = $\frac{6}{10}$	0.2 = $\frac{1}{5}$	0.8 = $\frac{4}{5}$
0.1 = $\frac{1}{10}$	0.7 = $\frac{7}{10}$	0.3 = $\frac{3}{10}$	0.4 = $\frac{2}{5}$
0.2 = $\frac{2}{10}$	0.5 = $\frac{1}{2}$	0.6 = $\frac{3}{5}$	0.75 = $\frac{3}{4}$

Write the answer in the box.

Which two of the fractions above are
the same as 0.5? $\frac{1}{2}$, $\frac{5}{10}$

Which two of the fractions above are
the same as 0.4? $\frac{4}{10}$, $\frac{2}{5}$

Which two of the fractions above are
the same as 0.6? $\frac{6}{10}$, $\frac{3}{5}$

Which two of the fractions above are
the same as 0.2? $\frac{2}{10}$, $\frac{1}{5}$

Children should realize that $1/10$ is equvalent to 0.1.
If necessary, help them understand that $2/10$ is
equivalent to 0.2, and so on. Children also need
to know the decimal equivalents of $1/4$ and $3/4$.

137

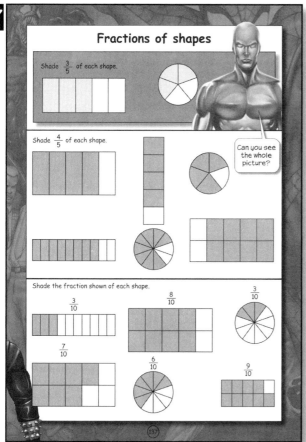

Children may shade in any combinations of the sections as long as the shaded area represents the correct fraction.

138

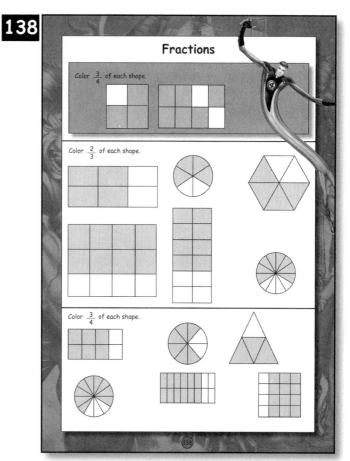

Children may shade in any combination of the sections as long as the shaded area represents the correct fraction.

139

Reading timetables

	Harbor	Hightown	Barker Plaza	Princess St.
Redline bus	8:10	8:15	8:25	8:35
Blueline tram	8:15	no stop	no stop	8:30
City taxi	8:30	8:35	8:45	8:55
Greenline trolley	8:16	no stop	8:21	8:24

The timetable shows the times it takes to travel between different places in Madripoor, using different transport companies.

Write the answer in the box.

How long does the Redline bus take to travel from the Harbor to Princess Street?	25 minutes
When does the City taxi arrive at Barker Plaza?	8:45
Where is the Greenline trolley at 8:21?	Barker Plaza
Where does the trolley not stop?	Hightown
Does the tram stop at Barker Plaza?	no
How long does the tram take to travel between the Harbor and Princess Street?	15 minutes
Which is the fastest trip between the Harbor and Princess Street?	Greenline trolley
Which service arrives at Princess Street at 8:30?	Blueline tram
How long does the City taxi take to get from Hightown to Barker Plaza?	10 minutes
Where is the City taxi at 8:35?	Hightown

Children should find this exercise straightforward. If they have difficulty, help them read across the rows and down the columns to find the information they need.

140

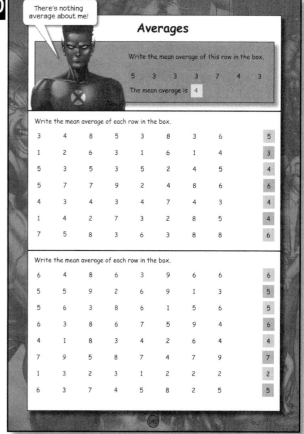

If necessary, remind children that the mean average of a set of quantities is the sum of the quantities divided by the total number of quantities.

141

Multiplying larger numbers by ones

Write the product for each problem.

Time to run!

$$\begin{array}{r} 529 \\ \times\ 4 \\ \hline 2{,}116 \end{array} \qquad \begin{array}{r} 1{,}273 \\ \times\ 5 \\ \hline 6{,}365 \end{array}$$

Write the product for each problem.

$$\begin{array}{r} 724 \\ \times\ 2 \\ \hline 1{,}448 \end{array} \qquad \begin{array}{r} 831 \\ \times\ 3 \\ \hline 2{,}493 \end{array} \qquad \begin{array}{r} 126 \\ \times\ 3 \\ \hline 378 \end{array} \qquad \begin{array}{r} 455 \\ \times\ 4 \\ \hline 1{,}820 \end{array}$$

$$\begin{array}{r} 261 \\ \times\ 4 \\ \hline 1{,}044 \end{array} \qquad \begin{array}{r} 182 \\ \times\ 5 \\ \hline 910 \end{array} \qquad \begin{array}{r} 449 \\ \times\ 5 \\ \hline 2{,}245 \end{array} \qquad \begin{array}{r} 253 \\ \times\ 6 \\ \hline 1{,}518 \end{array}$$

$$\begin{array}{r} 328 \\ \times\ 6 \\ \hline 1{,}968 \end{array} \qquad \begin{array}{r} 465 \\ \times\ 6 \\ \hline 2{,}790 \end{array} \qquad \begin{array}{r} 105 \\ \times\ 4 \\ \hline 420 \end{array} \qquad \begin{array}{r} 562 \\ \times\ 4 \\ \hline 2{,}248 \end{array}$$

Write the product for each problem.

$$\begin{array}{r} 4{,}268 \\ \times\ 3 \\ \hline 12{,}804 \end{array} \qquad \begin{array}{r} 1{,}582 \\ \times\ 3 \\ \hline 4{,}746 \end{array} \qquad \begin{array}{r} 3{,}612 \\ \times\ 4 \\ \hline 14{,}448 \end{array} \qquad \begin{array}{r} 4{,}284 \\ \times\ 4 \\ \hline 17{,}136 \end{array}$$

$$\begin{array}{r} 4{,}907 \\ \times\ 5 \\ \hline 24{,}535 \end{array} \qquad \begin{array}{r} 1{,}263 \\ \times\ 5 \\ \hline 6{,}315 \end{array} \qquad \begin{array}{r} 1{,}303 \\ \times\ 6 \\ \hline 7{,}818 \end{array} \qquad \begin{array}{r} 1{,}467 \\ \times\ 6 \\ \hline 8{,}802 \end{array}$$

$$\begin{array}{r} 5{,}521 \\ \times\ 6 \\ \hline 33{,}126 \end{array} \qquad \begin{array}{r} 8{,}436 \\ \times\ 6 \\ \hline 50{,}616 \end{array} \qquad \begin{array}{r} 1{,}599 \\ \times\ 6 \\ \hline 9{,}594 \end{array} \qquad \begin{array}{r} 3{,}761 \\ \times\ 6 \\ \hline 22{,}566 \end{array}$$

$$\begin{array}{r} 6{,}837 \\ \times\ 4 \\ \hline 27{,}348 \end{array} \qquad \begin{array}{r} 6{,}394 \\ \times\ 5 \\ \hline 31{,}970 \end{array} \qquad \begin{array}{r} 8{,}124 \\ \times\ 6 \\ \hline 48{,}744 \end{array} \qquad \begin{array}{r} 3{,}914 \\ \times\ 6 \\ \hline 23{,}484 \end{array}$$

Children should understand the convention of multiplication problems, i.e. to multiply the ones first and work left, regrouping when necessary. Problems on this page will highlight gaps in knowledge of the 2, 3, 4, 5, and 6 times tables.

142

Multiplying larger numbers by ones

Write the product for each problem.

Smash through these sums!

$$\begin{array}{r} 417 \\ \times\ 7 \\ \hline 2{,}919 \end{array} \qquad \begin{array}{r} 2{,}185 \\ \times\ 9 \\ \hline 19{,}665 \end{array}$$

Write the answer to each problem.

$$\begin{array}{r} 604 \\ \times\ 7 \\ \hline 4{,}228 \end{array} \qquad \begin{array}{r} 413 \\ \times\ 7 \\ \hline 2{,}891 \end{array} \qquad \begin{array}{r} 682 \\ \times\ 8 \\ \hline 5{,}456 \end{array} \qquad \begin{array}{r} 327 \\ \times\ 7 \\ \hline 2{,}289 \end{array}$$

$$\begin{array}{r} 436 \\ \times\ 8 \\ \hline 3{,}488 \end{array} \qquad \begin{array}{r} 171 \\ \times\ 9 \\ \hline 1{,}539 \end{array} \qquad \begin{array}{r} 715 \\ \times\ 8 \\ \hline 5{,}720 \end{array} \qquad \begin{array}{r} 254 \\ \times\ 8 \\ \hline 2{,}032 \end{array}$$

$$\begin{array}{r} 235 \\ \times\ 8 \\ \hline 1{,}880 \end{array} \qquad \begin{array}{r} 319 \\ \times\ 9 \\ \hline 2{,}871 \end{array} \qquad \begin{array}{r} 581 \\ \times\ 9 \\ \hline 5{,}299 \end{array} \qquad \begin{array}{r} 999 \\ \times\ 9 \\ \hline 8{,}991 \end{array}$$

Work out the answer to each problem.

$$\begin{array}{r} 2{,}816 \\ \times\ 7 \\ \hline 19{,}712 \end{array} \qquad \begin{array}{r} 4{,}331 \\ \times\ 7 \\ \hline 30{,}317 \end{array} \qquad \begin{array}{r} 2{,}617 \\ \times\ 8 \\ \hline 20{,}936 \end{array} \qquad \begin{array}{r} 1{,}439 \\ \times\ 8 \\ \hline 11{,}512 \end{array}$$

$$\begin{array}{r} 4{,}022 \\ \times\ 8 \\ \hline 32{,}176 \end{array} \qquad \begin{array}{r} 3{,}104 \\ \times\ 8 \\ \hline 24{,}832 \end{array} \qquad \begin{array}{r} 2{,}591 \\ \times\ 9 \\ \hline 23{,}319 \end{array} \qquad \begin{array}{r} 4{,}361 \\ \times\ 9 \\ \hline 39{,}249 \end{array}$$

$$\begin{array}{r} 4{,}361 \\ \times\ 9 \\ \hline 39{,}249 \end{array} \qquad \begin{array}{r} 3{,}002 \\ \times\ 8 \\ \hline 24{,}016 \end{array} \qquad \begin{array}{r} 2{,}567 \\ \times\ 7 \\ \hline 17{,}969 \end{array} \qquad \begin{array}{r} 1{,}514 \\ \times\ 8 \\ \hline 12{,}112 \end{array}$$

$$\begin{array}{r} 4{,}624 \\ \times\ 7 \\ \hline 32{,}368 \end{array} \qquad \begin{array}{r} 3{,}894 \\ \times\ 8 \\ \hline 31{,}152 \end{array} \qquad \begin{array}{r} 2{,}993 \\ \times\ 8 \\ \hline 23{,}944 \end{array} \qquad \begin{array}{r} 1{,}710 \\ \times\ 9 \\ \hline 15{,}390 \end{array}$$

Any problems encountered on this page will be similar to those of the previous page. Gaps in the child's knowledge of 7, 8, and 9 times tables will be highlighted here.

143

Real-life multiplication problems

There are 157 gamma-chargers in each box. How many will there be in three boxes?

471 gamma-chargers

$$\begin{array}{r} \overset{1\ 2}{157} \\ \times\ 3 \\ \hline 471 \end{array}$$

Each of Doctor Strange's disk holders can hold 660 disks. If he has 5 holders, how many will they hold altogether?

3,300

$$\begin{array}{r} \overset{3}{660} \\ \times\ 5 \\ \hline 3{,}300 \end{array}$$

A train that runs across District X can take 425 passengers. How many can it take on five trips?

2,125 passengers

$$\begin{array}{r} \overset{1\ 2}{425} \\ \times\ 5 \\ \hline 2{,}125 \end{array}$$

Bullseye puts $278 into the bank every month. How much will he have put in after 6 months?

$1,668

$$\begin{array}{r} \overset{4\ 4}{278} \\ \times\ 6 \\ \hline 1{,}668 \end{array}$$

Hightown theater can seat 4,536 people. If a play runs for 7 days, what is the maximum number of people who will be able to see the play?

31,752 people

$$\begin{array}{r} \overset{3\ 2\ 4}{4{,}536} \\ \times\ 7 \\ \hline 31{,}752 \end{array}$$

Punisher's motorcycle costs $35,956. How much will it cost the X-Men to buy 4 new motorcycles?

$143,824

$$\begin{array}{r} \overset{2\ 3\ \ 2\ 2}{35{,}956} \\ \times\ 4 \\ \hline 143{,}824 \end{array}$$

The Blackbird flies at a steady speed of 1,550 mph. How far will the plane travel in 6 hours?

9,300 miles

$$\begin{array}{r} \overset{3}{1{,}550} \\ \times\ 6 \\ \hline 9{,}300 \end{array}$$

This page provides an opportunity for children to apply their skills of multiplication to real-life problems. As with previous multiplication work, gaps in their knowledge of multiplication facts will be highlighted here.

144

Area of rectangles and squares

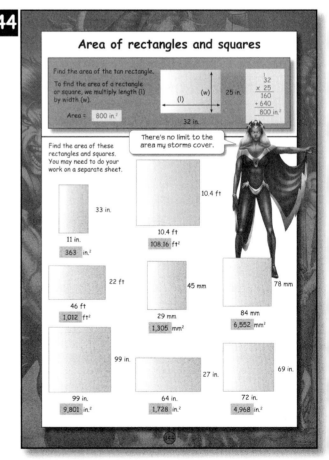

Find the area of the tan rectangle.

To find the area of a rectangle or square, we multiply length (l) by width (w).

Area = 800 in.²

25 in.

32 in.

$$\begin{array}{r} \overset{1}{32} \\ \times\ 25 \\ \hline 160 \\ +\ 640 \\ \hline 800 \end{array} \text{ in.}^2$$

Find the area of these rectangles and squares. You may need to do your work on a separate sheet.

There's no limit to the area my storms cover.

33 in.
11 in.
363 in.²

10.4 ft
10.4 ft
108.16 ft²

22 ft
46 ft
1,012 ft²

45 mm
29 mm
1,305 mm²

78 mm
84 mm
6,552 mm²

99 in.
99 in.
9,801 in.²

27 in.
64 in.
1,728 in.²

69 in.
72 in.
4,968 in.²

Children may confuse area and perimeter, and add the sides together instead of multiplying the two sides to arrive at the area. If any answers are wrong, check the long multiplication, and if necessary, revise the method.

Perimeter of shapes

Find the perimeter of this brown rectangle. To find the perimeter of a rectangle or square, we add the two lengths and the two widths together.

13.3 in.

25.4 in.

77.4 in.

13.3
13.3
25.4
+25.4
77.4

Find the perimeter of these rectangles and squares. You may need to do your work on an extra sheet.

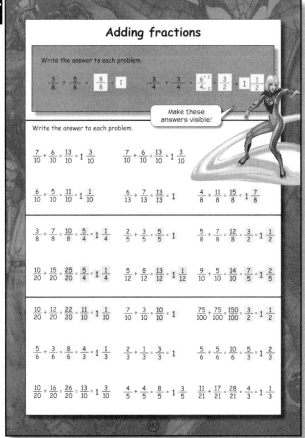

20.6 ft / 20.6 ft — 82.4 ft

28.9 ft / 48.3 ft — 154.4 ft

134 mm / 134 mm — 536 mm

25 mm / 55 mm — 160 mm

35.6 ft / 18.2 ft — 107.6 ft

50.5 ft / 50.5 ft — 202 ft

17 in. / 35 in. — 104 in.

35 mm / 19 mm — 108 mm

On this page and the next, the most likely problem will be confusion with the area work done on the previous page. Remind children to add the four sides together.

Adding fractions

Work out the answer to the problem.

$$\frac{1}{5} + \frac{3}{5} = \frac{4}{5} \qquad \frac{4}{9} + \frac{2}{9} = \frac{6 \div 2}{9 \div 3} = \frac{2}{3}$$

Add the numerators but keep the denominators when they are the same.

Remember to reduce to simplest form if you need to.

$\frac{2}{9} + \frac{5}{9} = \frac{7}{9}$ $\frac{2}{7} + \frac{3}{7} = \frac{5}{7}$ $\frac{1}{3} + \frac{1}{3} = \frac{2}{3}$

$\frac{2}{9} + \frac{3}{9} = \frac{5}{9}$ $\frac{2}{8} + \frac{1}{8} = \frac{3}{8}$ $\frac{3}{10} + \frac{6}{10} = \frac{9}{10}$

$\frac{4}{20} + \frac{5}{20} = \frac{9}{20}$ $\frac{1}{100} + \frac{16}{100} = \frac{17}{100}$ $\frac{7}{10} + \frac{2}{10} = \frac{9}{10}$

$\frac{2}{5} + \frac{1}{5} = \frac{3}{5}$ $\frac{1}{7} + \frac{3}{7} = \frac{4}{7}$ $\frac{4}{9} + \frac{1}{9} = \frac{5}{9}$

$\frac{1}{6} + \frac{2}{6} = \frac{3}{6} = \frac{1}{2}$ $\frac{19}{100} + \frac{31}{100} = \frac{50}{100} = \frac{1}{2}$ $\frac{5}{20} + \frac{10}{20} = \frac{15}{20} = \frac{3}{4}$

$\frac{4}{10} + \frac{4}{10} = \frac{8}{10} = \frac{4}{5}$ $\frac{3}{12} + \frac{6}{12} = \frac{9}{12} = \frac{3}{4}$ $\frac{2}{6} + \frac{2}{6} = \frac{4}{6} = \frac{2}{3}$

$\frac{3}{8} + \frac{3}{8} = \frac{6}{8} = \frac{3}{4}$ $\frac{1}{8} + \frac{3}{8} = \frac{4}{8} = \frac{1}{2}$ $\frac{5}{12} + \frac{1}{12} = \frac{6}{12} = \frac{1}{2}$

$\frac{1}{4} + \frac{1}{4} = \frac{2}{4} = \frac{1}{2}$ $\frac{4}{20} + \frac{1}{20} = \frac{5}{20} = \frac{1}{4}$ $\frac{1}{6} + \frac{3}{6} = \frac{4}{6} = \frac{2}{3}$

$\frac{3}{7} + \frac{3}{7} = \frac{6}{7}$ $\frac{2}{9} + \frac{2}{9} = \frac{4}{9}$ $\frac{13}{20} + \frac{5}{20} = \frac{18}{20} = \frac{9}{10}$

$\frac{81}{100} + \frac{9}{100} = \frac{90}{100} = \frac{9}{10}$ $\frac{5}{20} + \frac{8}{20} = \frac{13}{20}$ $\frac{2}{8} + \frac{3}{8} = \frac{5}{8}$

$\frac{6}{10} + \frac{2}{10} = \frac{8}{10} = \frac{4}{5}$ $\frac{28}{100} + \frac{47}{100} = \frac{75}{100} = \frac{3}{4}$ $\frac{72}{100} + \frac{18}{100} = \frac{90}{100} = \frac{9}{10}$

Difficulty in reducing the sum to its simplest form points to a weakness in finding common factors of the numerator and denominator. Children can reduce the answer in stages, first looking at whether 2 is a common factor, then 3, and so on.

Adding fractions

Write the answer to each problem.

$$\frac{3}{8} + \frac{5}{8} = \frac{8}{8} = 1 \qquad \frac{3}{4} + \frac{3}{4} = \frac{6 \div 2}{4 \div 2} = \frac{3}{2} = 1\frac{1}{2}$$

Make these answers visible!

Write the answer to each problem.

$\frac{7}{10} + \frac{6}{10} = \frac{13}{10} = 1\frac{3}{10}$ $\frac{7}{10} + \frac{6}{10} = \frac{13}{10} = 1\frac{3}{10}$

$\frac{6}{10} + \frac{5}{10} = \frac{11}{10} = 1\frac{1}{10}$ $\frac{6}{13} + \frac{7}{13} = \frac{13}{13} = 1$ $\frac{4}{8} + \frac{11}{8} = \frac{15}{8} = 1\frac{7}{8}$

$\frac{3}{8} + \frac{7}{8} = \frac{10}{8} = \frac{5}{4} = 1\frac{1}{4}$ $\frac{2}{5} + \frac{3}{5} = \frac{5}{5} = 1$ $\frac{5}{8} + \frac{7}{8} = \frac{12}{8} = \frac{3}{2} = 1\frac{1}{2}$

$\frac{10}{20} + \frac{15}{20} = \frac{25}{20} = \frac{5}{4} = 1\frac{1}{4}$ $\frac{5}{12} + \frac{8}{12} = \frac{13}{12} = 1\frac{1}{12}$ $\frac{9}{10} + \frac{5}{10} = \frac{14}{10} = \frac{7}{5} = 1\frac{2}{5}$

$\frac{10}{20} + \frac{12}{20} = \frac{22}{20} = \frac{11}{10} = 1\frac{1}{10}$ $\frac{7}{10} + \frac{3}{10} = \frac{10}{10} = 1$ $\frac{75}{100} + \frac{75}{100} = \frac{150}{100} = \frac{3}{2} = 1\frac{1}{2}$

$\frac{5}{6} + \frac{3}{6} = \frac{8}{6} = \frac{4}{3} = 1\frac{1}{3}$ $\frac{2}{3} + \frac{1}{3} = \frac{3}{3} = 1$ $\frac{5}{6} + \frac{5}{6} = \frac{10}{6} = \frac{5}{3} = 1\frac{2}{3}$

$\frac{10}{20} + \frac{16}{20} = \frac{26}{20} = \frac{13}{10} = 1\frac{3}{10}$ $\frac{4}{5} + \frac{4}{5} = \frac{8}{5} = 1\frac{3}{5}$ $\frac{11}{21} + \frac{17}{21} = \frac{28}{21} = \frac{4}{3} = 1\frac{1}{3}$

If children leave the answer as a fraction or do not reduce it, they are completing only one of the two steps to finding the simplest form. Have them first write the answer as a mixed number, and then reduce the fraction part.

Subtracting fractions

Write the answer to each problem.

$$\frac{4}{5} - \frac{2}{5} = \frac{2}{5} \qquad \frac{8}{9} - \frac{5}{9} = \frac{3 \div 3}{9 \div 3} = \frac{1}{3}$$

Subtract the numerators but keep the denominators when they are the same.

No one takes anything from me.

Find the difference of each problem.

$\frac{4}{5} - \frac{1}{5} = \frac{3}{5}$ $\frac{5}{7} - \frac{2}{7} = \frac{3}{7}$

$\frac{5}{10} - \frac{4}{10} = \frac{1}{10}$ $\frac{6}{9} - \frac{2}{9} = \frac{4}{9}$

$\frac{7}{8} - \frac{3}{8} = \frac{4}{8} = \frac{1}{2}$ $\frac{14}{20} - \frac{8}{20} = \frac{6}{20} = \frac{3}{10}$ $\frac{4}{6} - \frac{1}{6} = \frac{3}{6} = \frac{1}{2}$

$\frac{11}{12} - \frac{7}{12} = \frac{4}{12} = \frac{1}{3}$ $\frac{17}{20} - \frac{12}{20} = \frac{5}{20} = \frac{1}{4}$ $\frac{8}{12} - \frac{2}{12} = \frac{6}{12} = \frac{1}{2}$

$\frac{8}{9} - \frac{2}{9} = \frac{6}{9} = \frac{2}{3}$ $\frac{12}{12} - \frac{2}{12} = \frac{10}{12} = \frac{5}{6}$ $\frac{8}{10} - \frac{3}{10} = \frac{5}{10} = \frac{1}{2}$

$\frac{6}{10} - \frac{4}{10} = \frac{2}{10} = \frac{1}{5}$ $\frac{6}{8} - \frac{4}{8} = \frac{2}{8} = \frac{1}{4}$ $\frac{9}{12} - \frac{5}{12} = \frac{4}{12} = \frac{1}{3}$

$\frac{3}{4} - \frac{2}{4} = \frac{1}{4}$ $\frac{6}{8} - \frac{1}{8} = \frac{5}{8}$ $\frac{18}{20} - \frac{4}{20} = \frac{14}{20} = \frac{7}{10}$

$\frac{4}{6} - \frac{2}{6} = \frac{2}{6} = \frac{1}{3}$ $\frac{7}{12} - \frac{6}{12} = \frac{1}{12}$ $\frac{5}{8} - \frac{2}{8} = \frac{3}{8}$

$\frac{5}{7} - \frac{1}{7} = \frac{4}{7}$ $\frac{5}{16} - \frac{1}{16} = \frac{4}{16} = \frac{1}{4}$ $\frac{70}{100} - \frac{60}{100} = \frac{10}{100} = \frac{1}{10}$

See the notes for the previous page.

Showing decimals

Write the decimals on the number line.
0.4, 0.5, 0.6, 0.8, 0.9, 0.25, 0.45, 0.63

| 0 | 0.25 | 0.45 | 0.65 | 1 |

0.1 0.2 0.3 0.4 0.5 0.6 0.7 0.8 0.9

Write the decimals on the number line.

0.1, 0.2, 0.45, 0.6, 0.85, 0.95

0   0.25   0.5   0.75   1

0.1 0.2   0.45   0.6   0.85 0.95

Write the decimals on the number line.

1.2, 1.3, 1.4, 1.7, 1.8, 1.95

1   1.25   1.5   1.75   2

1.2 1.3 1.4   1.7 1.8 1.95

Write the decimals on the number line.

2.2, 2.35, 2.6, 2.8, 2.85, 3.15

2   2.5   3

2.2 2.35   2.6   2.8 2.85 3.15

If children are confused as to where to place the hundredths, have them first fill in all of the tenths on the number line. Then ask them to find those tenths between which the hundredths fall.

Conversions: length

Units of length	
12 inches	1 foot
3 feet	1 yard
5,280 feet	1 mile
1,760 yards	1 mile

This conversion table shows how to convert inches, feet, yards, and miles.

Daredevil's stunt rope is 3 yards long. How many inches is that?

| 3 × 3 = 9 | 9 feet long |
| 9 × 12 = 108 | 108 inches |

Mister Fantastic stretches 120 inches. How many feet is that?

| 120 ÷ 12 = 10 | 10 feet long |

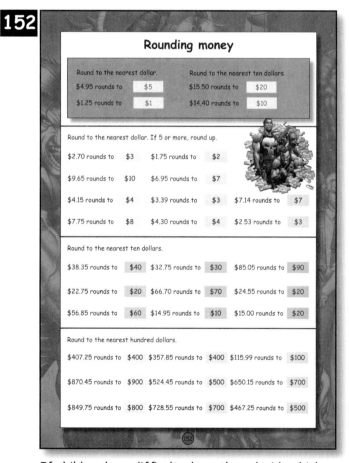

Convert each measurement to feet.

36 inches 36 ÷ 12 = 3	12 inches 12 ÷ 12 = 1	48 inches 48 ÷ 12 = 4
3 feet	1 foot	4 feet

Convert each measurement to yards.

6 feet 6 ÷ 3 = 2	12 feet 12 ÷ 3 = 4	27 feet 27 ÷ 3 = 9	36 feet 36 ÷ 3 = 12
2 yards	4 yards	9 yards	12 yards

Convert each measurement to inches.

4 feet 4 × 12 = 48	12 feet 12 × 12 = 144	8 feet 8 × 12 = 96	5 feet 5 × 12 = 60
48 inches	144 inches	96 inches	60 inches

Convert each measurement.

4 yards 4 × 3 = 12	5 yards 5 × 3 × 12 = 180	4 miles 4 × 5,280 = 20,120	1 mile 1 × 5,280 × 12
12 feet	180 inches	21,120 feet	63,360 inches
15,840 feet 15,840 ÷ 5,280 = 3	31,680 feet 31,680 ÷ 5,280 = 6	1,760 yards 1,760 ÷ 1,760 = 1	3,520 yards 3,520 ÷ 1,760 = 2
3 miles	6 miles	1 miles	2 miles

If children are confused whether to multiply or divide, ask them if the new unit is a longer or shorter unit. If the unit is longer, there will be fewer of them, so division would be the appropriate operation.

Conversions: capacity

Units of capacity	
8 fluid ounces	1 cup
2 cups	1 pint
2 pints	1 quart
4 quarts	1 gallon

This conversion table shows how to convert ounces, cups, pints, quarts, and gallons.

Wolverine's water bottle holds 6 cups. How many pints does it hold?

| 6 ÷ 2 = 3 | 3 pints |

Beast's water bottle holds 8 pints. How many cups does it hold?

| 8 × 2 = 16 | 16 cups |

Inventors have to know measures.

Convert each measurement to cups.

32 fluid ounces 36 ÷ 8 = 4	16 fluid ounces 16 ÷ 8 = 2	96 fluid ounces 96 ÷ 8 = 12
4 cups	2 cups	12 cups

Convert each measurement to pints.

6 cups 6 ÷ 2 = 3	12 cups 12 ÷ 2 = 6	30 quarts 30 × 2 = 60	6 quarts 6 × 2 = 12
3 pints	6 pints	60 pints	12 pints

Convert each measurement to gallons.

16 quarts 16 ÷ 4 = 4	32 quarts 32 ÷ 4 = 8	100 quarts 100 ÷ 4 = 25	20 quarts 20 ÷ 4 = 5
4 gallons	8 gallons	25 gallons	5 gallons

Convert each measurement.

3 gallons 3 × 8 = 24	5 quarts 5 × 4 = 20	36 cups 36 ÷ 4 = 9	72 pints 72 ÷ 8 = 9
24 pints	20 cups	9 quarts	9 gallons
1 quart 1 × 32 = 32	240 fluid ounces 240 ÷ 16 = 15	7 quarts 7 × 4 = 28	11 gallons 11 × 8 = 88
32 fluid ounces	15 pints	28 cups	88 pints

See the comments for the previous page.

Rounding money

Round to the nearest dollar.

$4.95 rounds to $5

$1.25 rounds to $1

Round to the nearest ten dollars.

$15.50 rounds to $20

$14.40 rounds to $10

Round to the nearest dollar. If 5 or more, round up.

$2.70 rounds to $3 $1.75 rounds to $2

$9.65 rounds to $10 $6.95 rounds to $7

$4.15 rounds to $4 $3.39 rounds to $3 $7.14 rounds to $7

$7.75 rounds to $8 $4.30 rounds to $4 $2.53 rounds to $3

Round to the nearest ten dollars.

$38.35 rounds to $40 $32.75 rounds to $30 $85.05 rounds to $90

$22.75 rounds to $20 $66.70 rounds to $70 $24.55 rounds to $20

$56.85 rounds to $60 $14.95 rounds to $10 $15.00 rounds to $20

Round to the nearest hundred dollars.

$407.25 rounds to $400 $357.85 rounds to $400 $115.99 rounds to $100

$870.45 rounds to $900 $524.45 rounds to $500 $650.15 rounds to $700

$849.75 rounds to $800 $728.55 rounds to $700 $467.25 rounds to $500

If children have difficulty, have them decide which are the two nearest dollars, tens of dollars, or hundreds dollars, and which of the two is closest to the number.

153

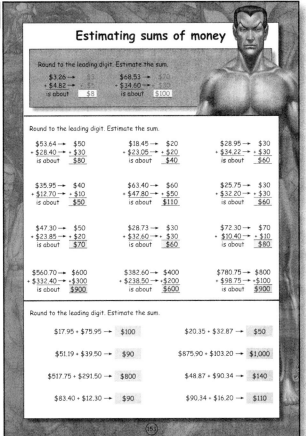

Estimating sums of money

Round to the leading digit. Estimate the sum.

$3.26 → $3
+ $4.82 → + $5
is about $8

$68.53 → $70
+ $34.60 → + $30
is about $100

Round to the leading digit. Estimate the sum.

$53.64 → $50
+ $28.40 → + $30
is about $80

$18.45 → $20
+ $23.05 → + $20
is about $40

$28.95 → $30
+ $34.22 → + $30
is about $60

$35.95 → $40
+ $12.70 → + $10
is about $50

$63.40 → $60
+ $47.80 → + $50
is about $110

$25.75 → $30
+ $32.20 → + $30
is about $60

$47.30 → $50
+ $23.85 → + $20
is about $70

$28.73 → $30
+ $32.60 → + $30
is about $60

$72.30 → $70
+ $10.40 → + $10
is about $80

$560.70 → $600
+ $332.40 → +$300
is about $900

$382.60 → $400
+ $238.50 → +$200
is about $600

$780.75 → $800
+ $98.75 → +$100
is about $900

Round to the leading digit. Estimate the sum.

$17.95 + $75.95 → $100

$20.35 + $32.87 → $50

$51.19 + $39.50 → $90

$875.90 + $103.20 → $1,000

$517.75 + $291.50 → $800

$48.87 + $90.34 → $140

$83.40 + $12.30 → $90

$90.34 + $16.20 → $110

In section 2, children need to estimate by rounding mentally. If they have trouble, have them write the rounded numbers above the originals, and then add them together.

154

Estimating differences of money

Round the numbers to the leading digit. Estimate the differences.

$8.75 → $9
- $4.83 → - $5
is about $4

$63.20 → $60
- $48.35 → - $50
is about $10

Round the numbers to the leading digit. Estimate the differences.

$27.80 → $30
- $11.90 → - $10
is about $20

$48.35 → $50
- $32.25 → - $30
is about $20

$89.20 → $90
- $22.40 → - $20
is about $70

$37.40 → $40
- $31.20 → - $30
is about $10

$58.20 → $60
- $17.30 → - $20
is about $40

$326.30 → $300
- $178.90 → - $200
is about $100

$54.10 → $50
- $33.80 → - $30
is about $20

$87.40 → $90
- $8.75 → - $10
is about $80

$783.90 → $800
- $417.60 → - $400
is about $400

Round the numbers to the leading digit. Estimate the differences.

$8.12 - $3.78
→ $8 - $4 = $4

$49.60 - $21.80
→ $50 - $20 = $30

$7.70 - $3.20
→ $8 - $3 = $5

$84.20 - $39.80
→ $80 - $40 = $40

$5.95 - $4.60
→ $6 - $5 = $1

$675.80 - $267.50
→ $700 - $300 = $400

$32.85 - $21.90
→ $30 - $20 = $10

$829.90 - $516.20
→ $800 - $500 = $300

$56.78 - $38.90
→ $60 - $40 = $20

$679.20 - $211.10
→ $700 - $200 = $500

See the comments for the previous page.

155

Estimating sums and differences

Round the numbers to the leading digit. Estimate the sum or difference.

3,762 → 4,000
+ 1,204 → 1,000
is about 5,000

287,257 → 300,000
- 98,592 → 100,000
is about 200,000

Round the numbers to the leading digit. Estimate the sum or difference.

587 → 600
+ 496 → + 500
is about 1,100

22,945 → 20,000
- 12,352 → - 10,000
is about 10,000

8,265 → 8,000
+ 2,156 → + 2,000
is about 10,000

685,271 → 700,000
+ 213,876 → + 200,000
is about 900,000

57,998 → 60,000
- 22,135 → - 20,000
is about 40,000

492,076 → 500,000
+ 237,631 → + 200,000
is about 700,000

23,957 → 20,000
+ 14,702 → + 10,000
is about 30,000

8,752 → 9,000
- 2,398 → - 2,000
is about 7,000

62,973 → 60,000
+ 21,482 → + 20,000
is about 80,000

5,294 → 5,000
+ 3,813 → + 4,000
is about 9,000

736 → 700
+ 829 → + 800
is about 1,500

33,729 → 30,000
- 19,372 → - 20,000
is about 10,000

Write > or < for each problem.

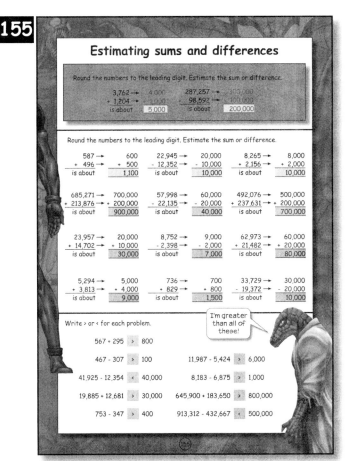

I'm greater than all of these!

567 + 295 > 800

467 - 307 > 100

11,987 - 5,424 > 6,000

41,925 - 12,354 < 40,000

8,183 - 6,875 > 1,000

19,885 + 12,681 > 30,000

645,900 + 183,650 > 800,000

753 - 347 > 400

913,312 - 432,667 < 500,000

In section 2, children need to think about their estimates more carefully if the estimate is very close to the number on the right side of the equation. Have them look at the digits in the next place to adjust their estimates up or down.

156

Conversion tables

Draw a table to convert dollars to cents.

$	Cents
1	100
2	200
3	300

Complete the conversion table.

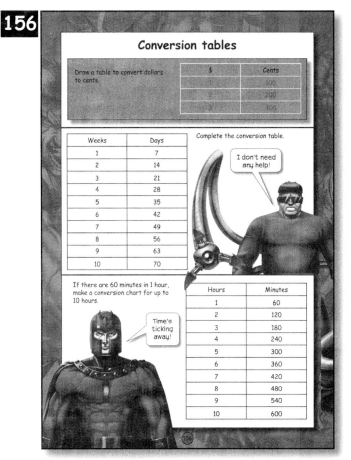

I don't need any help!

Weeks	Days
1	7
2	14
3	21
4	28
5	35
6	42
7	49
8	56
9	63
10	70

If there are 60 minutes in 1 hour, make a conversion chart for up to 10 hours.

Time's ticking away!

Hours	Minutes
1	60
2	120
3	180
4	240
5	300
6	360
7	420
8	480
9	540
10	600

Children will grasp that they are dealing in multiples of 7 and later 60. Any problems will be due to weaknesses in times tables or from missing numbers as they work down the chart. Encourage care and concentration.

LONDON, NEW YORK, MUNICH,
MELBOURNE, AND DELHI

First published in the United States in 2007 by DK Publishing
375 Hudson Street, New York, New York 10014

07 08 09 10 11 10 9 8 7 6 5 4 3 2 1
LD078 – 06/07

DK books are available at special discounts when purchased in bulk for sales promotions,
premiums, fund-raising, or educational use. For details, contact:
DK Publishing Special Markets, 375 Hudson Street, New York, New York 10014, or SpecialSales@dk.com
A catalog record for this book is available from the Library of Congress.

ISBN: 978-0-7566-2998-4

Reproduced by Icon Reproduction Ltd., UK
Printed and bound by Donnelley's, US

Discover more at
www.dk.com